PENGUIN 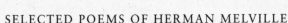 CLASSICS

SELECTED POEMS OF HERMAN MELVILLE

HERMAN MELVILLE was born in New York City on August 1, 1819, to Allan and Maria Gansevoort Melville. His paternal grandfather, Major Thomas Melville, had participated in the Boston Tea Party, and his maternal grandfather, General Peter Gansevoort, had defended Fort Stanwix in 1777. His father's importing business went bankrupt in 1830, and the family moved from Manhattan to Albany. After his father's death in 1832, Melville and his brother Gansevoort went to work to support the family; Herman attended the Albany Classical School.

After a failed effort at work as surveyor on the Erie Canal, he shipped as a cabin boy on a New York vessel bound for Liverpool, an experience later recounted in *Redburn, His First Voyage* (1849). After three years as a schoolteacher (1837–40), Melville sailed from New Bedford, Massachusetts, on the whaler *Achusnet* for an eighteen-month cruise in the South Pacific. He abandoned the ship in the Marquesas Islands and lived among the natives for several weeks, an experience that became the basis for his first books, *Typee: A Peep at Polynesian Life* (1846) and *Omoo: A Narrative of Adventures in the South Seas* (1847). Melville then shipped for Honolulu and joined the American frigate *United States* before returning home in 1844. Over the next six years, he would write *Typee, Omoo, Mardi: And a Voyage Thither* (1849), *Redburn*, and *White-Jacket: or, The World in a Man-of-War* (1850), initially achieving great fame with *Typee* as the man who lived among cannibals.

Melville married Elizabeth Shaw, the daughter of Massachusetts Supreme Court Chief Justice Lemuel Shaw, in 1847. In 1850, the Melvilles purchased Arrowhead, a farm in Pittsfield, Massachusetts, where they lived for thirteen years, raising their four children, and where Herman wrote *Moby-Dick, or the Whale* (1851), *Pierre: or, The Ambiguities* (1852), and *The Piazza Tales* (1856). There he befriended Nathaniel Hawthorne. He also wrote *Israel Potter: His Fifty Years of Exile* (1855) and *The Confidence-Man: His Masquerade* (1857). As his work suffered rapidly diminishing commercial and critical acclaim, Melville turned to lecturing at lyceums about his travels in the South Seas and about art and architecture based on his travels in Europe and the Middle East. As that venture proved unsuccessful, the Melvilles moved to New York City, where Herman secured a position as customs inspector, a job he held for nearly two decades. During those years, he continued to write, focusing almost exclusively on poetry, and published *Battle-Pieces and Aspects of the War* (1866), *Clarel* (1876), *John Marr and Other Sailors* (1888), and *Timoleon* (1891). At the time of his death on September 28, 1891, he left the manuscript of the novella *Billy Budd, Sailor: An Inside Narrative*, as well as another collection of poems, *Weeds and Wildings Chiefly: With a Rose or Two*.

ROBERT FAGGEN is the Barton Evans and H. Andrea Neves Professor of Literature at Claremont McKenna College. He is the author of *Robert Frost and the Challenge of Darwin* and the editor of *The Cambridge Companion to Robert Frost* and *Striving Towards Being: The Letters of Thomas Merton and Czeslaw Milosz*. He has also edited the Penguin Classics editions of the *Early Poems of Robert Frost* and the *Selected Poems* of Edwin Arlington Robinson.

HERMAN MELVILLE

Selected Poems

Edited with an Introduction and Notes by
ROBERT FAGGEN

PENGUIN BOOKS

PENGUIN BOOKS

Published by the Penguin Group

Penguin Group (USA) Inc., 375 Hudson Street, New York, New York 10014, U.S.A.

Penguin Group (Canada), 90 Eglinton Avenue East, Suite 700, Toronto, Ontario,
Canada M4P 2Y3 (a division of Pearson Penguin Canada Inc.)

Penguin Books Ltd, 80 Strand, London WC2R 0RL, England

Penguin Ireland, 25 St Stephen's Green, Dublin 2, Ireland
(a division of Pearson Australia Group Pty Ltd)

Penguin Books India Pvt Ltd, 11 Community Centre,
Panchsheel Park, New Delhi-110 017, India

Penguin Group (NZ), cnr Airborne and Rosedale Roads, Albany, Auckland 1310,
New Zealand (a division of Pearson New Zealand Ltd)

Penguin Books (South Africa) (Pty) Ltd, 24 Sturdee Avenue, Rosebank,
Johannesburg 2196, South Africa

Penguin Books Ltd, Registered Offices:
80 Strand, London WC2R 0RL, England

First published in Penguin Books 2006

1   3   5   7   9   10   8   6   4   2

Introduction and notes copyright © Robert Faggen, 2006
All rights reserved

LIBRARY OF CONGRESS CATALOGING IN PUBLICATION DATA
Melville, Herman, 1819–1891.
[Poems. Selections]
Selected poems/Herman Melville ; edited with an introduction and
notes by Robert Faggen.
p.   cm.
Includes bibliographical references and index.
ISBN 0 14 30.3903 2
1. Faggen, Robert.   11. Title.
PS2382.F34 2006
811'.3—dc22 20050558623

Printed in the United States of America

Contents

SELECTED POEMS

From *Battle-Pieces and Aspects of the War* (1866)

From *Clarel* (1876)

From *John Marr and Other Sailors* (1888)

From *Timoleon* (1891)

From *Weeds and Wildings Chiefly:*
With a Rose or Two (1924)

Miscellaneous Poems

Introduction

When Herman Melville committed himself to the art of poetry, he was already one of the grandest failures in the world of fiction. Upon the publication of his first book of poems, *Battle-Pieces and Aspects of the War*, in 1866, Melville was forty-five years old and had published eight novels including *Moby-Dick* (1851) and *Pierre: or, The Ambiguities* (1852) and one collection of short stories, *The Piazza Tales* (1856); several of his best books had sold only a few hundred copies. Reviews had ranged from mincing to severe; advances for new books were no longer a possibility because he owed his publishers unearned money on the old ones.

Melville had very much been a conscious participant in his own march into popular literary oblivion. After becoming one of America's first literary sex symbols at age twenty-five with the publication of *Typee*, his subsequent novels, *Omoo* and *Mardi*, tried the patience of his readers and eventually his publishers with their more sprawling metaphysical and allegorical narratives. In a chastened attempt to produce two books that were more marketable, the remarkably energetic Melville, at twenty-nine, produced in two months each *Redburn* and *White-Jacket*, the latter a glimpse of life on a "man-of-war" and a polemic against flogging in the navy. Writing in 1849 of these efforts to his father-in-law, the chief justice of the state of Massachusetts Lemuel Shaw, Melville confessed to this sympathetic benefactor "my only desire for their 'success' (as it is called) springs from my pocket & not from my heart. So far as I am individually concerned, & independent of my pocket, it is my earnest desire to write those sort of books which are said to 'fail.'—Pardon this egotism."

By 1851, Melville was in the midst of pursuing his white whale, and made it clear to Nathaniel Hawthorne that he knew that the marketplace could not go where he wanted to take his literary interests: "Dollars damn me; and the malicious Devil is forever grinning in on me, holding the door ajar. . . . What I feel most moved to write, that is banned, it will not pay. Yet, altogether, write the *other* way I cannot. So the product is final hash, and all my books are botches." Melville's reputation as the famed author of *Typee* haunted him as much as the demand of the marketplace as he continued in his lament to Hawthorne: "All Fame is patronage. Let me be infamous: there is no patronage in *that*. . . . Think of it! To go down to posterity is bad enough, any way; but to go down as 'a man who lived among the cannibals'!"

Melville worked hard and enthusiastically to rid himself of his early popularity and to engage fully with those preoccupations of his heart, however dark, that led to the end of his career, if such a mundane word could be used to describe Melville's endeavors in fiction. The great strain of his monumental literary achievement entwined with its predictable critical failure had left Melville exhausted and in poor health. With great stress in his marriage making bad matters worse, his father-in-law underwrote the one remedy that seemed to work: travel. A grand tour through Europe and then Palestine in 1856 found Melville exploring art and archaeology the way he had whaling and libraries in previous decades. Much of what he observed would become the subject matter of his journals and later of his most ambitious poetry. *The Confidence-Man: His Masquerade* (1857), a surreal adventure aboard a Mississippi steamboat, found Melville disappearing behind a shapeshifter narrator and an array of characters who challenge the reader's faith and fundamental sense of the real. Its cool, sometimes sophistic dialogues concluded with only the open-ended possibility that "something further may follow of this Masquerade." But for the next few years, the only literary opportunity that remained for Melville was the masquerade of public lectures.

He made use of his travels for a brief new career as lecturer, first trying out such topics as "The Statues of Rome" and then realizing that audiences would much rather hear more about the old adventures in "The South Seas." For three seasons, Melville was willing to oblige. Reviews were mixed, and the criticisms often leveled at the speaker's unwillingness at times to lift his head sufficiently from his text. But the public loved great sermons, and they loved Emerson. Melville could soar in exploring the tensions of Puritanism in the sermons of Father Mapple of *Moby-Dick* or Plotinus Plinlimmon's pamphlet in *Pierre: or, The Ambiguities*. But those explorations of the worldly and unworldly were for his fiction and for his private shelf. On the lecture circuit, Melville kept to travel topics and only with moderate success.

Melville had been writing poetry intensely during his years of lecturing. In 1860, he gave up the lecture circuit for a journey to California on the clipper ship *Meteor* with his brother Thomas at the helm, and he left a book of poems with his wife Lizzie to send out to publishers. Both ventures failed. The terrors of rounding Cape Horn left Melville unnerved, and he returned via Panama to New York without his brother. And the book did not find a publisher. Elizabeth Melville had asked Herman's friend and editor Everett Duyckinck for his opinion of the book and for his help in finding a publisher. Though he thought highly of the work, a response from an editor at Scribners reveals what one might expect for any first-time author of a volume of poetry:

> I have looked over Melville's Poems. I have no doubt they are excellent, they seem so to me, and I have confidence in your judgment—But I have not the heart to publish them—I doubt whether they would more than pay expenses, and as I have issued two volumes of Poems [by E. C. Stedman & G. P. Morris] this season and the prospect is that neither of them will pay I don't feel like making another venture in that line.

It is unlikely that we will ever know what was in that first volume, though we may speculate that some of the poems later formed the section of *Timoleon*, which Melville published privately in 1891 in an edition of twenty-five copies, entitled *Fruit of Travel Long Ago.* But it may never be possible to explain why or how Melville made the transition from prose to formal verse. With the very notable exception of Thomas Hardy (whose *The Dynasts* has often been compared with Melville's *Clarel*), few modern novelists working in English have successfully made a transition from prose to poetry. One could hardly accuse Melville's fiction of failing to be poetic, if what one means by that term is the evocation of a figurative and symbolic realm. In his fiction Melville had taken the greatest risks and given the world the most remarkable variety of rhetoric and rhythms—from sermons to aphorisms to rhapsody. Where other fiction writers may have been inspired, Melville was possessed by the "blasts resistless." Where other writers had exhibited skill and craft, Melville had given us the "fine hammered steel of woe." But would he wish his divinely extravagant energy to fit the confines of formal verse? Did the change in form herald a change in Melville's subject matter?

By the late 1850s Melville was writing and reading a great deal of poetry; his library reveals volumes of poets—Collins, Cowper, Emerson, Thomson, Heine, Hood, Chaucer, Moore, Arnold, Byron—all annotated and underscored from those years. Poetry was about as far from the fame of *Typee* as Melville could go, and as indifferent to the marketplace. A short lyric of Melville's in response to the Greek architecture he saw on his travels in the late 1850s suggests the pleasure he took in classical form and, perhaps, a rejection of the extravagances of romantic expansiveness. The poem could be taken either as an observation or a resolution of a formalist poetics, an architecture toward which Melville aspired in his own poetry:

> Not magnitude, not lavishness,
>   But Form—the Site;
> Not innovating wilfullness,
>   But reverence for the Archetype.

By the outbreak of the Civil War, Melville's employment and health difficulties had grown only worse. In 1861, he sought a

consular post in Washington and even met Lincoln briefly at the
White House but received no position. There was some suspi-
cion that his father-in-law's enforcement of fugitive slave laws
had cast a shadow on his reputation. But Lemuel Shaw died
that March. Later in the year Melville severely injured his back
when he was thrown from a wagon. Unable to handle life at his
farm in Arrowhead, he eventually purchased his brother's home
on East 26th Street in New York City where he would live until
his death in 1891. Hawthorne's death in 1864 was the likely—
though by no means certain—inspiration for "Monody,"
which gives us a glimpse into Melville's isolation.

> To have known him, to have loved him
> After loneness long;
> And then to be estranged in life,
> And neither in the wrong;
> And now for death to set his seal—
> Ease me, a little ease, my song!

> By wintry hills his hermit-mound
> The sheeted snow-drifts drape,
> And houseless there the snow-bird flits
> Beneath the fir-trees' crape:
> Glazed now with ice the cloistral vine
> That hid the shyest grape.

Though Melville's efforts at poetry increased greatly just be-
fore the outbreak and at the beginning of the Civil War, his de-
cision to assemble an entire volume on the subject, he tells us in
the brief but fascinating preface to *Battle-Pieces*, "originated in
an impulse imparted by the fall of Richmond." If we take him
at his word, then, it was not until April of 1865, when the po-
litical center of the military effort to destroy the Union had
failed, that Melville could see the way to assemble his pieces
into a whole. Several years earlier, after the Emancipation
Proclamation, Lincoln had declared, "We are like the whalers
who have been on long chase. We have at last got the harpoon
into the monster, but we must now look how to steer, or with

one flop of his tail he will send us all into eternity." No one could have better appreciated the poignancy of Lincoln's words than Melville. The unfolding events of April 1865 and beyond would make them even more ironic. Melville's *Battle-Pieces and Aspects of the War* provides in seventy-two poems a deeply conflicted, ambiguous portrait of the nation marching through an uncertain, incomprehensible war and hovering on the edge of a bitter and dark peace.

Battle-Pieces is a rich and varied book of elegies, odes, marches, dialogues, and a ballad depicting an episode of guerrilla warfare. Despite Edmund Wilson's claim that Melville's book is "versified journalism; a chronicle of the patriotic feelings of an anxious, middle-aged non-combatant, as day by day he reads the bulletins from the front," only about a third of the poems focus on actual battles. The rest can be said to be in other senses "aspects" of the war, mostly philosophical, dramatic, imaginative, and historical-political viewed from many planes of regard. But the book can hardly be characterized in a simple way as expressing "patriotic feelings"; its moods and voices are varied and, as one might expect from its author and its subject matter, multifaceted. Though the poems are arranged chronologically according to the history of the war, Melville was surely being selective about that history. When Melville was in pursuit of a whale, he loved to digress, and digression is among his greatest gifts. No doubt Melville regarded the Civil War as a significant subject, but it is striking how different a poetic he adopted for it from the one proclaimed in *Moby-Dick*. There Ishmael declares, "One often hears of writers that rise and swell with their subject, though often it may seem an ordinary one. . . . Such, and, so magnifying, is the virtue of a large and liberal theme! We expand to its bulk. To produce a mighty book, you must choose a mighty theme." In treating the Civil War, Melville exhibits a great deal of restraint, tact, and reserve in reaction to the awesome loss that had been experienced.

Melville cultivated a poetic language suited to a new kind of war and consciousness of war, one in which the heroism of individuals became subsumed in the instrumentality of brutal

machinery. Melville gave dignified and sometimes elegiac por-
traits of individual heroes such as "Stonewall Jackson" and "A
Dirge for McPherson," but otherwise he depicted humanity in
Battle-Pieces as marching or crushed beyond the hopes of Or-
phic fame. At one moment in the book, Melville contrasts the
beautiful wooden warship of old, the *Temeraire* (as painted by
Turner),—"But Fame has nailed your battle-flags—/Your ghost
it sails before:/O, the navies old and oaken,/O, the Temeraire
no more!"—with the new machinery in "A Utilitarian View of
the *Monitor*'s Fight." "Grimed war" demands a different use,
perhaps a different language in contrast to "rhyme's barbaric
cymbal":

> Plain be the phrase, yet apt the verse,
>   More ponderous than nimble;
> For since grimed War here laid aside
> His Orient pomp, 'twould ill befit
>   Overmuch to ply
> The rhyme's barbaric cymbal.

This war introduces a new machinery, yet it is one that this poet
can hail because its

> . . . plain mechanic power
> Plied cogently in War now placed—
>   Where War belongs—
> Among the trades and artisans.

Technical and barbaric, it is indeed what war *is*, and Melville
can find a language appropriate for its inhuman "calculations":

> Yet this was battle, and intense—
>   Beyond the strife of fleets heroic;
> Deadlier, closer, calm 'mid storm;
> No passion; all went on by crank,
>   Pivot, and screw,
> And calculations of caloric.

The conclusion heralds the clarification that this conflict has brought to the nature of warfare: "War yet shall be, but warriors / Are now but operatives." "The Portent," the lyric in striking trochees that begins the book, presents the mysterious figure of the executed John Brown *"Hanging from the beam, / Slowing swaying (such the law), / Gaunt the shadow on your green, / Shenandoah!"* His presence appears almost an embodiment of the conflict of rebellion and the law of state played out against the implacable consequences of time in the peaceful valley. His *"streaming beard is shown / (Weird John Brown), / the meteor of the war."* Shown by whom or what we are never told. Brown appears as another operative or instrument in fated, "wyrd," history without canonization as saint or demon that was common at the time. This detachment and the accompanying sense that hundreds of thousands were being killed and maimed by forces far beyond anything comprehensible and for ends that could be reasonably justified haunt *Battle-Pieces* and, no doubt, has troubled readers since its publication.

Melville enthusiastically personified the war machine as avenging deity in his ballad-lyric "The Swamp Angel," a poem about a Union cannon that repeatedly fired on and contributed greatly to the destruction of Charleston. The divine and natural fuse ironically in this engine that also embodies an avenging slave, not unlike Babo of *Benito Cereno:*

> There is a coal-black Angel
>   With a thick Afric lip,
> And he dwells (like the hunted and harried)
>   In a swamp where the green frogs dip.
> But his face is against a City
>   Which is over a bay of the sea,
> And he breathes with a breath that is blastment,
>   And dooms by a far decree.

In the almost relentless, energetic drive of its anapestic trimeter, the poem builds over five stanzas, taking great delight in the

destruction this black engine wreaks on the Southern city and
its traditional Christian angels and icons:

> Is this the proud City? the scorner
>   Which never would yield the ground?
> Which mocked at the coal-black Angel?
>   The cup of despair goes round.
> Vainly she calls upon Michael
>   (The white man's seraph was he),
> For Michael has fled from the tower
>   To the Angel over the sea.

Yet, the concluding quatrain contains at first a couplet that may
be taken as dismissal of pity, given "our guilty kind," while the
second couplet, with its extra metrical beat, does, perhaps, sug-
gest an exhortation about having gone too far in cruelty:

> Who weeps for the woeful City
>   Let him weep for our guilty kind;
> Who joys at her wild despairing—
>   Christ, the Forgiver, convert his mind.

It may seem somewhat sardonic for Melville to invoke
"Christ" given the predominant figure of the poem or, perhaps,
in light of the warrior God in the opening stanza of "The Battle
for Mississippi." Julia Ward Howe's *Battle Hymn of the Re-
public*, one of the most popular poems of the day, provided an
image of God with a scythe killing and as a redeemer dying:

> In the beauty of the lilies Christ was born across the sea,
> With a glory in his bosom that transfigures you and me:
> As he died to make men holy, let us die to make men free,
>   While God is marching on.

In "On the Slain Collegians," Melville provides what seems
an almost direct counter to her thrilling logic with the elegiac
reflection that the young of both North and South "went forth

with blessings given / By priests and mothers in the name of Heaven; / And honor in both was chief. / Warred one for right Right, and one for Wrong? So be it; but they both were young—/ Each grape to his cluster clung, / All their elegies are sung." In the hush of "Shiloh," perhaps the greatest of *Battle-Pieces,* the already dissipated groans and prayers of dead soldiers from both sides converge under the haunting swallows circling the battlefield. Shiloh, a name that sounds like a sigh and also means "peace with God," is not only the location of one of the bloodiest battles of the Civil War. It also evokes the biblical place where God once spoke to Eli the priest and Hannah's son Samuel but eventually became the corrupt city of the Israelites that God caused to be defeated and eventually utterly destroyed. Melville's single-sentence elegiac utterance—punctuated by the chilling parenthetical interjection "What like a bullet can undeceive!"—points to the silence in which "friend and foe" are stripped of pride of victory and resentment of loss. The bullet ironically becomes the liberating technological angel of war, and war itself does the work that religion cannot. Nature embodied in the swallows "wheeling" above the dead completes its smooth cycles, indifferent to the momentary noise of human history. All forces seem to lose before a God that has withdrawn into silence, an awful and indifferent silence Melville had been pointing toward in *Moby-Dick,* "Bartleby," and *Pierre.*

Melville followed closely accounts of the battles from *The Rebellion Record* and often sought to view the front lines. He finally saw some action in April of 1864. Traveling with his brother Allen to Washington, D.C., he went to inspect cousin Henry Gansevoort's regiment in Vienna, Virginia. They met the camp commander, Colonel Charles Russell Lowell, and his young wife, Josephine, who was pregnant. Lowell was planning a scouting party to rout the Confederate guerrillas known as "Mosby's Raiders," named for their commander, George P. Mosby, who staged commando raids on Union supply lines. Ever the adventurer, Melville joined the cavalry patrol as they made their way toward Aldie, Virginia. The resulting ballad, the penultimate poem of *Battle-Pieces,* gives us a frightening portrait

of chance and death in the display of would-be heroism and ad-
venture. "The weakest thing is lustihood," and the young colo-
nel's heroics are met only by "a ball through the heart."

Melville's battle scenes differ strikingly from those of his con-
temporaries, particularly Whitman's. Though Whitman had
never seen battle, he offers a vivid and sentimental snapshot of
one in "The Artilleryman's Vision." Melville's contemplation of
battle remains elegiac, trying to imagine the incomprehensible
suffering and bewilderment of those who died, wondering if the
immense sacrifice of life could possibly be justified. Melville at-
tempts to unify through contemplation of the undeceived dead;
Whitman through sympathy with the wounded, whom he had
tended extensively as a psychological nurse in Washington hos-
pitals. Whitman's *Drum-Taps* expresses an optimism that the
war will lead to a more transcendent unity through death. *Battle-
Pieces*, riddled with Melville's sense of irony and dark vision of
human nature, points, if anything, toward great prudence and
restraint in the North's handling of its power and the glory ac-
corded to its victorious warriors.

The extent of Melville's irony can be measured from the ded-
ication of the volume, the rhetoric of which would be suited to
the very grandest of nineteenth-century war monuments: "The
Battle-Pieces in this Volume are Dedicated to the Memory of
the Three Hundred Thousand who in the War for the Mainte-
nance of the Union Fell Devotedly Under the Flag of Their Fa-
thers." Melville's language for the war and in referring only to
the Union dead clearly shows his allegiances. But reading the
ambiguities and contradictions of the poems that follow cer-
tainly mitigates any sense of triumphal celebration. His invo-
cation of the immense number of dead as well as the religious
overtone of "devotedly" in the context of "flag of their fa-
thers" becomes more pointedly and painfully ironic, a kind of
idolatrous self-sacrifice of blind Isaacs following blind Abra-
hams, in light of such poems memorable poems as "The March
into Virginia":

> Youth must its ignorant impulse lend—
> Age finds place in the rear.

> All wars are boyish, and are fought by boys,
> The champions and enthusiasts of the state:
> Turbid ardors and vain joys
>   Not barrenly abate—
> Stimulants to the power mature,
>   Preparatives of fate.

The stanza typifies the way Melville's somewhat gnarled syntax forces us to reflect on the elusiveness of agency and power in war; the "turbid ardors" of the boys "abate" (intransitively) only to become the mysterious "stimulants" to a more elusive "power mature" and "fate." Melville gives us more than anything a sharp dirge for the young boys unwittingly destroyed at what he cruelly puns as a "berrying party," for "The College Colonel" who though alive embodies "A still rigidity and pale—/An Indian aloofness lones his brow;/He has lived a thousand years/Compressed in battle's pains and prayers,/Marches and watches slow." His poignant and ambivalent attitude toward war and an uncertain future, expressed in often terse phrases, harsh diction, off-rhymes, strange meters, and odd syntax, seemed unpoetic to critics looking for the rhetorical lather of a James Russell Lowell.

This is not to say that Melville cannot and does not grant nobility to the warriors. He does so in a way that allows for the incomprehensibility of suffering without imposing upon that suffering with grave truths, as in "The College Colonel":

> It is not that a leg is lost,
>   It is not that an arm is maimed,
> It is not that the fever has racked—
>   Self he has long disclaimed.
>
> But all through the Seven Days' Fight,
>   And deep in the Wilderness grim,
> And in the field-hospital tent,
>   And Petersburg crater, and dim
> Lean brooding in Libby, there came—
>   Ah heaven!—what *truth* to him.

Melville's perception of worldly manliness and virtue in sol-
diers creates an erotic bond of union, though less personal and
more detached than in Whitman, as he presented it in "On the
Photograph of a Corps Commander":

> Nothing can lift the heart of man
>   Like manhood in a fellow-man.
> The thought of heaven's great King afar
>   But humbles us—too weak to scan;
> But manly greatness men can span,
>   And feel the bonds that draw.

Worldly virtue in *Battle-Pieces* remains, nevertheless, severely
circumscribed. "Commemorative of a Naval Victory" begins
with a vision of sailors of "the gentlest breed" and "sworded
noblemen" but concludes with an emblem of primordial dark-
ness that shadows Melville's work:

> But seldom the laurel wreath is seen
>   Unmixed with pensive pansies dark;
> There's a light and a shadow on every man
>   Who at last attains his lifted mark—
>   Nursing through night the ethereal spark.
> Elate he never can be;
> He feels that spirits which glad had hailed his worth,
>   Sleep in oblivion.—The shark
> Glides white through the phosphorous sea.

Here, as elsewhere in Melville's writing, the shark appears to
represent not only those elusive forces that govern the destruc-
tion of matter but also the private rapacity that moves stealth-
ily beneath the public surfaces of civic virtue and honor.

Battle-Pieces is a "civil" book in so far as Melville exhibits ele-
giac restraint. The narrative presence is remote and, in some
sense, almost Virgilian and statesmanlike, especially in the "sup-
plement," the only overt piece of political prose that Melville
ever wrote except for the chapter in *White-Jacket* condemning

flogging in the navy and his polemics against the racism of Christian missionaries in *Omoo*. Rhetorically, it is a subtle plea for restraint, a Machiavellian argument for Christian forgiveness in the interest of the future of the Union. The detachment and perspective conveyed in the poems give them a great deal of their power; they are anything but jingoistic or nationalistic. When the book appears to be on the verge of becoming so, Melville introduces an odd reversal or irony that more often than not leaves the reader startled or baffled. After the section of the book entitled "Verses Inscriptive and Memorial," Melville takes us back into bloodshed with the chilling ballad "The Scout Toward Aldie," which he follows with "Lee in the Capitol." The final poem, "A Meditation," spoken by a Northern veteran, asks:

> If men for new agreement yearn,
>   Then old upraiding best forbear:
> *"The South's the sinner!"* Well, so let it be;
> But shall the North sin worse, and stand the Pharisee?

Battle-Pieces remains a varied music of ambiguities and neither a panoramic journalistic record nor a triumphal march in celebration of the Union victory or of peace.

Some critics have puzzled that Melville's Civil War poems were not more outspoken about slavery. First, it should be noted that one of the finest poems in the book, "Formerly a Slave," inspired by a painting by Elihu Vedder, gives prophetic vision to the sense of loss—past, present, and far future—from slavery. "The March to the Sea" and "The Swamp Angel" represent blacks joining the forces that crush the South. Of all nineteenth-century American writers, Melville ranks among the least sentimental and condescending in his depiction of blacks. The author who gave us condemnations of flogging, satires on the condescending assumptions of Christan missionaries, and such a penetrating and prophetic story as *Benito Cereno*, with its final, brutally ironic image of Babo's—the leader of the slave insurrection—head displayed opposite St. Bartholomew's Church (named for a Christian martyr who was also beheaded), did not need to write antislavery broadsides poem to prove his contempt.

But by the end of the war, Melville was less concerned about slavery than about the problem of peace and Reconstruction and about the ability of the North to forgive the South. Melville's profound distrust of human nature on both sides of the civil divide withered his hopes for the republic beyond the institution of slavery. Distrust of the mob tempered his faith in democracy. In one of the fine poems of the book, "The House-top," the narrator witnesses from a city roof the New York draft riots of July 1863 in which blacks were tortured and lynched and sees "All civil charms / And priestly spells which late held hearts in awe— / Fear-bound, subjected to a better sway / Than sway of self; these like a dream dissolve, / And man rebounds whole aeons back in nature." Yet the poem concludes with an equally dark depiction of the imposition of the military and, worse, the city's eager welcome of the draconian measures taken to quell the riots:

> Wise Draco comes, deep in the midnight roll
> Of black artillery; he comes, though late;
> In code corroborating Calvin's creed
> And cynic tyrannies of honest kings;
> He comes, nor parlies; and the Town, redeemed,
> Gives thanks devout; nor, being thankful, heeds
> The grimy slur on the Republic's faith implied,
> Which holds that Man is naturally good,
> And—more—is Nature's Roman, never to be scourged.

The idea of "redemption" or thanks "devout" could not be more ironic in terms of the general corrosion of faith, the "grimy slur" on human nature that the riots and the war in general have created. Melville underscores the irony by changing the pentameter blank verse to Virgilian (Roman) hexameter in the final line, as if to emphasize in the dignity of meter what cannot be found in life. When in "Misgivings" Melville refers to "the world's fairest hope linked with man's foulest crime," he may have meant not only slavery but fratricide, which in

"On the Slain Collegians" he calls "the mask of Cain." At the moment of the publication of *Battle-Pieces* in 1866, it was *that* crime that Melville felt most needed underscoring to keep the ship of state afloat.

The political moment of the book, thus, cannot be ignored. Melville does not have a simple political aim, but his "pieces" and "aspects" appeared calculated to create a sense of commonality precisely by not providing an overarching symbolic or epic structure. He wanted to provide a variety of voices and perspectives as though to cool the kind of universal claim to truth and justice that would make the peace intolerable for many, particularly in the South. Though the Civil War was a grand subject, Melville approached it with detachment. The very title of the book suggests the approach not of realism but of paintings or specific scenes, and, as in a gallery, perspectives, underscored by the subtitle, "Aspects of the War." Melville combines specific detail and historical reference to particular battles, while other poems are metaphysical in their characterization of the general conflict. He was especially attentive to the problem of fragmentary knowledge. In "Donelson," for example, Melville uses pieces of different newspapers accounts precisely to show the limited perspectives of the ongoing conflict. Although he regularly collected information about the war, the word "pieces" suggests a fragmentation of perspective not to mention the shattering of consciousness, if not conscience, that came with the war. In "The Armies of the Wilderness":

> None can narrate that strife in the pines,
>   A seal is on it—Sabaean lore!
> Obscure as the wood, the entangled rhyme
>   But hints at the maze of war—
> Vivid glimpses or livid through peopled gloom,
>   And fires which creep and char—
> A riddle of death, of which the slain
>   Sole solvers are.

Melville's poetry paradoxically gives us a sense of the grand immensity, confusion, and horror of the war precisely by allowing us only to have ruins, "aspects," "pieces," however well-honed the shrapnel.

Melville no doubt remained alert to the nation's need to make sense of its division and suffering in terms of religious epic and theodicy, a war of good versus evil. Attentive readers have noted not only the biblical but especially Miltonic allusions haunting *Battle-Pieces* (and, of course, Melville generally), particularly phrases and passages from the War in Heaven of *Paradise Lost* Book VI. It may appear as though Milton provided a mythic point of departure for an otherwise fragmented history. It should not be in the least surprising that Melville would reflect on the great Puritan poem of the English Civil War as he contemplated his nation's own civil strife, a struggle that many sought to understand in terms of theodicy and divine plan. "The Conflict of Convictions," a lyric with varying stanza forms and choruses, invokes many of the great theological questions of free will and divine providence as well as many of the great Miltonic heroes and figures in the Christian mythic pantheon:

> On starry heights
>   A bugle wails the long recall;
> Derision stirs the deep abyss,
>   Heaven's ominous silence over all.
> Return, return, O eager Hope,
>   And face man's latter fall.
> Events, they make the dreamers quail;
> Satan's old age is strong and hale,
> A disciplined captain, gray in skill,
> And Raphael a white enthusiast still;
> Dashed aims, at which Christ's martyrs pale,
> Shall Mammon's slaves fulfill?

Milton's warring angels in this, "man's latter fall," have become strikingly human, "a disciplined captain" and "a white enthusiast." Melville adds the damning suggestion here that all warring factions may be "Mammon's slaves," beholden to the corruptions of greed. Melville's own nationalism would continue to remain skeptical and limited long after the war.

God in Melville seems invoked almost as a rhetorical prop; the Miltonic allusions become what one might expect from a late romantic writer—a perception that Milton's theodicy was not convincing and that God was either "a man of war" or quite absent from human affairs altogether. He gives us "Gettysburg: The Check" in which God defeats Dagon only to follow that poem with the utterly depraved vision of the North in "The House-top." Melville concludes "The Fall of Richmond" with "But God is in Heaven, and Grant in the Town,/And Right through the might is Law—/ *God's way adore*"; some readers have justifiably detected a sardonic grin behind the jingoistic theology. Melville allowed other voices than the triumphant voices of the North into the book. "The March to the Sea," a poem about Sherman's horrific campaign (each stanza ends with sardonic couplet "It was glorious glad marching,/ That marching to the sea"), precedes "The Frenzy in the Wake," spoken by a Confederate soldier. He reflects on the brutality of Sherman's march and contemplates the possibility someday of retribution:

> We were sore deceived—an awful host!
>   They move like a roaring wind.
> Have we gamed and lost? but even despair
>   Shall never our hate rescind.

Melville has allowed him an unmistakable echo from Satan's speech in Hell of *Paradise Lost* Book I: "What though the field be lost?/ all is not lost; th' unconquerable will,/ And study of revenge, immortal hate. And courage never to submit or yield." In his note to the poem, Melville attempted to make it clear that the views of the speaker are not necessarily those of the author and that the poem, for example, could not be held responsible for "the historic tragedy of the 14th of April," namely the assassination of Lincoln. Melville also compared Sherman's tactics of destruction unfavorably with the restraint of Pompey during the Roman Civil War but concludes that differences in geography might account for Sherman's "sweeping measure." But he adds, "After consideration, it [the poem] was allowed to remain."

Why he allowed the poem to remain despite its volatile and subversive rhetoric goes to the heart of the dark side of Melville and his vision of the war as well as his struggle with Milton and theodicy. The second stanza of "The Frenzy of the Wake" provides a more revealing analogy, particularly from the standpoint of Milton (and, in terms of the flag, revealing the poignancy of the dedication of the *Battle-Pieces*). Here the speaker invokes the biblical Jael of Judges, the woman who killed Sisera by driving a stake through his temple:

> Shall Time, avenging every woe,
>   To us that jot allot
> Which Israel thrilled when Sisera's brow
>   Showed gaunt and showed the clot?
>   Curse on their foreheads, cheeks, and eyes—
>   The Northern faces—true
>   To the flag we hate, the flag whose stars
>   Like planets strike us through.

This impassioned lyric curse has more power than the analogies to victorious Israel in the opening stanza of "The Battle for the Mississippi." But it was precisely the use of this analogy to Jael's murder of Sisera by Milton in *Samson Agonistes* that provoked some of Melville's most interesting speculation about Milton's mind. In his copy of Milton's *Samson Agonistes*, Melville marked Delila's rebuke to the blind, imprisoned Samson, in which she proclaimed that she will be "not less renown'd than in Mount *Ephraim*, / Jael, who with inhospitable guile / Smote *Sisera* sleeping through the temples nail'd." Certainly there was dark irony in Delila invoking Jael, a hero of Israel, as a model for herself as she taunts Samson. Melville's marginal comment seizes upon the irony and refers to his initial suspicions about Milton's entire "intent": "There is basis for the doubt expressed by A. Marvell in his lines to Milton on the publication of P. Lost. There was a *twist* in Milton. From its place, the above marked has an interesting significance." Melville refers, of course, to Andrew Marvell's prefatory poem to *Paradise Lost* in which he wrote that "the argument / Held me awhile misdoubting his intent,/That he would ruine (for I saw him strong) the sacred truths to Fable and old song." Melville had marked *that* passage in *Paradise Lost* and wrote (as if Marvell were having a brandy with him): "It is still misdoubted by some. First impressions are generally true, too, Andrew." What did Melville misdoubt? At the very least, he probably doubted how far one could justify violence and punishment in the name of God while remaining *exempt* from culpability.

In "Lee in the Capitol," Melville gives the defeated general questions urgent for the future of the Union and that would haunt Reconstruction:

> Foreboding, cleaved to the natural part—
> Was this the unforgivable sin?
> These noble spirits are yet yours to win.
> Shall the great North go Sylla's way?
> Proscribe? prolong the evil day?
> Confirm the curse? infix the hate?
> In Union's name forever alienate?
> From reason who can urge the plea—
> Freemen conquerors of the free?
> When blood returns to the shrunken vein,
> Shall the wound of the Nation bleed again?

Though clearly a Unionist, Melville has given more dramatic voice and presence to Lee and the Southern defeated. His psyche, though not his politics, went with those who said no in thunder to great force and who had suffered galling defeat at its hands. Questions of sin, history, and power in a democracy continued to trouble Melville as he moved from the wounded of *Battle-Pieces* to the spiritually wounded pilgrims, most particularly Mortmain and Ungar, of *Clarel*.

The Civil War was not for the nation a wholly purifying event; nor was *Battle-Pieces* for Melville a cathartic, poetic tragedy. The fiasco of Reconstruction and the grossness of the ensuing Gilded Age left Melville as ever the wanderer seeking newer landscapes in which to test and purify the self. Melville's marriage had begun to undergo its worst strain. For the first time,

Elizabeth considered legal separation, and her minister, Henry Bellows, proposed a kidnapping scheme to provide her sanctuary from her husband with relatives in Boston (the plan was scrapped at the urging of her family). The Melvilles then suffered an enormous shock. Late in 1866 their oldest son, Malcolm, had come home late one night and not come out of his room the next morning. Herman broke down his door and found his son dead with a gunshot wound to the head. Though ruled a suicide, Melville and his wife believed it was an accident.

Not long after, Melville began work on a narrative poem that would consume him for nearly six years, more than any other work of his life. *Clarel: A Poem and Pilgrimage in the Holy Land*. Melville gives some of his most profound expression to his doubt and fears of the future of democracy through such characters as Ungar, an ex-Confederate and part Indian and Catholic. Biographers focusing strongly on Melville's life have ignored the immense richness of the poem as response to an epoch and a new, though less dramatic war: the warfare between science and religion. The epilogue to *Clarel* begins with a question that frames the effect of four centuries of challenge to faith. "If Luther's Day expands to Darwin's year / shall that exclude the hope—foreclose the fear?" Where has the great Protestant pilgrim found himself after four hundred years of wandering? In 1874, two years before the publication of *Clarel*, John Draper, the eminent historian of the Civil War and president of Cornell University, published his landmark *History of the Conflict between Religion and Science*, a book that established the "warfare" metaphor to describe the relations of religion and science. Draper was reacting to the Vatican Encyclical of 1870, establishing papal infallibility as part of the threat of material science. The world was one thing and faith another realm, something that became increasingly problematic, though, in the realm of politics. Draper feared that Protestantism could follow the model of Vatican control. Melville found the theological reactions to science unsatisfying. And he no doubt had his own profound attractions to the world of nature.

The poem is written in iambic tetrameter, and Melville saw the flexibility that meter had given Whittier in his highly successful and popular *Snowbound* of 1866. However, Melville entertained no such audience for this eighteen thousand-line poem. Lord Byron's *The Giaour*, *The Siege of Corinth*, and *Mazeppa*, as well as Sir Walter Scott's *The Lady of the Lake* and *The Lay of the Last Minstrel*, would also be likely precedents. He no doubt had in mind Butler's satiric *Hudibras*, itself a satire on Spenser's *Faerie Queen* and all pretenses of puritanical pilgrimage. Melville was in a philosophical and not satirical mode, and although *Clarel*'s pilgrims quest and companions often verge on becoming unmasked as merely mad, the quest never erodes nor becomes cynical. Difficult and demanding, the poem is also hauntingly beautiful and mysterious because Melville struggles so deeply with conflict of reason and faith.

A decade earlier Melville himself had set out on his own tour through the Holy Land; he saw Hawthorne for the last time in Lancashire, England, and took a walk by the shore. Hawthorne's journal entry imagines Melville as a nomad of imponderable theological problems:

> . . . we took a pretty long walk together, and sat down in a hollow among the sand hills (sheltering ourselves from the high, cool wind) and smoked a cigar. Melville, as he always does, began to reason of Providence and futurity, and of everything that lies beyond human ken, and informed me that he had "pretty much made up his mind to be annihilated"; but still he does not seem to rest in that anticipation; and, I think, will never rest until he gets a hold of a definite belief. It is strange how he persists—and has persisted ever since I knew him, and probably long before—in wandering to and fro over these deserts, as dismal and monotonous as the sand hills amid which we were sitting. He can neither believe, nor be comfortable in his unbelief; and he is too honest and courageous not to try to do one or the other. If he were a religious man, he would be one of the most truly religious and reverential; he has a very high and noble nature, and better worth immortality than most of us.

Clarel, then, is the full embodiment of Melville's "wandering to and fro over the deserts of faith," and the search for belief in a

world dominated by materialism, history, and science. Devoted
readers of Melville's fiction will find a continuation and not a
radical departure from his earlier quest. If Captain Ahab sought
to strike through the pasteboard mask of the whale and reach be-
yond the wall to the "inscrutable thing," in this desert quest we
find Clarel seeking to understand what faith, if any, lies behind
the masks of his fellow pilgrims, and what spirit, if any, haunts
the stony ruins, rubble, and dust of Palestine. But Clarel's first
search is to find faith through love. He is betrothed to Ruth, a
Jew, before his pilgrimage, and we see a conflict between desires
of the kind Melville once described in the story "The Piazza,"
where Fidele pines away because her lover is out wandering.
Clarel, though, imagines Luke being led by Jesus to Emmaus:

> Sudden I came in random play
> "Here to Emmaus is the way;"
> And Luke's narration straight recurred,
> How two falterers' hearts were stirred
> Meeting the arisen (then unknown)
> And listening to his lucid word
> As here in place they traveled on.
>   That scene in Clarel's temper, bred
> A novel sympathy, which said—
> I, too, I too; could *I* but meet
> Some stranger of a lore replete,
> Who, marking how my looks betray
> The dumb thoughts clogging here my feet,
> Would question me, expound and prove,
> And make my heart to burn with love—
> Emmaus were no dream to-day!

So, Clarel seeks that love, and he seeks it in his strange and mys-
terious fellow travelers, whose monologues and dialogues both
reveal and conceal their souls' aspirations and deep wounds.
Though Clarel's desire appears to be for *agape*, divine love, it
grows more apparent that it is a confused erotic love. Through-
out the poem we discover in particular the intensity of that desire
in relation to several of the other pilgrims, in particular, Vine,

whom Melville biographers, from Newton Arvin to Hershel
Parker, have discussed in great detail as a portrait of Hawthorne.

In many ways, the fractured student that was the Ishmael of
Moby-Dick is at the center of *Clarel*, seeking not only to believe
but to find an individual in whom to believe. The object of
belief—the whale—and nature become less important in this
poem than the souls of the pilgrims themselves. And they are a
fascinating array presented in dialogue and conflict, sometimes
representing particular aspects of the nineteenth-century intellec-
tual scene. There is Margoth, for example, a geologist who re-
lentlessly adheres to a reductive materialist position. He is a
particularly important figure in the overall drama of the poem,
given the symbolic emphasis on rock and stone as the foundation
of old faith, though not as important psychologically as the
darkly wounded figures of Agath and Mortmain. Agath, an old
Greek timoneer, provides a relentless and brutal vision of Pales-
tine as a bleak volcanic island where the only survivng life is a
tortoise; it is one of the most poetically haunting sections of the
poem, and goes to the heart of the Darwinian challenge to faith.
Mortmain, a Swede who has seen the limits of human evil in the
revolutions of 1848, sings brilliant apocalyptic hymns to the
Wormwood Star, an idealistic revolutionary who has collapsed
into a prophet of darkness. From the Civil War, Melville gives us
Ungar, a wounded Southern Indian and Catholic, "a wandering
Ishmael from the West," who in his own tortured way searches
for religious truth. These characters, powerful and sometimes
searing in their doubt, stand in contrast to another group of more
sanguine, if slightly naive and literal-minded, pilgrim-wanderers:
Derwent, a pleasant Anglican with a benign view of God and na-
ture, and Nehemiah, an evangelist and millenarian who provides
a window into American sectarian orthodoxy.

The pilgrimage has really much more to do with how these
characters spin their faith and doubts against the world and
each other. Sacred places in the Holy Land only serve to under-
score that faith and perhaps can no longer be found in the relics
and ruins of the past nor in nature but only tentatively within
the self.

The terrors of the ocean that haunted *Moby-Dick* have given way to the terrors of the desert, and Melville's poetic descriptions are among the greatest we have:

> Sands immense
> Impart the oceanic sense:
> The flying grit like scud is made:
> Pillars of sand which whirl about
> Or arc along in colonnade,
> True kin to the water-spout.
> Yonder on the horizon, red
> With storm, see there the caravan
> Struggling long-drawn, dispirited;
> Mark how it labors like a fleet
> Dismasted, which like the cross-winds fan
> In crippled disaster of retreat from
> From battle.—

The analogy between ocean and desert, "true kin," underlies a fundamental awareness in the poem of the geological forces that change the shape of the earth and threaten to change the nature of faith, itself in retreat.

Clarel observes the dialogues between the pilgrims over the relative value of nature and scripture, books or the material forces that erode the books. Beyond that, he observes the characters themselves, looking for what drives them to their beliefs, and these are the psychological moments that make the poem particularly fascinating. Not since *Moby-Dick* does Melville allow us to observe his characters in such unguarded moments, as they fall away from themselves in silent glimpses. Melville is capable of embracing as many forms of skepticism as possible on the way to faith, but he is most attracted to the way not only of doubt but of suffering, the way of the cross. But as is often the case in Melville, the more intense and darker characters appear more compelling—particularly Mortmain and Ungar.

What amid all of the discourse can we glean of Melville's theological concerns? He certainly has them. We find the narrator, for example, telling in summary a dialogue of all the pilgrims in a canto entitled "The High Desert," in which the retreat of faith and the challenge of science appear to reanimate the more ancient heresies of Gnosticism with its privileging of knowledge over faith and its dualistic vision of a wicked demiurge God of the world in conflict with an utterly transcendent God of peace:

> Here in apt review
> They call to mind Abel and Cain—
> Ormuzd involved with Ahriman
> In deadly lock. Were those gods gone?
> Or under other names lived on?
> The theme they started. 'Twas averred
> That, in old Gnostic pages blurred,
> Jehovah was construed to be
> Author of evil, yea, its god;
> And Christ divine His contrary:
> A god was held against a god,
> But Christ revered alone. Herefrom,
> If inference availeth aught
> (For still the topic pressed they home)
> The twofold Testaments become
> Transmitters of Chaldaic thought
> By implication. If no more
> Those Gnostic heretics prevail
> Which shook the East from shore to shore,
> Their strife forgotten now and pale;
> Yet, with the sects, that old revolt
> Now reappears, if in assault
> Less frank: none say Jehovah's evil,
> None gainsay that He bears the rod;
> Scarce that; but there's dismission civil,
> And Jesus is the indulgent God.
> This change, this dusking change that slips
> (Like the penumbra o'er the sun),
> Over the faith transmitted down;
> Foreshadows it complete eclipse?

Melville's refiguring of Gnosticism presents brilliantly the modern crisis of religious faith: a concern that if a good creator exists he must be something other than the God of the earth or matter. The God of the world may only be a demiurge of matter or a terrible fiction of the mind of man. What, then, of Jesus, and of faith through suffering? Playing with the figures of fear, petrification, and geology that pervade the poem he asks:

> But in her Protestant repose
> Snores faith toward her mortal close?
> Nay, like a sachem petrified,
> Encaved found in the mountain-side,
> Perfect in feature, true in limb,
> Life's full similitude in him,
> Yet all mere stone—is faith dead *now*,
> A petrification? Grant it so,
> Then what's in store? what shapeless birth?
> Reveal the doom reserved for earth?
> How far may seas retiring go?

Mortmain and Ungar, among the monomaniac characters of the poem and most lacking in Protestant repose, fall least readily into acceptance of any facile theodicy. Deeply suspicious of the motives and intentions of man in history, they have both found politics and the goals of revolution and democracy doomed by a profound depravity inherent in the nature of things. So we find Mortmain bitterly contemplating "the Wormwood Star" of the Apocalypse, revealing

> ". . . sins scarce scored as crimes
> In any statute known, or code—
> Nor now, nor in the former times:
> Things hard to prove: decorum's wile,
> Malice discreet, judicious guile;
> Good done with ill intent—reversed:
> Best deeds designed to serve the worst;
> And hate which under life's fair hue
> Prowls like the shark in sunned Pacific blue."

This is why we read Melville—for the sharks. Just when you thought nature could be explained, the creature justified, man rid of guilt, one of Melville's characters has it so that you just can't wiggle out the Piranesian prison of matter (hence Melville's wonderful meditation on Piranesi's "The Prisons" in the second part of *Clarel*). Not without a great deal of suffering. Not without nearly perishing first. So we can be reminded of "the shark that glides white through the phosphorous sea" of "Commemorative of a Naval Victory" or what the Old Fleece, the black cook, says in his sermon to the sharks in *Moby-Dick*: "You is sharks, sartin; but if you gobern de shark in you, why den you be angel; for all angel is not'ing more dan de shark well goberned." Yet Old Fleece concludes his sermon with the grimmest of benedictions: "Cussed fellow-critters! Kick up de damndest row as ever you can; fill your dam bellies 'till dey bust—an den die."

Having tried out many of the religious and philosophical claims of its era, the poem does not disavow faith; rather Melville's poetry appears continually to seek. The wounds of his most tortured characters produce the blood of faith, the inspiration that this Jobian poet uses to write poetry amid the ruins of old religion:

> Unmoved by all the claims our times avow,
> The ancient Sphinx still keeps the porch of shade
> And comes Despair, whom not her calm may cow,
> And coldly on that adamantine brow
> Scrawls undeterred his bitter pasquinade.
> But Faith (who from the scrawl indignant turns),
> With blood warm oozing from her wounded trust,
> Inscribes even on her shards of broken urns
> The sign o' the cross—*the spirit above the dust!*

After the experience of a poem of such complexity and richness, what, we might wonder, does Melville mean, breaking suddenly into pentameters, by "the sign o' the cross"? What are the shards of broken urns? Where, indeed, is Melville amid the chaos of failed theodicies and theologies? If it is to a pilgrim-poet such as Melville that we look with great interest because of the failure of religion to provide any real defense of faith or humanity against science or any real defense of humanity against fundamentalist religion, in what regions is Melville looking? It would be wrong to assume that Melville the poet has become belletristic. The poetry itself, rather, becomes for Melville a merging of form and content or an attempt to wrestle with form and matter, opposites that threaten to become dangerous opposites in a world he has strong tendencies to see as emanating from a wicked God. Both Gnosticism and Kabbalism posit the moment of creation with the breaking of the vessels (no doubt a reference, too, to Job). To inscribe something on those broken vessels is to recover from the initial diabolical catastrophe, the fractured "splintered glass" of creation that Melville obliquely suggests in toasting "the sub-sub" librarian at the opening of *Moby-Dick*. It is a vestige of the fraternal feeling he once conveyed in a letter to Hawthorne saying, "I feel that the Godhead is broken up like the bread at the [Last] Supper, and that we are the pieces."

So in reading Melville's late poetry, we come upon remarkable works that say something about how he was thinking about the vexed problem of whether the God of the Hebrew Bible and the God of the New Testament were the same God, projections of the human mind, or creations of the devil. In his architecture poems, Melville looks not only at form but at the idea that form is an inescapable instrument of nature, using men to work its logic. During his visit to Egypt in 1857, Melville was terrified by the pyramids, not only by their general sublimity but because he conceived that it was in their presence that the Hebrew mind conceived of Jehovah:

Oppressed by the massiveness & mystery of the pyramids. I myself too. A feeling of awe and terror came over me. Dread of the Arabs. Offering to lead me into a side-hole. The Dust. Long arched way,—then down as in a coal shaft. Then as in mines. Under the sea (At one moment seeming in the Mammoth Cave. Subterranean gorges, & c.) The stooping & doubling. I shudder at the idea of the ancient Egyptians. It was in these pyramids that was conceived the idea of Jehovah. Terrible mixture of the cunning and awful.

Melville then wrote "The Great Pyramid," which he included as the penultimate poem of *Timoleon*, that concludes

> Craftsmen, in dateless quarries dim,
> Stones formless into form did trim,
> Usurped on Nature's self with Art,
> And bade this dumb I AM to start,
>   Imposing him.

The terse, quite literally cryptic lines excavate the origins of monotheism and wed it forever to architecture and art. Did religion, perhaps a dangerous imposition of the ego, begin from these rituals of art and, more important, submission to worldly power? Were such rituals nothing more than those punishments Israel Potter experiences at the hands of the Master-at-Arms who "to no end" "keep[s] leading him about because he has no final destination"?

Perhaps, then, the depiction of "brutal matter" in "Fragments of a Lost Gnostic Poem of the Twelfth Century," published in *Timoleon*, offers a chilling answer to the question of the value or worth of human industry:

> Found a family, build a state,
> The pledged event is still the same:
> Matter in end will never abate
> His ancient brutal claim.
>   * * * *
> Indolence is heaven's ally here,
> And energy the child of hell:
> The Good Man pouring from his pitcher clear,
> But brims the poisoned well.

The vessel, the pitcher, should remain broken, and a poem such as this provides something of a gloss on why "Bartleby" may be not simply a story of despair but a vision from a certain stand-point of how one is to lead one's life: in a Gnostic universe in which the world is of the devil, perhaps it is best to do nothing except wait.

A haunting and almost eerily funny sense of Fate attends to some of Melville's best late verse—"The Maldive Shark," "The Haglets," and the poem that was really the genesis of the novella *Billy Budd*, "Billy in the Darbies." Melville seemed to return from the desert to the sea and to nature with a resigned sense of the inexplicable cunning and awful mythic Fates as the spinners and the inevitable source of inequity: one can do little to avoid them but accept their presence with grim certitude. The Good Man pouring from his pitcher clear may not be much different from those "pilot fish" of "The Maldive Shark" that alert in attendance be but "never partake of the treat." Instead they are simply a guide to "the dotard lethargic and dull" who is also "pale ravener of horrible meat." One need not go too far into the political to sense that Melville sees this as an emblem of the banality of evil and of the willingness of individuals to par-ticipate in a larger evil that they cannot even quite comprehend or see, not unlike the many conscripted to build a pyramid.

Clarel put an enormous strain on Melville's family. Elizabeth wrote to her mother shortly before its completion, "Herman is pretty well and very busy—pray do not mention to *any* one that he is writing poetry—you know how such things spread and he would be very angry if he knew I had spoken of it—and of course I have not, except in confidence to you and the family. We have been in much fear lest his pay should be reduced, as so many others have, but it has not been so far—it is hard enough to get along at all—" *Clarel* was published by Putnam's with a subvention by Melville's uncle Peter Gansevoort; it received at best respectful but mostly puzzled notices upon publication. Melville finally resigned from his position as a customs inspec-tor nine years later in 1885, though no doubt he had been busy in those years writing the poems that would become *John Marr and Other Sailors* in a private edition of only twenty-five copies after receiving a bequest of $3,000 from his sister Frances Priscilla. "John Marr," as well as other memorable poems in the volume such as "Tom Deadlight" and "Jack Roy," are broadside ballads of sailors who perished, saturnine but not morbid. "John Marr" in particular points to an aspect of Melville's style of composition and to his final efforts in poetry and prose. The poem "John Marr" seems to have been a prelude to what became a much longer headnote.

The same appears to be true of "Billy in the Darbies," Melville's brilliant broadside ballad, left at his death in 1891, along with the very long, unfinished headnote that became *Billy Budd, Sailor*. After reading the mysterious and now famous novella of the handsome and stuttering sailor, it is remarkable to read the ballad that was its genesis. For in the poem, Billy speaks, if not sings, clearly and beautifully and humorously in his dying. If we have been led to think about Billy as a Christlike figure—and Melville had always been brilliant at tweaking our allegorical noses—then here Jesus (as a great song goes) is simply a sailor, as he was when he began his ministry. And here, instead of walking on water, he tells us "Fathoms down, fathoms down, how I'll dream fast asleep." Perhaps for Melville this is not so bad an ending, for as Ishmael once told us, "I love all men who dive." But of course, Billy, caught in the horrible machinery of justice, will merely drop. Out of the tragedy of the story of Billy Budd comes the strange Prospero-like utterance of this late ballad. We can almost hear ancient Melville ready to be unshackled from the darbies of this life and given back to mysterious embrace of nature:

> Sentry, are you there?
> Just ease these darbies at the wrist,
> And roll me over fair.
> I am sleepy and the oozy weeds about me twist.

A number of Melville's late poems seem to embrace the weeds and flowers of earth rather than the symbols of the religious imagination. So in "Pebbles," concluding *John Marr*, the speaker turns from "Christ on the Mount, and the dove in her nest," to the rare weeds of the ocean: "Healed of my hurt, I laud the inhuman Sea—/ Yea, bless the Angels that there convene;/

For healed I am even by their pitiless breath/Distilled in wholesome dew named rosmarine." It were as though he wished transfiguration in the most common breath of the earth. In his last decade Melville took up the cultivation of roses and would present bouquets and dried petals to his close friends. Roses became the subject of some of these mysterious poems of his last years, published posthumously in *Weeds and Wildings Chiefly: With a Rose or Two*. One of those poems, "The New Rosicrucians," is thus an amusing play on the seventeenth-century alchemist-Christian religious cult (whose symbol, after its founder's name, was actually the rose), with Melville affirming something of the sanctified sensuality of *The Rubaiayat* and the language of poetry beyond religion and Christianity:

> For all the preacher's din
> There is no mortal sin—
> No, none to us but Malice.
>
> Exempt from that, in blest recline
> We let life's billows toss;
> If sorrow come, anew we twine
> The Rose-Vine round the Cross.

At the end, there was beauty in the forms he would find and could still create.

ROBERT FAGGEN
Claremont McKenna College

Suggestions for Further Reading

Aaron, Daniel. *The Unwritten War: American Writers and the Civil War*. Madison: University of Wisconsin Press, 1973.

Cohen, Henig, ed. *The Battle-Pieces of Herman Melville*. New York: Thomas Yoseloff, 1964.

Cox, Richard H., and Paul Dowling. "Herman Melville's Civil War: Lincolnian Prudence in Poetry." *Political Science Reviewer* 29 (2000): 192–295.

Dillingham, William B. *Melville and His Circle: The Last Years*. Athens: University of Georgia Press, 1996.

Garner, Stanton. *The Civil War World of Herman Melville*. Lawrence: University of Kansas Press, 1993.

Grey, Robin, and Douglas Robillard, in consultation with Hershel Parker. "Melville's Milton: A Transcription of Melville's Marginalia in His Copy of *The Poetical Works of John Milton*." *Leviathan* 4 (March and October 2002): 117–204.

Melville, Herman. *Clarel, A Poem and a Pilgrimage in the Holy Land*. Edited by Harrison Hayford, Alma A. MacDougal, Hershel Parker, and G. Thomas Tanselle. Evanston and Chicago: Northwestern University Press and the Newberry Library, 1991.

Milder, Robert, ed. *Critical Essays on Melville's Billy Budd, Sailor*. Boston: G. K. Hall & Co., 1989.

Parker, Hershel. *Herman Melville, A Biography, Volume II, 1851–1891*. Baltimore: Johns Hopkins University Press, 2002.

Philbrick, Nathaniel. "Hawthorne, Maria Mitchell, and Melville's 'After the Pleasure Party'." *ESQ* 37 (1991): 291–308.

Shurr, William B. *The Mystery of Iniquity: Melville as Poet, 1857–1891*. Lexington: University of Kentucky Press, 1972.

Spengemann, William C. "Melville the Poet." *American Literary History* 11, no. 4 (winter, 1999): 569–609.

Stein, William B. *The Poetry of Melville's Late Years: Time, Myth, and Religion*. Albany: State University of New York Press, 1970.

Vendler, Helen. "Melville and the Lyric of History." *Southern Review* 35, 3 (summer 1999): 579–94.

Warren, Robert Penn. "Melville the Poet." *Kenyon Review* 8 (1946): 208–23.

Warren, Rosanna. "Dark Knowledge: Melville's Poems of the Civil War." *Raritan* 19, 1 (summer 1999): 100–21.

A Note on the Texts

The texts of *Battle-Pieces and Aspects of the War* (Harper and Brothers, 1866), *John Marr and Other Sailors* (The Devine Press, 1888), and *Timoleon, Etc.* (The Caxton Press, 1891) are based on facsimiles of the first editions that have been compared with Melville's own corrected copies. Two copies of *Battle-Pieces and Aspects of the War* (1866) with corrections in Melville's and his wife's hand are in the Houghton Library at Harvard University. A corrected copy in Melville's hand of *John Marr and Other Sailors* is held at the New York Public Library. There is no manuscript of *Battle-Pieces* but the manuscripts of *John Marr and Other Sailors*; *Timoleon*; and *Weeds and Wildings Chiefly: With a Rose or Two* are also at the Houghton Library. Houghton Library also holds a corrected copy in Melville's hand of *Clarel: A Poem and Pilgrimage in the Holy Land* (Putnam, 1876). I have used the 1924 John Constable Standard Edition of Melville's work for the texts of both unpublished and uncollected poems as well as for *Clarel*.

Selected Poems of
Herman Melville

FROM
BATTLE-PIECES AND ASPECTS OF THE WAR

THE BATTLE-PIECES IN THIS VOLUME
ARE DEDICATED
TO THE MEMORY OF THE
THREE HUNDRED THOUSAND
WHO IN THE WAR FOR THE MAINTENANCE
OF THE UNION FELL DEVOTEDLY UNDER
THE FLAG OF THEIR FATHERS

[WITH few exceptions, the Pieces in this volume originated in an impulse imparted by the fall of Richmond. They were composed without reference to collective arrangement, but, being brought together in review, naturally fall into the order assumed.

The events and incidents of the conflict—making up a whole, in varied amplitude, corresponding with the geographical area covered by the war—from these but a few themes have been taken, such as for any cause chanced to imprint themselves upon the mind.

The aspects which the strife as a memory assumes are as manifold as are the moods of involuntary meditation—moods variable, and at times widely at variance. Yielding instinctively, one after another, to feelings not inspired from any one source exclusively, and unmindful, without purposing to be, of consistency, I seem, in most of these verses, to have but placed a harp in a window, and noted the contrasted airs which wayward winds have played upon the strings.]

THE PORTENT

(1859)

Hanging from the beam,
   Slowly swaying (such the law),
Gaunt the shadow on your green,
   Shenandoah!
The cut is on the crown
(Lo, John Brown),
And the stabs shall heal no more.

Hidden in the cap
   Is the anguish none can draw;
So your future veils its face,
   Shenandoah!
But the streaming beard is shown
(Weird John Brown),
The meteor of the war.

MISGIVINGS

(1860)

WHEN ocean-clouds over inland hills
    Sweep storming in late autumn brown,
And horror the sodden valley fills,
    And the spire falls crashing in the town,
I muse upon my country's ills—
The tempest bursting from the waste of Time
On the world's fairest hope linked with man's foulest
      crime.

Nature's dark side is heeded now—
    (Ah! optimist-cheer disheartened flown)—
A child may read the moody brow
    Of yon black mountain lone.
With shouts the torrents down the gorges go,
And storms are formed behind the storm we feel:
The hemlock shakes in the rafter, the oak in the
      driving keel.

THE CONFLICT OF CONVICTIONS

(1860–61)

ON starry heights
   A bugle wails the long recall;
Derision stirs the deep abyss,
   Heaven's ominous silence over all.
Return, return, O eager Hope,
   And face man's latter fall.
Events, they make the dreamers quail;
Satan's old age is strong and hale,
A disciplined captain, gray in skill,
And Raphael a white enthusiast still;
Dashed aims, at which Christ's martyrs pale,
Shall Mammon's slaves fulfill?

> *(Dismantle the fort,*
> *Cut down the fleet—*
> *Battle no more shall be!*
> *While the fields for fight in æons to come*
> *Congeal beneath the sea.)*

The terrors of truth and dart of death
   To faith alike are vain;
Though comets, gone a thousand years,
     Return again,
Patient she stands—she can no more—
And waits, nor heeds she waxes hoar.

> *(At a stony gate,*
> *A statue of stone,*
> *Weed overgrown—*
> *Long 'twill wait!)*

But God His former mind retains,
    Confirms His old decree;
The generations are inured to pains,
    And strong Necessity
Surges, and heaps Time's strand with wrecks.
    The People spread like a weedy grass,
    The thing they will they bring to pass,
And prosper to the apoplex.
The rout it herds around the heart,
    The ghost is yielded in the gloom;
Kings wag their heads—Now save thyself
    Who wouldst rebuild the world in bloom.

> *(Tide-mark*
> *And top of the ages' strife,*
> *Verge where they called the world to come,*
> *The last advance of life—*
> *Ha ha, the rust on the Iron Dome!)*

Nay, but revere the hid event;
    In the cloud a sword is girded on,
I mark a twinkling in the tent
    Of Michael the warrior one.
Senior wisdom suits not now,
The light is on the youthful brow.

> *(Ay, in caves the miner see:*
> *His forehead bears a blinking light;*
> *Darkness so he feebly braves—*
> *A meager wight!)*

But He who rules is old—is old;
Ah! faith is warm, but heaven with age is cold.

> *(Ho ho, ho ho,*
> *The cloistered doubt*
> *Of olden times*
> *Is blurted out!)*

The Ancient of Days forever is young,
    Forever the scheme of Nature thrives;
I know a wind in purpose strong—
    It spins *against* the way it drives.
What if the gulfs their slimed foundations bare?
So deep must the stones be hurled
Whereon the throes of ages rear
The final empire and the happier world.

        (The poor old Past,
        The Future's slave,
        She drudged through pain and crime
        To bring about the blissful Prime,
        Then—perished. There's a grave!)

    Power unanointed may come—
Dominion (unsought by the free)
    And the Iron Dome,
Stronger for stress and strain,
Fling her huge shadow athwart the main;
But the Founders' dream shall flee.
Age after age shall be
As age after age has been,
(From man's changeless heart their way they win);
And death be busy with all who strive—
Death, with silent negative.

        YEA AND NAY—
        EACH HATH HIS SAY;
        BUT GOD HE KEEPS THE MIDDLE WAY.
        NONE WAS BY
        WHEN HE SPREAD THE SKY;
        WISDOM IS VAIN, AND PROPHESY.

APATHY AND ENTHUSIASM

(1860–61)

I

O THE clammy cold November,
   And the winter white and dead,
And the terror dumb with stupor,
   And the sky a sheet of lead;
And events that came resounding
   With the cry that *ALL WAS LOST*,
Like the thunder-cracks of massy ice
   In intensity of frost—
Bursting one upon another
   Through the horror of the calm.
   The paralysis of arm
In the anguish of the heart;
And the hollowness and dearth.
   The appealings of the mother
   To brother and to brother
Not in hatred so to part—
And the fissure in the hearth
   Growing momently more wide.
Then the glances 'tween the Fates,
   And the doubt on every side,
And the patience under gloom
In the stoniness that waits
The finality of doom.

II

So the winter died despairing,
   And the weary weeks of Lent;
And the ice-bound rivers melted,
   And the tomb of Faith was rent.
O, the rising of the People
   Came with springing of the grass,
They rebounded from dejection
   After Easter came to pass.
And the young were all elation
   Hearing Sumter's cannon roar,
And they thought how tame the Nation
   In the age that went before.
And Michael seemed gigantical,
   The Arch-fiend but a dwarf;
And at the towers of Erebus
   Our striplings flung the scoff.
But the elders with foreboding
   Mourned the days forever o'er,
And recalled the forest proverb,
   The Iroquois' old saw:
Grief to every graybeard
   When young Indians lead the war.

THE MARCH INTO VIRGINIA
Ending in the First Manassas
(July 1861)

DID all the lets and bars appear
   To every just or larger end,
Whence should come the trust and cheer?
   Youth must its ignorant impulse lend—
Age finds place in the rear.
    All wars are boyish, and are fought by boys,
The champions and enthusiasts of the state:
   Turbid ardors and vain joys
    Not barrenly abate—
   Stimulants to the power mature,
    Preparatives of fate.

Who here forecasteth the event?
What heart but spurns at precedent
And warnings of the wise,
Contemned foreclosures of surprise?
The banners play, the bugles call,
The air is blue and prodigal.
   No berrying party, pleasure-wooed,
No picnic party in the May,
Ever went less loth than they
   Into that leafy neighborhood.
In Bacchic glee they file toward Fate,
Moloch's uninitiate;
Expectancy, and glad surmise
Of battle's unknown mysteries.
All they feel is this: 'tis glory,
A rapture sharp, though transitory,
Yet lasting in belaurelled story.

So they gaily go to fight,
Chatting left and laughing right.

But some who this blithe mood present,
   As on in lightsome files they fare,
Shall die experienced ere three days are spent—
   Perish, enlightened by the volleyed glare;
Or shame survive, and, like to adamant,
   The throe of Second Manassas share.

BALL'S BLUFF
A Reverie
(October 1861)

ONE noonday, at my window in the town,
   I saw a sight—saddest that eyes can see—
   Young soldiers marching lustily
      Unto the wars,
With fifes, and flags in mottoed pageantry;
     While all the porches, walks, and doors
Were rich with ladies cheering royally.

They moved like Juny morning on the wave,
   Their hearts were fresh as clover in its prime
   (It was the breezy summer-time),
      Life throbbed so strong,
How should they dream that Death in a rosy clime
     Would come to thin their shining throng?
Youth feels immortal, like the gods sublime.

Weeks passed; and at my window, leaving bed,
   By night I mused, of easeful sleep bereft,
   On those brave boys (Ah War! thy theft);
      Some marching feet
Found pause at last by cliffs Potomac cleft;
     Wakeful I mused, while in the street
Far footfalls died away till none were left.

DuPONT'S ROUND FIGHT

(November 1861)

IN time and measure perfect moves
  All Art whose aim is sure;
Evolving rhyme and stars divine
  Have rules, and they endure.

Nor less the Fleet that warred for Right,
  And, warring so, prevailed,
In geometric beauty curved,
  And in an orbit sailed.

The rebel at Port Royal felt
  The Unity overawe,
And rued the spell. A type was here,
  And victory of LAW.

DONELSON

(February 1862)

THE bitter cup
    Of that hard countermand
Which gave the Envoys up,
Still was wormwood in the mouth,
    And clouds involved the land,
When, pelted by sleet in the icy street,
    About the bulletin-board a band
Of eager, anxious people met,
And every wakeful heart was set
On latest news from West or South.
"No seeing here," cries one—"don't crowd"—
"You tall man, pray you, read aloud."

IMPORTANT.

        We learn that General Grant,
        Marching from Henry overland,
    And joined by a force up the Cumberland sent
        (Some thirty thousand the command),
    On Wednesday a good position won—
    Began the siege of Donelson.

    This stronghold crowns a river-bluff,
        A good broad mile of leveled top;
    Inland the ground rolls off
        Deep-gorged, and rocky, and broken up—
    A wilderness of trees and brush.
        The spaded summit shows the roods
    Of fixed entrenchments in their hush;

Breastworks and rifle-pits in woods
Perplex the base.—
                    The welcome weather
Is clear and mild; 'tis much like May.
The ancient boughs that lace together
Along the stream, and hang far forth,
    Strange with green mistletoe, betray
A dreamy contrast to the North.

Our troops are full of spirits—say
    The siege won't prove a creeping one.
They purpose not the lingering stay
Of old beleaguerers; not that way;
    But, full of vim *from Western prairies won,*
    They'll make, ere long, a dash at Donelson.
Washed by the storm till the paper grew
Every shade of a streaky blue,
That bulletin stood. The next day brought
A second.

LATER FROM THE FORT.

Grant's investment is complete—
    A semicircular one.
Both wings the Cumberland's margin meet,
Then, backward curving, clasp the rebel seat.
    On Wednesday this good work was done;
    But of the doers some lie prone.
Each wood, each hill, each glen was fought for,
The bold enclosing line we wrought for
Flamed with sharpshooters. Each cliff cost
A limb or life. But back we forced
Reserves and all; made good our hold;
And so we rest.
                Events unfold.
On Thursday added ground was won,
    A long bold steep: we near the Den.

Later the foe came shouting down
    In sortie, which was quelled; and then
We stormed them on their left.
A chilly change in the afternoon;
The sky, late clear, is now bereft
Of sun. Last night the ground froze hard—
Rings to the enemy as they run
Within their works. A ramrod bites
The lip it meets. The cold incites
To swinging of arms with brisk rebound.
Smart blows 'gainst lusty chests resound.

Along the outer line we ward
    A crackle of skirmishing goes on.
Our lads creep round on hand and knee,
    They fight from behind each trunk and stone;
    And sometimes, flying for refuge, one
Finds 'tis an enemy shares the tree.
Some scores are maimed by boughs shot off
    In the glades by the Fort's big gun.
    We mourn the loss of Colonel Morrison,
    Killed while cheering his regiment on.
Their far sharpshooters try our stuff;
And ours return them puff for puff:
'Tis diamond-cutting-diamond work.
    Woe on the rebel cannoneer
Who shows his head. Our fellows lurk
    Like Indians that waylay the deer
By the wild salt-spring.—The sky is dun,
Foredooming the fall of Donelson.
Stern weather is all unwonted here.
    The people of the country own
We brought it. Yea, the earnest North
Has elementally issued forth
    To storm this Donelson.

FURTHER.

A yelling rout
Of ragamuffins broke profuse
To-day from out the Fort.
Sole uniform they wore, a sort
Of patch, or white badge (as you choose)
Upon the arm. But leading these,
Or mingling, were men of face
And bearing of patrician race,
Splendid in courage and gold lace—
The officers. Before the breeze
Made by their charge, down went our line;
But, rallying, charged back in force,
And broke the sally; yet with loss.
This on the left; upon the right
Meanwhile there was an answering fight;
Assailants and assailed reversed.
The charge too upward, and not down—
Up a steep ridge-side, toward its crown,
A strong redoubt. But they who first
Gained the fort's base, and marked the trees
Felled, heaped in horned perplexities,
And shagged with brush; and swarming there
Fierce wasps whose sting was present death—
They faltered, drawing bated breath,
And felt it was in vain to dare;
Yet still, perforce, returned the ball,
Firing into the tangled wall
Till ordered to come down. They came;
But left some comrades in their fame,
Red on the ridge in icy wreath
And hanging gardens of cold Death.
But not quite unavenged these fell;
Our ranks once out of range, a blast
Of shrapnel and quick shell

Burst on the rebel horde, still massed,
   Scattering them pell-mell.
       (This fighting—judging what we read—
       Both charge and countercharge,
       Would seem but Thursday's told at large,
       Before in brief reported.—Ed.)
Night closed in about the Den
   Murky and lowering. Ere long, chill rains.
A night not soon to be forgot,
   Reviving old rheumatic pains
And longings for a cot.
   No blankets, overcoats, or tents.
Coats thrown aside on the warm march here—
We looked not then for changeful cheer;
Tents, coats, and blankets too much care.
   No fires; a fire a mark presents;
   Near by, the trees show bullet-dents.
Rations were eaten cold and raw.
   The men well soaked, came snow; and more—
A midnight sally. Small sleeping done—
      But such is war;
No matter, we'll have Fort Donelson.

        "Ugh! ugh!
'Twill drag along—drag along,"
Growled a cross patriot in the throng,
His battered umbrella like an ambulance-cover
Riddled with bullet-holes, spattered all over.
"Hurrah for Grant!" cried a stripling shrill;
Three urchins joined him with a will,
And some of taller stature cheered.
Meantime a Copperhead passed; he sneered.
   "Win or lose," he pausing said,
"Caps fly the same; all boys, mere boys;
Anything to make a noise.
   Like to see the list of the dead;
   These 'craven Southerners' hold out;

Ay, ay, they'll give you many a bout."
   "We'll beat in the end, sir,"
Firmly said one in staid rebuke,
A solid merchant, square and stout.
   "And do you think it? that way tend, sir?"
Asked the lean Copperhead, with a look
Of splenetic pity. "Yes, I do."
His yellow death's-head the croaker shook:
"The country's ruined, that I know."
A shower of broken ice and snow,
   In lieu of words, confuted him;
They saw him hustled round the corner go,
   And each bystander said—Well suited him.

Next day another crowd was seen
In the dark weather's sleety spleen.
Bald-headed to the storm came out
A man, who, 'mid a joyous shout,
Silently posted this brief sheet:

   GLORIOUS VICTORY OF THE FLEET!

   FRIDAY'S GREAT EVENT!

   THE ENEMY'S WATER-BATTERIES BEAT!

   WE SILENCED EVERY GUN!

   THE OLD COMMODORE'S COMPLIMENTS SENT

   PLUMP INTO DONELSON!

"Well, well, go on!" exclaimed the crowd
To him who thus much read aloud.
"That's all," he said. "What! nothing more?"
"Enough for a cheer, though—hip, hurrah!
But here's old Baldy come again—
More news!"—And now a different strain.

   (*Our own reporter a dispatch compiles,*
      As best he may, from varied sources.)

Large reinforcements have arrived—
*   Munitions, men, and horses—*
For Grant, and all debarked, with stores.

*   The enemy's field-works extend six miles—*
The gate still hid; so well contrived.

*   Yesterday stung us; frozen shores*
*   Snow-clad, and through the drear defiles*
And over the desolate ridges blew
A Lapland wind.
*   The main affair*
*   Was a good two hours' steady fight*
Between our gunboats and the Fort.
*   The* Louisville's *wheel was smashed outright.*
A hundred-and-twenty-eight-pound ball
Came planet-like through a starboard port,
Killing three men, and wounding all
The rest of that gun's crew,
(The captain of the gun was cut in two);
Then splintering and ripping went—
Nothing could be its continent.

*   In the narrow stream the* Louisville,
Unhelmed, grew lawless; swung around,
*   And would have thumped and drifted, till*
All the fleet was driven aground,
But for the timely order to retire.

Some damage from our fire, 'tis thought,
Was done the water-batteries of the Fort.

Little else took place that day,
*   Except the field artillery in line*
Would now and then—for love, they say—
*   Exchange a valentine.*
The old sharpshooting going on,

Some plan afoot as yet unknown;
So Friday closed round Donelson.

LATER.

      Great suffering through the night—
A stinging one. Our heedless boys
   Were nipped like blossoms. Some dozen
   Hapless wounded men were frozen.
During day being struck down out of sight,
And help-cries drowned in roaring noise,
They were left just where the skirmish shifted—
Left in dense underbrush snow-drifted.
Some, seeking to crawl in crippled plight,
So stiffened—perished.
               Yet in spite
Of pangs for these, no heart is lost.
Hungry, and clothing stiff with frost,
Our men declare a nearing sun
Shall see the fall of Donelson.

   And this they say, yet not disown
The dark redoubts round Donelson,
   And ice-glazed corpses, each a stone—
     A sacrifice to Donelson;
They swear it, and swerve not, gazing on
A flag, deemed black, flying from Donelson.

Some of the wounded in the wood
   Were cared for by the foe last night,
Though he could do them little needed good,
   Himself being all in shivering plight.
The rebel is wrong, but human yet;
He's got a heart, and thrusts a bayonet.
He gives us battle with wondrous will—
This bluff's a perverted Bunker Hill.

The stillness stealing through the throng
The silent thought and dismal fear revealed;
    They turned and went,
     Musing on right and wrong
     And mysteries dimly sealed—
Breasting the storm in daring discontent;
The storm, whose black flag showed in heaven,
As if to say no quarter there was given
     To wounded men in wood,
    Or true hearts yearning for the good—
All fatherless seemed the human soul.
But next day brought a bitterer bowl—
    On the bulletin-board this stood:

     Saturday morning at 3 A.M.
      A stir within the Fort betrayed
     That the rebels were getting under arms;
      Some plot these early birds had laid.

But a lancing sleet cut him who stared
Into the storm. After some vague alarms,
Which left our lads unscared,
Out sallied the enemy at dim of dawn,
    With cavalry and artillery, and went
    In fury at our environment.
Under cover of shot and shell
    Three columns of infantry rolled on,
    Vomited out of Donelson—
Rolled down the slopes like rivers of hell,
    Surged at our line, and swelled and poured
Like breaking surf. But unsubmerged
    Our men stood up, except where roared
The enemy through one gap. We urged
Our all of manhood to the stress,
But still showed shattered in our desperateness.
     Back set the tide,
But soon afresh rolled in;

And so it swayed from side to side—
Far batteries joining in the din,
Though sharing in another fray—
   Till all became an Indian fight,
Intricate, dusky, stretching far away,
Yet not without spontaneous plan
   However tangled showed the plight:
Duels all over 'tween man and man,
Duels on cliff-side, and down in ravine,
   Duels at long range, and bone to bone;
Duels everywhere flitting and half unseen.
   Only by courage good as their own,
And strength outlasting theirs,
   Did our boys at last drive the rebels off.
Yet they went not back to their distant lairs
   In stronghold, but loud in scoff
Maintained themselves on conquered ground—
Uplands; built works, or stalked around.
Our right wing bore this onset. Noon
Brought calm to Donelson.

The reader ceased; the storm beat hard;
   'Twas day, but the office-gas was lit;
   Nature retained her sulking-fit,
      In her hand the shard.
Flitting faces took the hue
Of that washed bulletin-board in view,
And seemed to bear the public grief
As private, and uncertain of relief;
Yea, many an earnest heart was won,
   As broodingly he plodded on,
To find in himself some bitter thing,
Some hardness in his lot as harrowing
      As Donelson.
That night the board stood barren there,
   Oft eyed by wistful people passing,
   Who nothing saw but the rain-beads chasing

Each other down the wafered square,
As down some storm-beat graveyard stone.
But next day showed—

MORE NEWS LAST NIGHT.

STORY OF SATURDAY AFTERNOON.

VICISSITUDES OF THE WAR.

The damaged gunboats can't wage fight
For days; so says the Commodore.
Thus no diversion can be had.
Under a sunless sky of lead
    Our grim-faced boys in blackened plight
Gaze toward the ground they held before,
And then on Grant. He marks their mood,
And hails it, and will turn the same to good.
Spite all that they have undergone,
Their desperate hearts are set upon
This winter fort, this stubborn fort,
This castle of the last resort,
        This Donelson.

1 P.M.

        An order given
     Requires withdrawal from the front
     Of regiments that bore the brunt
Of morning's fray. Their ranks all riven
Are being replaced by fresh, strong men.
Great vigilance in the foeman's Den;
He snuffs the stormers. Need it is
That for that fell assault of his,
That rout inflicted, and self-scorn—
Immoderate in noble natures, torn
By sense of being through slackness overborne—

The rebel be given a quick return:
The kindest face looks now half-stern.
Balked of their prey in airs that freeze,
Some fierce ones glare like savages.
And yet, and yet, strange moments are—
Well—blood, and tears, and anguished War!
The morning's battle-ground is seen
    In lifted glades, like meadows rare;
    The blood-drops on the snow-crust there
Like clover in the white-weed show—
    Flushed fields of death, that call again—
    Call to our men, and not in vain,
For that way must the stormers go.

3 P.M.

                    The work begins.
Light drifts of men thrown forward, fade
    In skirmish-line along the slope,
Where some dislodgments must be made
    Ere the stormer with the stronghold cope.

Lew Wallace, moving to retake
The heights late lost—
                    (Herewith a break.
    Storms at the West derange the wires.
Doubtless, ere morning, we shall hear
The end; we look for news to cheer—
    Let Hope fan all her fires.)

Next day in large bold hand was seen
The closing bulletin:

Victory!
                Our troops have retrieved the day
By one grand surge along the line;
The spirit that urged them was divine.

The first works flooded, naught could stay
The stormers: on! still on!
Bayonets for Donelson!
Over the ground that morning lost
Rolled the blue billows, tempest-tossed,
    Following a hat on the point of a sword.
Spite shell and round-shot, grape and canister,
Up they climbed without rail or banister—
    Up the steep hill-sides long and broad,
Driving the rebel deep within his works.
'Tis nightfall; not an enemy lurks
    In sight. The chafing men
        Fret for more fight:
    "To-night, to-night let us take the Den!"
But night is treacherous, Grant is wary;
Of brave blood be a little chary.
Patience! the Fort is good as won;
To-morrow, and into Donelson.

LATER AND LAST.

THE FORT IS OURS.

    A flag came out at early morn
Bringing surrender. From their towers
    Floats out the banner late their scorn.
In Dover, hut and house are full
    Of rebels dead or dying.
    The National flag is flying
From the crammed court-house pinnacle.
Great boat-loads of our wounded go
To-day to Nashville. The sleet-winds blow;
But all is right: the fight is won,
The winter-fight for Donelson.
            Hurrah!
The spell of old defeat is broke,
    The habit of victory begun;

Grant strikes the war's first sounding stroke
At Donelson.

For lists of killed and wounded, see
The morrow's dispatch: to-day 'tis victory.

The man who read this to the crowd
    Shouted as the end he gained;
    And though the unflagging tempest rained,
        They answered him aloud.
And hand grasped hand, and glances met
In happy triumph; eyes grew wet.
O, to the punches brewed that night
Went little water. Windows bright
Beamed rosy on the sleet without,
And from the deep street came the frequent shout;
While some in prayer, as these in glee,
Blessed heaven for the winter-victory.
But others were who wakeful laid
    In midnight beds, and early rose,
    And, feverish in the foggy snows,
Snatched the damp paper—wife and maid.
    The death-list like a river flows
        Down the pale sheet,
And there the whelming waters meet.

    Ah God! may Time with happy haste
    Bring wail and triumph to a waste,
        And war be done;
    The battle flag-staff fall athwart
    The curs'd ravine, and wither; naught
        Be left of trench or gun;
    The bastion, let it ebb away,
    Washed with the river bed; and Day
        In vain seek Donelson.

IN THE TURRET

(March 1862)

YOUR honest heart of duty, Worden,
    So helped you that in fame you dwell;
You bore the first iron battle's burden
    Sealed as in a diving-bell.
Alcides, groping into haunted hell
To bring forth King Admetus' bride,
Braved naught more vaguely direful and untried.
    What poet shall uplift his charm,
Bold Sailor, to your height of daring,
    And interblend therewith the calm,
And build a goodly style upon your bearing.

Escaped the gale of outer ocean—
    Cribbed in a craft which like a log
Was washed by every billow's motion—
    By night you heard of Og
The huge; nor felt your courage clog
At tokens of his onset grim:
You marked the sunk ship's flag-staff slim,
    Lit by her burning sister's heart;
You marked and mused: "Day brings the trial:
    Then be it proved if I have part
With men whose manhood never took denial."

A prayer went up—a champion's. Morning
    Beheld you in the Turret walled
By adamant, where a spirit forewarning
    And all-deriding called:
"Man, darest thou—desperate, unappalled—
Be first to lock thee in the armored tower?

I have thee now; and what the battle-hour
    To me shall bring—heed well—thou 'lt share;
This plot-work, planned to be the foeman's terror,
    To thee may prove a goblin-snare;
Its very strength and cunning—monstrous error!"

"Stand up, my heart; be strong; what matter
    If here thou seest thy welded tomb?
And let huge Og with thunders batter—
    Duty be still my doom,
Though drowning come in liquid gloom;
First duty, duty next, and duty last;
Ay, Turret, rivet me here to duty fast!"—
    So nerved, you fought, wisely and well;
And live, twice live in life and story;
    But over your Monitor dirges swell,
In wind and wave that keep the rites of glory.

THE *TEMERAIRE*

(Supposed to have been suggested to an Englishman of the old order by the fight of the Monitor *and* Merrimac.)

THE gloomy hulls, in armor grim,
    Like clouds o'er moors have met,
And prove that oak, and iron, and man
    Are tough in fiber yet.

But Splendors wane. The sea-fight yields
    No front of old display;
The garniture, emblazonment,
    And heraldry all decay.

Towering afar in parting light,
    The fleets like Albion's forelands shine—
The full-sailed fleets, the shrouded show
    Of Ships-of-the-Line.

The fighting *Temeraire,*
    Built of a thousand trees,
Lunging out her lightnings,
    And beetling o'er the seas—
O Ship, how brave and fair,
    That fought so oft and well,
On open decks you manned the gun
        Armorial.
What cheerings did you share,
    Impulsive in the van,
When down upon leagued France and Spain
    We English ran—

The freshet at your bowsprit
   Like the foam upon the can.
Bickering, your colors
   Licked up the Spanish air,
You flapped with flames of battle-flags—
   Your challenge, *Temeraire!*
The rear ones of our fleet
   They yearned to share your place,
Still vying with the *Victory*
   Throughout that earnest race—
The *Victory,* whose Admiral,
   With orders nobly won,
Shone in the globe of the battle glow—
   The angel in that sun.

Parallel in story,
   Lo, the stately pair,
As late in grapple ranging,
   The foe between them there—
When four great hulls lay tiered,
And the fiery tempest cleared,
And your prizes twain appeared,
              Temeraire!

But Trafalgar is over now,
   The quarter-deck undone;
The carved and castled navies fire
   Their evening-gun.
O, Titan *Temeraire,*
   Your stern-lights fade away;
Your bulwarks to the years must yield,
   And heart-of-oak decay.
A pigmy steam-tug tows you,
   Gigantic, to the shore—
Dismantled of your guns and spars,
   And sweeping wings of war.
The rivets clinch the ironclads,

Men learn a deadlier lore;
But Fame has nailed your battle-flags—
    Your ghost it sails before:
O, the navies old and oaken,
    O, the *Temeraire* no more!

A UTILITARIAN VIEW OF
THE *MONITOR*'S FIGHT

PLAIN be the phrase, yet apt the verse,
   More ponderous than nimble;
For since grimed War here laid aside
His Orient pomp, 'twould ill befit
     Overmuch to ply
   The rhyme's barbaric cymbal.

Hail to victory without the gaud
   Of glory; zeal that needs no fans
Of banners; plain mechanic power
Plied cogently in War now placed—
     Where War belongs—
   Among the trades and artisans.

Yet this was battle, and intense—
   Beyond the strife of fleets heroic;
Deadlier, closer, calm 'mid storm;
No passion; all went on by crank,
     Pivot, and screw,
   And calculations of caloric.

Needless to dwell; the story's known.
   The ringing of those plates on plates
Still ringeth round the world—
The clangor of that blacksmiths' fray.
     The anvil-din
   Resounds this message from the Fates:

War shall yet be, and to the end;
   But war-paint shows the streaks of weather;
War yet shall be, but warriors
Are now but operatives; War's made
     Less grand than Peace,
   And a singe runs through lace and feather.

SHILOH
A Requiem
(April 1862)

SKIMMING lightly, wheeling still,
   The swallows fly low
Over the field in clouded days,
   The forest-field of Shiloh—
Over the field where April rain
Solaced the parched one stretched in pain
Through the pause of night
That followed the Sunday fight
   Around the church of Shiloh—
The church so lone, the log-built one,
That echoed to many a parting groan
     And natural prayer
   Of dying foemen mingled there—
Foemen at morn, but friends at eve—
   Fame or country least their care:
(What like a bullet can undeceive!)
   But now they lie low,
While over them the swallows skim
   And all is hushed at Shiloh.

BATTLE OF STONE RIVER, TENNESSEE
A View from Oxford Cloisters

(January 1863)

WITH Tewksbury and Barnet heath
   In days to come the field shall blend,
The story dim and date obscure;
   In legend all shall end.
Even now, involved in forest shade
   A Druid-dream the strife appears,
The fray of yesterday assumes
   The haziness of years.
         In North and South still beats the vein
         Of Yorkist and Lancastrian.

Our rival Roses warred for Sway—
   For Sway, but named the name of Right;
And Passion, scorning pain and death,
   Lent sacred fervor to the fight.
Each lifted up a broidered cross,
   While crossing blades profaned the sign;
Monks blessed the fratricidal lance,
   And sisters scarfs could twine.
         Do North and South the sin retain
         Of Yorkist and Lancastrian?

But Rosecrans in the cedarn glade,
   And, deep in denser cypress gloom,
Dark Breckinridge, shall fade away
   Or thinly loom.
The pale throngs who in forest cowed
   Before the spell of battle's pause,

Forefelt the stillness that shall dwell
   On them and on their wars.
        North and South shall join the train
        Of Yorkist and Lancastrian.

But where the sword has plunged so deep,
   And then been turned within the wound
By deadly Hate; where Climes contend
      On vasty ground—
No warning Alps or seas between,
   And small the curb of creed or law,
And blood is quick, and quick the brain;
   Shall North and South their rage deplore,
      And reunited thrive amain
      Like Yorkist and Lancastrian?

THE HOUSE-TOP
A Night Piece

(July 1863)

No sleep. The sultriness pervades the air
And binds the brain—a dense oppression, such
As tawny tigers feel in matted shades,
Vexing their blood and making apt for ravage.
Beneath the stars the roofy desert spreads
Vacant as Libya. All is hushed near by.
Yet fitfully from far breaks a mixed surf
Of muffled sound, the Atheist roar of riot.
Yonder, where parching Sirius set in drought,
Balefully glares red Arson—there—and there.
The Town is taken by its rats—ship-rats
And rats of the wharves. All civil charms
And priestly spells which late held hearts in awe—
Fear-bound, subjected to a better sway
Than sway of self; these like a dream dissolve,
And man rebounds whole aeons back in nature.
Hail to the low dull rumble, dull and dead,
And ponderous drag that shakes the wall.
Wise Draco comes, deep in the midnight roll
Of black artillery; he comes, though late;
In code corroborating Calvin's creed
And cynic tyrannies of honest kings;
He comes, nor parleys; and the Town, redeemed,
Gives thanks devout; nor, being thankful, heeds
The grimy slur on the Republic's faith implied,
Which holds that Man is naturally good,
And—more—is Nature's Roman, never to be scourged.

THE ARMIES OF THE WILDERNESS

(1863–64)

I

LIKE snows the camps on Southern hills
    Lay all the winter long,
Our levies there in patience stood—
    They stood in patience strong.
On fronting slopes gleamed other camps
    Where faith as firmly clung:
Ah, froward kin! so brave amiss—
    The zealots of the Wrong.

> *In this strife of brothers*
>   *(God, hear their country call),*
> *However it be, whatever betide,*
>   *Let not the just one fall.*

Through the pointed glass our soldiers saw
    The base-ball bounding sent;
They could have joined them in their sport
    But for the vale's deep rent.
And others turned the reddish soil,
    Like diggers of graves they bent:
The reddish soil and trenching toil
    Begat presentiment.

> *Did the Fathers feel mistrust?*
>   *Can no final good be wrought?*
> *Over and over, again and again*
>   *Must the fight for the Right be fought?*

They lead a Gray-back to the crag:
    "Your earthworks yonder—tell us, man!"
"A prisoner—no deserter, I,
    Nor one of the tell-tale clan."
His rags they mark: "True-blue like you
    Should wear the color—your Country's, man!"
He grinds his teeth: "However that be,
    Yon earthworks have their plan."

> *Such brave ones, foully snared*
>   *By Belial's wily plea,*
> *Were faithful unto the evil end—*
>   *Feudal fidelity.*

"Well, then, your camps—come, tell the names!"
    Freely he leveled his finger then:
"Yonder—see—are our Georgians; on the crest,
    The Carolinians; lower, past the glen,
Virginians—Alabamians—Mississippians—Kentuckians
    (Follow my finger)—Tennesseeans; and the ten
Camps *there*—ask your grave-pits; they'll tell.
    Halloa! I see the picket-hut, the den
Where I last night lay." "Where's Lee?"
    "In the hearts and bayonets of all yon men!"

> *The tribes swarm up to war*
>   *As in ages long ago,*
> *Ere the palm of promise leaved*
>   *And the lily of Christ did blow.*

Their mounted pickets for miles are spied
    Dotting the lowland plain,
The nearer ones in their veteran-rags—
    Loutish they loll in lazy disdain.
But ours in perilous places bide
    With rifles ready and eyes that strain
Deep through the dim suspected wood
    Where the Rapidan rolls amain.

> *The Indian has passed away,*
> > *But creeping comes another—*
> *Deadlier far. Picket,*
> > *Take heed—take heed of thy brother!*

From a wood-hung height, an outpost lone,
  Crowned with a woodman's fort,
The sentinel looks on a land of dole,
  Like Paran, all amort.
Black chimneys, gigantic in moor-like wastes,
  The scowl of the clouded sky retort;
The hearth is a houseless stone again—
  Ah! where shall the people be sought?

> *Since the venom such blastment deals,*
> > *The South should have paused, and thrice,*
> *Ere with heat of her hate she hatched*
> > *The egg with the cockatrice.*

A path down the mountain winds to the glade
  Where the dead of the Moonlight Fight lie low;
A hand reaches out of the thin-laid mould
  As begging help which none can bestow.
But the field-mouse small and busy ant
  Heap their hillocks, to hide if they may the woe:
By the bubbling spring lies the rusted canteen,
  And the drum which the drummer-boy dying let go.

> *Dust to dust, and blood for blood—*
> > *Passion and pangs! Has Time*
> *Gone back? or is this the Age*
> > *Of the world's great Prime?*

The wagon mired and cannon dragged
  Have trenched their scar; the plain
Tramped like the cindery beach of the damned—
  A site for the city of Cain.
And stumps of forests for dreary leagues

Like a massacre show. The armies have lain
By fires where gums and balms did burn,
    And the seeds of Summer's reign.

            Where are the birds and boys?
                Who shall go chestnutting when
            October returns? The nuts—
                O, long ere they grow again.

They snug their huts with the chapel-pews,
    In court-houses stable their steeds—
Kindle their fires with indentures and bonds,
    And old Lord Fairfax's parchment deeds;
And Virginian gentlemen's libraries old—
    Books which only the scholar heeds—
Are flung to his kennel. It is ravage and range,
    And gardens are left to weeds.

            Turned adrift into war
                Man runs wild on the plain,
            Like the jennets let loose
                On the Pampas—zebras again.

Like the Pleiads dim, see the tents through the storm—
    Aloft by the hill-side hamlet's graves,
On a head-stone used for a hearth-stone there
    The water is bubbling for punch for our braves.
What if the night be drear, and the blast
    Ghostly shrieks? their rollicking staves
Make frolic the heart; beating time with their swords,
    What care they if Winter raves?

            Is life but a dream? and so,
                In the dream do men laugh aloud?
            So strange seems mirth in a camp,
                So like a white tent to a shroud.

II

The May-weed springs; and comes a Man
    And mounts our Signal Hill;
A quiet Man, and plain in garb—
    Briefly he looks his fill,
Then drops his gray eye on the ground,
    Like a loaded mortar he is still:
Meekness and grimness meet in him—
    The silent General.

> *Were men but strong and wise,*
>   *Honest as Grant, and calm,*
> *War would be left to the red and black ants,*
>   *And the happy world disarm.*

That eve a stir was in the camps,
    Forerunning quiet soon to come
Among the streets of beechen huts
    No more to know the drum.
The weed shall choke the lowly door,
    And foxes peer within the gloom,
Till scared perchance by Mosby's prowling men,
    Who ride in the rear of doom.

> *Far West, and farther South,*
>   *Wherever the sword has been,*
> *Deserted camps are met,*
>   *And desert graves are seen.*

The livelong night they ford the flood;
    With guns held high they silent press,
Till shimmers the grass in their bayonets' sheen—
    On Morning's banks their ranks they dress;
Then by the forests lightly wind,
    Whose waving boughs the pennons seem to bless,
Borne by the cavalry scouting on—
    Sounding the Wilderness.

Like shoals of fish in spring
  That visit Crusoe's isle,
The host in the lonesome place—
  The hundred thousand file.

The foe that held his guarded hills
  Must speed to woods afar;
For the scheme that was nursed by the Culpepper hearth
  With the slowly-smoked cigar—
The scheme that smouldered through winter long
  Now bursts into act—into war—
The resolute scheme of a heart as calm
  As the Cyclone's core.

      The fight for the city is fought
        In Nature's old domain;
      Man goes out to the wilds,
        And Orpheus' charm is vain.

In glades they meet skull after skull
  Where pine-cones lay—the rusted gun,
Green shoes full of bones, the moldering coat
  And cuddled-up skeleton;
And scores of such. Some start as in dreams,
  And comrades lost bemoan:
By the edge of those wilds Stonewall had charged—
  But the Year and the Man were gone.

      At the height of their madness
        The night winds pause,
      Recollecting themselves;
        But no lull in these wars.

A gleam!—a volley! And who shall go
  Storming the swarmers in jungles dread?
No cannon-ball answers, no proxies are sent—
  They rush in the shrapnel's stead.

Plume and sash are vanities now—
    Let them deck the pall of the dead;
They go where the shade is, perhaps into Hades,
    Where the brave of all times have led.

> *There's a dust of hurrying feet,*
>   *Bitten lips and bated breath,*
> *And drums that challenge to the grave,*
>   *And faces fixed, forefeeling death.*

What husky huzzahs in the hazy groves—
    What flying encounters fell;
Pursuer and pursued like ghosts disappear
    In gloomed shade—their end who shall tell?
The crippled, a ragged-barked stick for a crutch,
    Limp to some elfin dell—
Hobble from the sight of dead faces—white
    As pebbles in a well.

> *Few burial rites shall be;*
>   *No priest with book and band*
> *Shall come to the secret place*
>   *Of the corpse in the foeman's land.*

Watch and fast, march and fight—clutch your gun!
    Day-fights and night-fights; sore is the stress;
Look, through the pines what line comes on?
    Longstreet slants through the hauntedness!
'Tis charge for charge, and shout for yell:
    Such battles on battles oppress—
But Heaven lent strength, the Right strove well,
    And emerged from the Wilderness.

> *Emerged, for the way was won;*
>   *But the Pillar of Smoke that led*
> *Was brand-like with ghosts that went up*
>   *Ashy and red.*

None can narrate that strife in the pines,
  A seal is on it—Sabæan lore!
Obscure as the wood, the entangled rhyme
  But hints at the maze of war—
Vivid glimpses or livid through peopled gloom,
  And fires which creep and char—
A riddle of death, of which the slain
      Sole solvers are.

  Long they withhold the roll
    Of the shroudless dead. It is right;
  Not yet can we bear the flare
    Of the funeral light.

ON THE PHOTOGRAPH OF A CORPS COMMANDER

Ay, man is manly. Here you see
   The warrior-carriage of the head,
And brave dilation of the frame;
   And lighting all, the soul that led
In Spottsylvania's charge to victory,
   Which justifies his fame.

A cheering picture. It is good
   To look upon a Chief like this,
In whom the spirit molds the form.
   Here favoring Nature, oft remiss,
With eagle mien expressive has endued
   A man to kindle strains that warm.

Trace back his lineage, and his sires,
   Yeoman or noble, you shall find
Enrolled with men of Agincourt,
   Heroes who shared great Harry's mind,
Down to us come the knightly Norman fires,
   And front the Templars bore.

Nothing can lift the heart of man
   Like manhood in a fellow-man.
The thought of heaven's great King afar
   But humbles us—too weak to scan;
But manly greatness men can span,
   And feel the bonds that draw.

THE SWAMP ANGEL

THERE is a coal-black Angel
    With a thick Afric lip,
And he dwells (like the hunted and harried)
    In a swamp where the green frogs dip.
But his face is against a City
    Which is over a bay of the sea,
And he breathes with a breath that is blastment,
    And dooms by a far decree.

By night there is fear in the City,
    Through the darkness a star soareth on;
There's a scream that screams up to the zenith,
    Then the poise of a meteor lone—
Lighting far the pale fright of the faces,
    And downward the coming is seen;
Then the rush, and the burst, and the havoc,
    And wails and shrieks between.

It comes like the thief in the gloaming;
    It comes, and none may foretell
The place of the coming—the glaring;
    They live in a sleepless spell
That wizens, and withers, and whitens;
    It ages the young, and the bloom
Of the maiden is ashes of roses—
    The Swamp Angel broods in his gloom.

Swift is his messengers' going,
    But slowly he saps their halls,
As if by delay deluding.
    They move from their crumbling walls

Farther and farther away;
  But the Angel sends after and after,
By night with the flame of his ray—
    By night with the voice of his screaming—
Sends after them, stone by stone,
    And farther walls fall, farther portals,
And weed follows weed through the Town.

Is this the proud City? the scorner
    Which never would yield the ground?
Which mocked at the coal-black Angel?
    The cup of despair goes round.
Vainly she calls upon Michael
    (The white man's seraph was he),
For Michael has fled from his tower
    To the Angel over the sea.

Who weeps for the woeful City
    Let him weep for our guilty kind;
Who joys at her wild despairing—
    Christ, the Forgiver, convert his mind.

SHERIDAN AT CEDAR CREEK

(October 1864)

SHOE the steed with silver
　　That bore him to the fray,
When he heard the guns at dawning—
　　　　Miles away;
When he heard them calling, calling—
　　　　Mount! nor stay:
　　　　　Quick, or all is lost;
　　　　　They've surprised and stormed the post,
　　　　　They push your routed host—
　　Gallop! retrieve the day.

House the horse in ermine—
　　For the foam-flake blew
White through the red October;
　　He thundered into view;
They cheered him in the looming,
　　Horseman and horse they knew.
　　　　　The turn of the tide began,
　　　　　The rally of bugles ran,
　　　　　He swung his hat in the van;
　　The electric hoof-spark flew.

Wreathe the steed and lead him—
　　For the charge he led
Touched and turned the cypress
　　Into amaranths for the head
Of Philip, king of riders,
　　Who raised them from the dead.
　　　　　The camp (at dawning lost),

By eve, recovered—forced,
 Rang with laughter of the host
At belated Early fled.

Shroud the horse in sable—
 For the mounds they heap!
There is firing in the Valley,
 And yet no strife they keep;
It is the parting volley,
 It is the pathos deep.
   There is glory for the brave
   Who lead, and noblys ave,
   But no knowledge in the grave
Where the nameless followers sleep.

THE COLLEGE COLONEL

He rides at their head;
   A crutch by his saddle just slants in view,
One slung arm is in splints, you see,
   Yet he guides his strong steed—how coldly too.

He brings his regiment home—
   Not as they filed two years before,
But a remnant half-tattered, and battered, and worn,
Like castaway sailors, who—stunned
     By the surf's loud roar,
   Their mates dragged back and seen no more—
Again and again breast the surge,
   And at last crawl, spent, to shore.

A still rigidity and pale—
   An Indian aloofness lones his brow;
He has lived a thousand years
Compressed in battle's pains and prayers,
   Marches and watches slow.

There are welcoming shouts, and flags;
   Old men off hat to the Boy,
Wreaths from gay balconies fall at his feet,
   But to *him*—there comes alloy.

It is not that a leg is lost,
   It is not that an arm is maimed,
It is not that the fever has racked—
   Self he has long disclaimed.

But all through the Seven Days' Fight,
    And deep in the Wilderness grim,
And in the field-hospital tent,
    And Petersburg crater, and dim
Lean brooding in Libby, there came—
    Ah heaven!—what *truth* to him.

A DIRGE FOR McPHERSON
Killed in Front of Atlanta
(July 1864)

ARMS reversed and banners craped—
    Muffled drums;
Snowy horses sable-draped—
    McPherson comes.

> *But, tell us, shall we know him more,*
> *Lost-Mountain and lone Kenesaw?*

Brave the sword upon the pall—
    A gleam in gloom;
    So a bright name lighteth all
    McPherson's doom.

Bear him through the chapel-door—
    Let priest in stole
Pace before the warrior
    Who led. Bell—toll!

Lay him down within the nave,
    The Lesson read—
Man is noble, man is brave,
    But man's—a weed.

Take him up again and wend
    Graveward, nor weep:
There's a trumpet that shall rend
    This Soldier's sleep.

Pass the ropes the coffin round,
   And let descend;
Prayer and volley—let it sound
   McPherson's end.

True fame is his, for life is o'er—
Sarpedon of the mighty war.

AT THE CANNON'S MOUTH

Destruction of the *Ram Albemarle* by the Torpedo-Launch

(October 1864)

PALELY intent, he urged his keel
　　Full on the guns, and touched the spring;
Himself involved in the bolt he drove
Timed with the armed hull's shot that stove
His shallop—die or do!
Into the flood his life he threw,
　　Yet lives—unscathed—a breathing thing
To marvel at.

　　　　　　　　He has his fame;
But that mad dash at death, how name?

Had Earth no charm to stay the Boy
　　From the martyr-passion? Could he dare
Disdain the Paradise of opening joy
　　Which beckons the fresh heart everywhere?
Life has more lures than any girl
　　For youth and strength; puts forth a share
Of beauty, hinting of yet rarer store;
And ever with unfathomable eyes,
　　　　　Which bafflingly entice,
Still strangely does Adonis draw.
And life once over, who shall tell the rest?
Life is, of all we know, God's best.
What imps these eagles then, that they
Fling disrespect on life by that proud way
In which they soar above our lower clay.

Pretence of wonderment and doubt unblest:
   In Cushing's eager deed was shown
   A spirit which brave poets own—
That scorn of life which earns life's crown;
   Earns, but not always wins; but *he*—
   The star ascended in his nativity.

THE MARCH TO THE SEA

(December 1864)

Not Kenesaw high-arching,
   Nor Allatoona's glen—
Though there the graves lie parching—
   Stayed Sherman's miles of men;
From charred Atlanta marching
   They launched the sword again.
        The columns streamed like rivers
          Which in their course agree,
        And they streamed until their flashing
          Met the flashing of the sea:
             It was glorious glad marching,
             That marching to the sea.

They brushed the foe before them
   (Shall gnats impede the bull?);
Their own good bridges bore them
   Over swamps or torrents full,
And the grand pines waving o'er them
   Bowed to axes keen and cool.
        The columns grooved their channels,
          Enforced their own decree,
        And their power met nothing larger
          Until it met the sea:
             It was glorious glad marching,
             A marching glad and free.

Kilpatrick's snare of riders
   In zigzags mazed the land,
Perplexed the pale Southsiders
   With feints on every hand;

Vague menace awed the hiders
   In forts beyond command.
               To Sherman's shifting problem
                  No foeman knew the key;
               But onward went the marching
                  Unpausing to the sea:
                     It was glorious glad marching,
                     The swinging step was free.

The flankers ranged like pigeons
   In clouds through field or wood;
The flocks of all those regions,
   The herds and horses good,
Poured in and swelled the legions,
   For they caught the marching mood.
               A volley ahead! They hear it;
                  And they hear the repartee:
               Fighting was but frolic
                  In that marching to the sea:
                     It was glorious glad marching,
                     A marching bold and free.

All nature felt their coming,
   The birds like couriers flew,
And the banners brightly blooming
   The slaves by thousands drew,
And they marched beside the drumming,
   And they joined the armies blue.
               The cocks crowed from the cannon
                  (Pets named from Grant and Lee),
               Plumed fighters and campaigners
                  In that marching to the sea:
                     It was glorious glad marching,
                     For every man was free.

The foragers through calm lands
   Swept in tempest gay,

And they breathed the air of balm-lands
   Where rolled savannas lay,
And they helped themselves from farm-lands—
   As who should say them nay?
      The regiments uproarious
        Laughed in Plenty's glee;
      And they marched till their broad laughter
        Met the laughter of the sea:
          It was glorious glad marching,
          That marching to the sea.

The grain of endless acres
   Was threshed (as in the East)
By the trampling of the Takers,
   Strong march of man and beast;
The flails of those earth-shakers
   Left a famine where they ceased.
      The arsenals were yielded;
        The sword (that was to be),
      Arrested in the forging,
        Rued that marching to the sea:
          It was glorious glad marching,
          But ah, the stern decree!

For behind they left a wailing,
   A terror and a ban,
And blazing cinders sailing,
   And houseless households wan,
Wide zones of counties paling,
   And towns where maniacs ran.
      Was it Treason's retribution—
        Necessity the plea?
      They will long remember Sherman
        And his streaming columns free—
          They will long remember Sherman
          Marching to the sea.

THE FRENZY IN THE WAKE
Sherman's Advance through the Carolinas

(February 1865)

So strong to suffer, shall we be
   Weak to contend, and break
The sinews of the Oppressor's knee
   That grinds upon the neck?
      O, the garments rolled in blood
        Scorch in cities wrapped in flame,
      And the African—the imp!
        He gibbers, imputing shame.

Shall Time, avenging every woe,
   To us that joy allot
Which Israel thrilled when Sisera's brow
   Showed gaunt and showed the clot?
      Curse on their foreheads, cheeks, and eyes—
        The Northern faces—true
      To the flag we hate, the flag whose stars
        Like planets strike us through.

From frozen Maine they come,
   Far Minnesota too;
They come to a sun whose rays disown—
   May it wither them as the dew!
      The ghosts of our slain appeal:
        "Vain shall our victories be?"
      But back from its ebb the flood recoils—
        Back in a whelming sea.

With burning woods our skies are brass,
   The pillars of dust are seen;

The live-long day their cavalry pass—
No crossing the road between.
We were sore deceived—an awful host!
They move like a roaring wind,
Have we gamed and lost? but even despair
Shall never our hate rescind.

THE SURRENDER AT APPOMATTOX

(April 1865)

As billows upon billows roll,
   On victory victory breaks;
Ere yet seven days from Richmond's fall
   And crowning triumph wakes
The loud joy-gun, whose thunders run
   By sea-shore, streams, and lakes.
      The hope and great event agree
      In the sword that Grant received from Lee.

The warring eagles fold the wing,
   But not in Cæsar's sway;
Not Rome o'ercome by Roman arms we sing,
   As on Pharsalia's day,
But Treason thrown, though a giant grown,
   And Freedom's larger play.
      All human tribes glad token see
      In the close of the wars of Grant and Lee.

A CANTICLE

Significant of the National Exaltation of Enthusiasm at the Close of the War

O THE precipice Titanic
  Of the congregated Fall,
And the angle oceanic
  Where the deepening thunders call—
    And the Gorge so grim,
    And the firmamental rim!
Multitudinously thronging
  The waters all converge,
Then they sweep adown in sloping
  Solidity of surge.

      The Nation, in her impulse
        Mysterious as the Tide,
      In emotion like an ocean
        Moves in power, not in pride;
      And is deep in her devotion
        As Humanity is wide.
      Thou Lord of hosts victorious,
        The confluence Thou hast twined;
      By a wondrous way and glorious
        A passage Thou dost find—
        A passage Thou dost find:
      Hosanna to the Lord of hosts,
        The hosts of human kind.

Stable in its baselessness
  When calm is in the air,
The Iris half in tracelessness
  Hovers faintly fair.
Fitfully assailing it

A wind from heaven blows,
Shivering and paling it
    To blankness of the snows;
While, incessant in renewal,
    The Arch rekindled grows,
Till again the gem and jewel
    Whirl in blinding overthrows—
Till, prevailing and transcending,
    Lo, the Glory perfect there,
And the contest finds an ending,
    For repose is in the air.

But the foamy Deep unsounded,
    And the dim and dizzy ledge,
And the booming roar rebounded,
    And the gull that skims the edge!
        The Giant of the Pool
        Heaves his forehead white as wool—
Toward the Iris ever climbing
    From the Cataracts that call—
Irremovable vast arras
    Draping all the Wall.

        The Generations pouring
            From times of endless date,
        In their going, in their flowing
            Ever form the steadfast State;
        And Humanity is growing
            Toward the fullness of her fate.

        Thou Lord of hosts victorious,
            Fulfill the end designed;
        By a wondrous way and glorious
            A passage Thou dost find—
            A passage Thou dost find:
        Hosanna to the Lord of hosts.
            The hosts of human kind.

THE MARTYR

Indicative of the Passion of the People on the 15th of April 1865

GOOD FRIDAY was the day
  Of the prodigy and crime,
When they killed him in his pity,
  When they killed him in his prime
Of clemency and calm—
    When with yearning he was filled
    To redeem the evil-willed,
And, though conqueror, be kind;
    But they killed him in his kindness,
    In their madness and their blindness,
And they killed him from behind.

      There is sobbing of the strong,
        And a pall upon the land;
      But the People in their weeping
          Bare the iron hand:
      Beware the People weeping
        When they bare the iron hand.

He lieth in his blood—
  The father in his face;
They have killed him, the Forgiver—
  The Avenger takes his place,
The Avenger wisely stern,
    Who in righteousness shall do
    What the heavens call him to,
And the parricides remand;
    For they killed him in his kindness
    In their madness and their blindness,
And his blood is on their hand.

There is sobbing of the strong,
      And a pall upon the land;
But the People in their weeping
          Bare the iron hand:
Beware the People weeping
    When they bare the iron hand.

"THE COMING STORM"

A Picture by S. R. Gifford, and Owned by E. B. Included in the N. A. Exhibition, April 1865

ALL feeling hearts must feel for him
   Who felt this picture. Presage dim—
Dim inklings from the shadowy sphere
   Fixed him and fascinated here.

A demon-cloud like the mountain one
   Burst on a spirit as mild
As this urned lake, the home of shades,
   But Shakespeare's pensive child

Never the lines had lightly scanned,
   Steeped in fable, steeped in fate;
The Hamlet in his heart was 'ware,
   Such hearts can antedate.

No utter surprise can come to him
   Who reaches Shakespeare's core;
That which we seek and shun is there—
   Man's final lore.

REBEL COLOR-BEARERS AT SHILOH

A Plea Against the Vindictive Cry Raised by Civilians Shortly After the Surrender at Appomattox

THE color-bearers facing death
White in the whirling sulfurous wreath,
  Stand boldly out before the line;
Right and left their glances go,
Proud of each other, glorying in their show;
Their battle-flags about them blow,
  And fold them as in flame divine:
Such living robes are only seen
Round martyrs burning on the green—
And martyrs for the Wrong have been.

Perish their Cause! but mark the men—
Mark the planted statues, then
Draw trigger on them if you can.

The leader of a patriot-band
Even so could view rebels who so could stand;
  And this when peril pressed him sore,
Left aidless in the shivered front of war—
  Skulkers behind, defiant foes before,
And fighting with a broken brand.
The challenge in that courage rare—
Courage defenseless, proudly bare—
Never could tempt him; he could dare
Strike up the leveled rifle there.

Sunday at Shiloh, and the day
When Stonewall charged—McClellan's crimson May,
And Chickamauga's wave of death,

And of the Wilderness the cypress wreath—
    All these have passed away.
The life in the veins of Treason lags,
Her daring color-bearers drop their flags,
    And yield. *Now* shall we fire?
        Can poor spite be?
Shall nobleness in victory less aspire
Than in reverse? Spare Spleen her ire,
      And think how Grant met Lee.

THE MUSTER

Suggested by the Two Days' Review
at Washington

(May 1865)

THE Abrahamic river—
    Patriarch of floods,
Calls the roll of all his streams
    And watery multitudes:
           Torrent cries to torrent,
              The rapids hail the fall;
           With shouts the inland freshets
             Gather to the call.

The quotas of the Nation,
    Like the watershed of waves,
Muster into union—
    Eastern warriors, Western braves.

Martial strains are mingling,
    Though distant far the bands,
And the wheeling of the squadrons
    Is like surf upon the sands.

The bladed guns are gleaming—
    Drift in lengthened trim,
Files on files for hazy miles—
    Nebulously dim.

O Milky Way of armies—
    Star rising after star,
New banners of the Commonwealths
    And eagles of the War.

The Abrahamic river
  To sea-wide fullness fed,
Pouring from the thaw-lands
  By the God of floods is led:
        His deep enforcing current
          The streams of ocean own,
        And Europe's marge is evened
          By rills from Kansas lone.

"FORMERLY A SLAVE."

An idealized Portrait, by E. Vedder, in the Spring Exhibition of the National Academy, 1865.

THE sufferance of her race is shown,
    And retrospect of life,
Which now too late deliverance dawns upon;
    Yet is she not at strife.

Her children's children they shall know
    The good withheld from her;
And so her reverie takes prophetic cheer—
    In spirit she sees the stir

Far down the depth of thousand years,
    And marks the revel shine;
Her dusky face is lit with sober light,
    Sibylline, yet benign.

MAGNANIMITY BAFFLED

"SHARP words we had before the fight;
        But—now the fight is done—
Look, here's my hand," said the Victor bold,
        Take it—an honest one!
What, holding back? I mean you well;
    Though worsted, you strove stoutly, man;
The odds were great; I honor you;
        Man honors man.

"Still silent, friend? can grudges be?
        Yet am I held a foe?—
Turned to the wall, on his cot he lies—
        Never I'll leave him so!
Brave one! I here implore your hand;
    Dumb still? all fellowship fled?
Nay, then, I'll have this stubborn hand!"
        He snatched it—it was dead.

ON THE SLAIN COLLEGIANS

YOUTH is the time when hearts are large,
  And stirring wars
Appeal to the spirit which appeals in turn
  To the blade it draws.
If woman incite, and duty show
 (Though made the mask of Cain),
Or whether it be Truth's sacred cause,
  Who can aloof remain
That shares youth's ardor, uncooled by the snow
  Of wisdom or sordid gain?

The liberal arts and nurture sweet
Which give his gentleness to man—
 Train him to honor, lend him grace
Through bright examples meet—
That culture which makes never wan
 With underminings deep, but holds
  The surface still, its fitting place,
  And so gives sunniness to the face
And bravery to the heart; what troops
 Of generous boys in happiness thus bred—
 Saturnians through life's Tempe led,
Went from the North and came from the South,
With golden mottoes in the mouth,
 To lie down midway on a bloody bed.

Woe for the homes of the North,
And woe for the seats of the South:
All who felt life's spring in prime,
And were swept by the wind of their place and time—
 All lavish hearts, on whichever side,
Of birth urbane or courage high,

Armed them for the stirring wars—
Armed them—some to die.
  Apollo-like in pride,
Each would slay his Python—caught
The maxims in his temple taught—
 Aflame with sympathies whose blaze
Perforce enwrapped him—social laws,
 Friendship and kin, and bygone days—
Vows, kisses—every heart unmoors,
And launches into the seas of wars.
What could they else—North or South?
Each went forth with blessings given
By priests and mothers in the name of Heaven;
  And honor in both was chief.
Warred one for Right, and one for Wrong?
So be it; but they both were young—
Each grape to his cluster clung,
All their elegies are sung.

The anguish of maternal hearts
 Must search for balm divine;
But well the striplings bore their fated parts
 (The heavens all parts assign)—
Never felt life's care or cloy.
Each bloomed and died an unabated Boy;
Nor dreamed what death was—thought it mere
Sliding into some vernal sphere.
They knew the joy, but leaped the grief,
Like plants that flower ere comes the leaf—
Which storms lay low in kindly doom,
And kill them in their flush of bloom.

AMERICA

I

Where the wings of a sunny Dome expand
I saw a Banner in gladsome air—
Starry, like Berenice's Hair—
Afloat in broadened bravery there;
With undulating long-drawn flow,
As rolled Brazilian billows go
Voluminously o'er the Line.
The Land reposed in peace below;
    The children in their glee
Were folded to the exulting heart
    Of young Maternity.

II

Later, and it streamed in fight
    When tempest mingled with the fray,
And over the spear-point of the shaft
    I saw the ambiguous lightning play.
Valor with Valor strove, and died:
Fierce was Despair, and cruel was Pride;
And the lorn Mother speechless stood,
Pale at the fury of her brood.

III

Yet later, and the silk did wind
        Her fair cold form;
Little availed the shining shroud,
    Though ruddy in hue, to cheer or warm.

A watcher looked upon her low, and said—
She sleeps, but sleeps, she is not dead.
    But in that sleep contortion showed
The terror of the vision there—
    A silent vision unavowed,
Revealing earth's foundation bare,
    And Gorgon in her hidden place.
It was a thing of fear to see
    So foul a dream upon so fair a face,
And the dreamer lying in that starry shroud.

IV

But from the trance she sudden broke—
    The trance, or death into promoted life;
At her feet a shivered yoke,
And in her aspect turned to heaven
    No trace of passion or of strife—
A clear calm look. It spake of pain,
But such as purifies from stain—
Sharp pangs that never come again—
    And triumph repressed by knowledge meet,
Power dedicate, and hope grown wise,
    And youth matured for age's seat—
Law on her brow and empire in her eyes.
    So she, with graver air and lifted flag;
While the shadow, chased by light,
Fled along the far-drawn height,
    And left her on the crag.

VERSES INSCRIPTIVE AND MEMORIAL

ON THE HOME GUARDS

Who Perished in the Defense of Lexington, Missouri

THE men who here in harness died
  Fell not in vain, though in defeat.
They by their end well fortified
  The Cause, and built retreat
(With memory of their valor tried)
For emulous hearts in many an after fray—
Hearts sore beset, which died at bay.

THE FORTITUDE OF THE NORTH

Under the Disaster of the Second Manassas

THEY take no shame for dark defeat
  While prizing yet each victory won,
Who fight for the Right through all retreat,
  Nor pause until their work is done.
The Cape-of-Storms is proof to every throe;
  Vainly against that foreland beat
Wild winds aloft and wilder waves below:
  The black cliffs gleam through rents in sleet
When the livid Antarctic storm-clouds glow.

AN UNINSCRIBED MONUMENT

On One of the Battle-Fields of the Wilderness

SILENCE and Solitude may hint
  (Whose home is in yon piney wood)

What I, though tableted, could never tell—
The din which here befell,
   The striving of the multitude.
The iron cones and spheres of death
   Set round me in their rust,
      These, too, if just,
Shall speak with more than animated breath.
   Thou who beholdest, if thy thought,
Not narrowed down to personal cheer,
Take in the import of the quiet here—
   The after-quiet—the calm full fraught;
Thou too wilt silent stand—
Silent as I, and lonesome as the land.

ON THE GRAVE

Of a Young Cavalry Officer Killed in the Valley of Virginia

BEAUTY and youth, with manners sweet, and friends—
   Gold, yet a mind not unenriched had he
Whom here low violets veil from eyes.
   But all these gifts transcended be:
His happier fortune in this mound you see.

ON A NATURAL MONUMENT

In a Field of Georgia

No trophy this—a Stone unhewn,
   And stands where here the field immures
The nameless brave whose palms are won.
Outcast they sleep; yet fame is nigh—
   Pure fame of deeds, not doers;
Nor deeds of men who bleeding die
   In cheer of hymns that round them float:

In happy dreams such close the eye.
But withering famine slowly wore,
 And slowly fell disease did gloat.
Even Nature's self did aid deny;
They choked in horror the pensive sigh.
 Yea, off from home sad Memory bore
(Though anguished Yearning heaved that way),
Lest wreck of reason might befall.
 As men in gales shun the lee shore,
Though there the homestead be, and call,
And thitherward winds and waters sway—
As such lorn mariners, so fared they.
But naught shall now their peace molest.
 Their fame is this: they did endure—
Endure, when fortitude was vain
To kindle any approving strain
Which they might hear. To these who rest,
 This healing sleep alone was sure.

COMMEMORATIVE OF

A NAVAL VICTORY

SAILORS there are of gentlest breed,
 Yet strong, like every goodly thing;
The discipline of arms refines,
 And the wave gives tempering.
 The damasked blade its beam can fling;
It lends the last grave grace:
The hawk, the hound, and sworded nobleman
 In Titian's picture for a king,
Are of hunter or warrior race.

In social halls a favored guest
 In years that follow victory won,
How sweet to feel your festal fame
 In woman's glance instinctive thrown:

Repose is yours—your deed is known,
It musks the amber wine;
It lives, and sheds a light from storied days
    Rich as October sunsets brown,
Which make the barren place to shine.

But seldom the laurel wreath is seen
    Unmixed with pensive pansies dark;
There's a light and a shadow on every man
    Who at last attains his lifted mark—
    Nursing through night the ethereal spark.
Elate he never can be;
He feels that spirits which glad had hailed his worth,
    Sleep in oblivion.—The shark
Glides white through the phosphorous sea.

THE SCOUT TOWARD ALDIE

THE cavalry-camp lies on the slope
   Of what was late a vernal hill,
But now like a pavement bare—
An outpost in the perilous wilds
    Which ever are lone and still;
       But Mosby's men are there—
       Of Mosby best beware.

Great trees the troopers felled, and leaned
   In antlered walls about their tents,
Strict watch they kept; 'twas *Hark!* and *Mark!*
Unarmed none cared to stir abroad
    For berries beyond their forest-fence:
       As glides in seas the shark,
       Rides Mosby through green dark.

All spake of him, but few had seen
   Except the maimed ones or the low;
Yet rumor made him everything—
A farmer—woodman—refugee—
    The man who crossed the field but now;
       A spell about his life did cling—
       Who to the ground shall Mosby bring?

The morning bugles lonely play,
   Lonely the evening bugle calls—
Unanswered voices in the wild;
The settled hush of birds in nest
    Becharms, and all the wood enthralls:
       Memory's self is so beguiled
       That Mosby seems a satyr's child.

They lived as in the Eerie Land—
  The fire-flies showed with fairy gleam;
And yet from pine-tops one might ken
The Capitol Dome—hazy—sublime—
    A vision breaking on a dream:
        So strange it was that Mosby's men
        Should dare to prowl where the Dome was seen.

A scout toward Aldie broke the spell.—
  The Leader lies before his tent
Gazing at heaven's all-cheering lamp
Through blandness of a morning rare;
    His thoughts on bitter-sweets are bent:
        His sunny bride is in the camp—
        But Mosby—graves are beds of damp!

The trumpet calls; he goes within;
  But none the prayer and sob may know:
Her hero he, but bridegroom too.
Ah, love in a tent is a queenly thing,
    And fame, be sure, refines the vow;
        But fame fond wives have lived to rue,
        And Mosby's men fell deeds can do.

Tan-tara! tan-tara! tan-tara!
  Mounted and armed he sits a king;
For pride she smiles if now she peep—
Elate he rides at the head of his men;
    He is young, and command is a boyish thing:
        They file out into the forest deep—
        Do Mosby and his rangers sleep?

The sun is gold, and the world is green,
  Opal the vapors of morning roll;
The champing horses lightly prance—
Full of caprice, and the riders too
    Curving in many a caricole.
        But marshaled soon, by fours advance—
        Mosby had checked that airy dance.

By the hospital tent the cripples stand—
　　Bandage, and crutch, and cane, and sling,
And palely eye the brave array;
The froth of the cup is gone for them
　　　(Caw! caw! the crows through the blueness wing):
　　　　　Yet these were late as bold, as gay;
　　　　　But Mosby—a clip, and grass is hay.

How strong they feel on their horses free,
　　Tingles the tendoned thigh with life;
Their cavalry jackets make boys of all—
With golden breasts like the oriole;
　　The chat, the jest, and laugh are rife.
　　　　　But word is passed from the front—a call
　　　　　For order: the wood is Mosby's hall.

To which behest one rider sly
　　(Spurred, but unarmed) gave little heed—
Of dexterous fun not slow or spare,
He teased his neighbors of touchy mood,
　　Into plungings he pricked his steed:
　　　　　A black-eyed man on a coal-black mare,
　　　　　Alive as Mosby in mountain air.

His limbs were long, and large, and round;
　　He whispered, winked—did all but shout:
A healthy man for the sick to view;
The taste in his mouth was sweet at morn;
　　Little of care he cared about.
　　　　　And yet of pains and pangs he knew—
　　　　　In others, maimed by Mosby's crew.

The Hospital Steward—even he
　　(Sacred in person as a priest),
And on his coat-sleeve broidered nice
Wore the caduceus, black and green.
　　No wonder he sat so light on his beast;

This cheery man in suit of price
Not even Mosby dared to slice.

They pass the picket by the pine
    And hollow log—a lonesome place;
His horse adroop, and pistol clean;
'Tis cocked—kept leveled toward the wood;
    Strained vigilance ages his childish face.
        Since midnight has that stripling been
        Peering for Mosby through the green.

Splashing they cross the freshet-flood,
    And up the muddy bank they strain;
A horse at a spectral white-ash shies—
One of the span of the ambulance,
    Black as a hearse. They give the rein:
        Silent speed on a scout were wise,
        Could cunning baffle Mosby's spies.

Rumor had come that a band was lodged
    In green retreats of hills that peer
By Aldie (famed for the swordless charge).
Much store they'd heaped of captured arms
    And, peradventure, pilfered cheer;
        For Mosby's lads oft hearts enlarge
        In revelry by some gorge's marge.

"Don't let your sabers rattle and ring;
    To his oat-bag let each man give heed—
There now, that fellow's bag's untied,
Sowing the road with the precious grain.
    Your carbines swing at hand—you need!
        Look to yourselves, and your nags beside,
        Men who after Mosby ride."

Picked lads and keen went sharp before—
    A guard, though scarce against surprise;

And rearmost rode an answering troop,
But flankers none to right or left.
  No bugle peals, no pennon flies:
      Silent they sweep, and fain would swoop
      On Mosby with an Indian whoop.

On, right on through the forest land,
  Nor man, nor maid, nor child was seen—
Not even a dog. The air was still;
The blackened hut they turned to see,
  And spied charred benches on the green;
      A squirrel sprang from the rotting mill
      Whence Mosby sallied late, brave blood to spill.

By worn-out fields they cantered on—
  Drear fields amid the woodlands wide;
By cross-roads of some olden time,
In which grew groves; by gate-stones down—
  Grassed ruins of secluded pride:
      A strange lone land, long past the prime,
      Fit land for Mosby or for crime.

The brook in the dell they pass. One peers
  Between the leaves: "Ay, there's the place—
There, on the oozy ledge—'twas there
We found the body (Blake's, you know);
  Such whirlings, gurglings round the face—
      Shot drinking! Well, in war all's fair—
      So Mosby says. The bough—take care!"

Hard by, a chapel. Flower-pot mold
  Danked and decayed the shaded roof;
The porch was punk; the clapboards spanned
With ruffled lichens gray or green;
  Red coral-moss was not aloof;
      And mid dry leaves green dead-man's-hand
      Groped toward that chapel in Mosby-land.

They leave the road and take the wood,
    And mark the trace of ridges there—
·A wood where once had slept the farm—
A wood where once tobacco grew
    Drowsily in the hazy air,
            And wrought in all kind things a calm—
            Such influence, Mosby! bids disarm.

To ease even yet the place did woo—
    To ease which pines unstirring share,
For ease the weary horses sighed:
Halting, and slackening girths, they feed,
    Their pipes they light, they loiter there;
            Then up, and urging still the Guide,
            On, and after Mosby ride.

This Guide in frowzy coat of brown,
    And beard of ancient growth and mold,
Bestrode a bony steed and strong,
As suited well with bulk he bore—
    A wheezy man with depth of hold
            Who jouncing went. A staff he swung—
            A wight whom Mosby's wasp had stung.

Burnt out and homeless—hunted long!
    That wheeze he caught in autumn-wood
Crouching (a fat man) for his life,
And spied his lean son 'mong the crew
    That probed the covert. Ah! black blood
            Was his 'gainst even child and wife—
            Fast friends to Mosby. Such the strife.

A lad, unhorsed by sliding girths,
    Strains hard to readjust his seat
Ere the main body show the gap
'Twixt them and the rearguard; scrub-oaks near
    He sidelong eyes, while hands move fleet;

Then mounts and spurs. One drops his cap—
"Let Mosby find!" nor heeds mishap.

A gable time-stained peeps through trees:
   "You mind the fight in the haunted house?
That's it; we clenched them in the room—
An ambuscade of ghosts, we thought,
   But proved sly rebels on a bouse!
      Luke lies in the yard." The chimneys loom:
      Some muse on Mosby—some on doom.

Less nimbly now through brakes they wind,
   And ford wild creeks where men have drowned;
They skirt the pool, avoid the fen,
And so till night, when down they lie,
   Their steeds still saddled, in wooded ground:
      Rein in hand they slumber then,
      Dreaming of Mosby's cedarn den.

But Colonel and Major friendly sat
   Where boughs deformed low made a seat.
The Young Man talked (all sworded and spurred)
Of the partisan's blade he longed to win,
   And frays in which he meant to beat.
      The grizzled Major smoked and heard:
      "But what's that—Mosby?" "No, a bird."

A contrast here like sire and son,
   Hope and Experience sage did meet;
The Youth was brave, the Senior too;
But through the Seven Days one had served,
   And gasped with the rearguard in retreat:
      So he smoked and smoked, and the wreath he
        blew—
      "Any *sure* news of Mosby's crew?"

He smoked and smoked, eyeing the while
   A huge tree hydra-like in growth—

Moon-tinged—with crook'd boughs rent or lopped—
Itself a haggard forest. "Come!"
    The Colonel cried, "to talk you're loath;
        D'ye hear? I say he must be stopped,
        This Mosby—caged, and hair close cropped."

"Of course; but what's that dangling there?"
    "Where?" "From the tree—that gallows-bough";
"A bit of frayed bark, is it not?"
"Ay—or a rope; did *we* hang last?—
    Don't like my neckerchief anyhow";
        He loosened it: "O ay, we'll stop
        This Mosby—but that vile jerk and drop!"

By peep of light they feed and ride,
    Gaining a grove's green edge at morn,
And mark the Aldie hills uprear
And five gigantic horsemen carved
    Clear-cut against the sky withdrawn;
        Are more behind? an open snare?
        Or Mosby's men but watchmen there?

The ravaged land was miles behind,
    And Loudon spread her landscape rare;
Orchards in pleasant lowlands stood,
Cows were feeding, a cock loud crew,
    But not a friend at need was there;
        The valley-folk were only good
        To Mosby and his wandering brood.

What best to do? what mean yon men?
    Colonel and Guide their minds compare;
Be sure some looked their Leader through;
Dismounted, on his sword he leaned
    As one who feigns an easy air;
        And yet perplexed he was they knew—
        Perplexed by Mosby's mountain crew.

The Major hemmed as he would speak,
   But checked himself, and left the ring
Of cavalrymen about their Chief—
Young courtiers mute who paid their court
   By looking with confidence on their king;
         They knew him brave, foresaw no grief—
         But Mosby—the time to think is brief.

The Surgeon (sashed in sacred green)
   Was glad 'twas not for *him* to say
What next should be; if a trooper bleeds,
Why he will do his best, as wont,
   And his partner in black will aid and pray;
         But judgment bides with him who leads,
         And Mosby many a problem breeds.

This Surgeon was the kindliest man
   That ever a callous trade professed;
He felt for him, that Leader young,
And offered medicine from his flask;
   The Colonel took it with marvelous zest.
         For such fine medicine good and strong
         Oft Mosby and his foresters long.

A charm of proof. "Ho, Major, come—
   Pounce on yon men! Take half your troop,
Through the thickets wind—pray speedy be—
And gain their rear. And, Captain Morn,
   Picket these roads—all travelers stop;
         The rest to the edge of this crest with me,
         That Mosby and his scouts may see."

Commanded and done. Ere the sun stood steep,
   Back came the Blues, with a troop of Grays,
Ten riding double—luckless ten!—
Five horses gone, and looped hats lost,
   And love-locks dancing in a maze—

Certes, but sophomores from the glen
Of Mosby—not his veteran men.

"Colonel," said the Major, touching his cap,
    "We've had our ride, and here they are."
"Well done! how many found you there?"
"As many as I bring you here."
        "And no one hurt?" "There'll be no scar—
            One fool was battered." "Find their lair?"
            "Why, Mosby's brood camp everywhere."

He sighed, and slid down from his horse,
    And limping went to a spring-head nigh.
"Why, bless me, Major, not hurt, I hope?"
"Battered my knee against a bar
    When the rush was made; all right by-and-by.—
        Halloa! they gave you too much rope—
        Go back to Mosby, eh? elope?"

Just by the low-hanging skirt of wood
    The guard, remiss, had given a chance
For a sudden sally into the cover—
But foiled the intent, nor fired a shot,
    Though the issue was a deadly trance;
        For, hurled 'gainst an oak that humped low over,
        Mosby's man fell, pale as a lover.

They pulled some grass his head to ease
    (Lined with blue shreds a ground-nest stirred).
The Surgeon came—"Here's a to-do!"
"Ah!" cried the Major, darting a glance,
    "This fellow's the one that fired and spurred
        Downhill, but met reserves below—
        My boys, not Mosby's—so we go!"

The Surgeon—bluff, red, goodly man—
    Kneeled by the hurt one; like a bee

He toiled. The pale young Chaplain too—
(Who went to the wars for cure of souls,
    And his own student-ailments)—he
        Bent over likewise; spite the two,
        Mosby's poor man more pallid grew.

Meanwhile the mounted captives near
    Jested; and yet they anxious showed;
Virginians; some of family pride,
And young, and full of fire, and fine
    In open feature and cheek that glowed;
        And here thralled vagabonds now they ride—
        But list! one speaks for Mosby's side.

"Why, three to one—your horses strong—
    Revolvers, rifles, and a surprise—
Surrender we account no shame!
We live, are gay, and life is hope;
    We'll fight again when fight is wise.
        There are plenty more from where we came;
        But go find Mosby—start the game!"

Yet one there was who looked but glum;
    In middle-age, a father he,
And this his first experience too;
"They shot at my heart when my hands were up—
    This fighting's crazy work, I see!"
        But noon is high; what next to do?
        The woods are mute, and Mosby is the foe.

"Save what we've got" the Major said;
    "Bad plan to make a scout too long;
The tide may turn, and drag them back,
And more beside. These rides I've been,
    And every time a mine was sprung.
        To rescue, mind, they won't be slack—
        Look out for Mosby's rifle-crack."

"We'll welcome it! give crack for crack!
    Peril, old lad, is what I seek."
"O then, there's plenty to be had—
By all means on, and have our fill!"
    With that, grotesque, he writhed his neck,
            Showing a scar by buck-shot made—
            Kind Mosby's Christmas gift, he said.

"But, Colonel, my prisoners—let a guard
    Make sure of them, and lead to camp.
That done, we're free for a dark-room fight
If so you say." The other laughed;
    "Trust me, Major, now throw a damp.
            But first to try a little sleight—
            Sure news of Mosby would suit me quite."

Herewith he turned—"Reb, have a dram?"
    Holding the Surgeon's flask with a smile
To a young scapegrace from the glen.
"O yes!" he eagerly replied,
    "And thank you, Colonel, but—any guile?
            For if you think we'll blab—why, then
            You don't know Mosby or his men."

The Leader's genial air relaxed.
    "Best give it up," a whisperer said.
"By heaven, I'll range their rebel den!"
"They'll treat you well," the captive cried;
    "They're all like us—handsome—well-bred:
            In wood or town, with sword or pen,
            Polite is Mosby, bland his men."

"Where were you, lads, last night?—come, tell!"
    "We?—at a wedding in the Vale—
The bridegroom our comrade; by his side
Belisent, my cousin—O, so proud
    Of her young love with old wounds pale—

A Virginian girl! God bless her pride—
Of a crippled Mosby-man the bride!"

"Four walls shall mend that saucy mood,
    And moping prisons tame him down,"
Said Captain Cloud. "God help that day,"
Cried Captain Morn, "and he so young.
    But hark, he sings—a madcap one!"
        *"O we multiply merrily in the May,
        The birds and Mosby's men, they say!"*

While echoes ran, a wagon old,
    Under stout guard of Corporal Chew
Came up; a lame horse, dingy white,
With clouted harness; ropes in hand,
    Cringed the humped driver, black in hue;
        By him (for Mosby's band a sight)
        A sister-rebel sat, her veil held tight.

"I picked them up," the Corporal said,
    "Crunching their way over stick and root,
Through yonder wood. The man here—Cuff—
Says they are going to Leesburg town."
    The Colonel's eye took in the group;
        The veiled one's hand he spied—enough!
        Not Mosby's. Spite the gown's poor stuff,

Off went his hat: "Lady, fear not;
    We soldiers do what we deplore—
I must detain you till we march."
The stranger nodded. Nettled now,
    He grew politer than before:—
        " 'Tis Mosby's fault, this halt and search":
        The lady stiffened in her starch.

"My duty, madam, bids me now
    Ask what may seem a little rude.

Pardon—that veil—withdraw it, please
(Corporal! make every man fall back);
   Pray, now, I do but what I should;
      Bethink you, 'tis in masks like these
      That Mosby haunts the villages."

Slowly the stranger drew her veil,
   And looked the Soldier in the eye—
A glance of mingled foul and fair;
Sad patience in a proud disdain,
   And more than quietude. A sigh
      She heaved, as if all unaware,
      And far seemed Mosby from her care.

She came from Yewton Place, her home,
   So ravaged by the war's wild play—
Campings, and foragings, and fires—
That now she sought an aunt's abode.
   Her kinsmen? In Lee's army, they.
      The black? A servant, late her sire's.
      And Mosby? Vainly he inquires.

He gazed, and sad she met his eye;
   "In the wood yonder were you lost?"
No; at the forks they left the road
Because of hoof-prints (thick they were—
   Thick as the words in notes thrice crossed),
      And fearful, made that episode.
      In fear of Mosby? None she showed.

Her poor attire again he scanned:
   "Lady, once more; I grieve to jar
On all sweet usage, but must plead
To have what peeps there from your dress;
   That letter—'tis justly prize of war."
      She started—gave it—she must need.
      " 'Tis not from Mosby? May I read?"

And straight such matter he perused
　　That with the Guide he went apart.
The Hospital Steward's turn began:
"Must squeeze this darkey; every tap
　　Of knowledge we are bound to start."
　　　　　"Garry," she said, "tell all you can
　　　　　Of Colonel Mosby—that brave man."

"Dun know much, sare; and missis here
　　Know less dan me. But dis I know—"
"Well, what?" "I dun know what I know."
"A knowing answer!" The humpback coughed,
　　Rubbing his yellowish wool like tow.
　　　　　"Come—Mosby—tell!" "O dun look so!
　　　　　My gal nursed missis—let we go."

"Go where?" demanded Captain Cloud;
　　"Back into bondage? Man, you're free!"
"Well, *let* we free!" The Captain's brow
Lowered; the Colonel came—had heard:
　　"Pooh! pooh! his simple heart I see—
　　　　　A faithful servant.—Lady" (a bow),
　　　　　"Mosby's abroad—with us you'll go."

"Guard! look to your prisoners; back to camp!
　　The man in the grass—can he mount and away?
Why, how he groans!" "Bad inward bruise—
Might lug him along in the ambulance."
　　"Coals to Newcastle! let him stay.
　　　　　Boots and saddles!—our pains we lose,
　　　　　Nor care I if Mosby hear the news!"

But word was sent to a house at hand,
　　And a flask was left by the hurt one's side.
They seized in that same house a man,
Neutral by day, by night a foe—
　　So charged his neighbor late, the Guide.

A grudge? Hate will do what it can;
Along he went for a Mosby-man.

No secrets now; the bugle calls;
    The open road they take, nor shun
The hill; retrace the weary way.
But one there was who whispered low,
    "This is a feint—we'll back anon;
        Young Hair-Brains don't retreat, they say;
        A brush with Mosby is the play!"

They rode till eve. Then on a farm
    That lay along a hill-side green,
Bivouacked. Fires were made, and then
Coffee was boiled; a cow was coaxed
    And killed, and savory roasts were seen;
        And under the lee of a cattle-pen
        The guard supped freely with Mosby's men.

The ball was bandied to and fro;
    Hits were given and hits were met:
"Chickamauga, Feds—take off your hat!"
"But the Fight in the Clouds repaid you, Rebs!"
    "Forgotten about Manassas yet?"
        Chatting and chaffing, and tit for tat,
        Mosby's clan with the troopers sat.

"Here comes the moon!" a captive cried;
    "A song! what say? Archy, my lad!"
Hailing the still one of the clan
(A boyish face with girlish hair),
    "Give us that thing poor Pansy made
        Last year." He brightened, and began;
        And this was the song of Mosby's man:

        Spring is come; she shows her pass—
            Wild violets cool!

South of woods a small close grass—
A vernal wool!
Leaves are a'bud on the sassafras—
They'll soon be full:
Blessings on the friendly screen—
I'm for the South! says the leafage green.

Robins! fly, and take your fill
Of out of doors—
Garden, orchard, meadow, hill,
Barns and bowers;
Take your fill, and have your will—
Virginia's yours!
But, bluebirds! keep away, and fear
The ambuscade in bushes here.

"A green song that," a sergeant said;
  "But where's poor Pansy? gone, I fear."
"Ay, mustered out at Ashby's Gap."
  "I see; now for a live man's song;
    Ditty for ditty—prepare to cheer.
      My bluebirds, you can fling a cap!
      You barehead Mosby-boys—why—clap!"

Nine Blue-coats went a-nutting
Slyly in Tennessee—
Not for chestnuts—better than that—
Hush, you bumble-bee!
Nutting, nutting—
All through the year there's nutting!

A tree they spied so yellow,
Rustling in motion queer;
In they fired, and down they dropped—
Butternuts, my dear!
Nutting, nutting—
Who'll 'list to go a-nutting?

Ah! why should good fellows foemen be?
   And who would dream that foes they were—
Larking and singing so friendly then—
A family likeness in every face.
   But Captain Cloud made sour demur:
      "Guard! keep your prisoners *in* the pen,
      And let none talk with Mosby's men."

That captain was a valorous one
   (No irony, but honest truth),
Yet down from his brain cold drops distilled,
Making stalactites in his heart—
   A conscientious soul, forsooth;
      And with a formal hate was filled
      Of Mosby's band; and some he'd killed.

Meantime the lady rueful sat,
   Watching the flicker of a fire
Where the Colonel played the outdoor host
In brave old hall of ancient Night.
   But ever the dame grew shyer and shyer,
      Seeming with private grief engrossed—
      Grief far from Mosby, housed or lost.

The ruddy embers showed her pale.
   The Soldier did his best devoir:
"Some coffee?—no?—a cracker?—one?"
Cared for her servant—sought to cheer:
   "I know, I know—a cruel war!
      But wait—even Mosby'll eat his bun;
      The Old Hearth—back to it anon!"

But cordial words no balm could bring;
   She sighed, and kept her inward chafe,
And seemed to hate the voice of glee—
Joyless and tearless. Soon he called
   An escort: "See this lady safe

In yonder house.—Madam, you're free.
And now for Mosby.—Guide! with me."

("A night-ride, eh?") "Tighten your girths!
  But, buglers! not a note from you.
Fling more rails on the fires—a blaze!"
("Sergeant, a feint—I told you so—
  Toward Aldie again. Bivouac, adieu!")
      After the cheery flames they gaze,
      Then back for Mosby through the maze.

The moon looked through the trees, and tipped
  The scabbards with her elfin beam;
The Leader backward cast his glance,
Proud of the cavalcade that came—
  A hundred horses, bay and cream:
      "Major! look how the lads advance—
      Mosby we'll have in the ambulance!"

"No doubt, no doubt:—was that a hare?—
  First catch, then cook; and cook him brown."
"Trust me to catch," the other cried—
"The lady's letter!—a dance, man, dance
  This night is given in Leesburg town!"
      "He'll be there, too!" wheezed out the Guide;
      "That Mosby loves a dance and ride!"

"The lady, ah!—the lady's letter—
  A *lady,* then, is in the case,"
Muttered the Major. "Ay, her aunt
Writes her to come by Friday eve
  (To-night), for people of the place,
      At Mosby's last fight jubilant,
      A party give, though table-cheer be scant."

The Major hemmed. "Then this night-ride
  We owe to her?—One lighted house

In a town else dark.—The moths, begar!
Are not quite yet all dead!" "How? how?"
    "A mute, meek, mournful little mouse!—
        Mosby has wiles which subtle are—
        But woman's wiles in wiles of war!"

"Tut, Major! by what craft or guile—"
    "Can't tell! but he'll be found in wait.
Softly we enter, say, the town—
Good! pickets post, and all so sure—
    When—crack! the rifles from every gate,
        The Gray-backs fire—dash up and down—
        Each alley unto Mosby known!"

"Now, Major, now—you take dark views
    Of a moonlight night." "Well, well, we'll see,"
And smoked as if each whiff were gain.
The other mused; then sudden asked,
    "What would you do in grand decree?"
        "I'd beat, if I could, Lee's armies—then
        Send constables after Mosby's men."

"Ay! ay!—you're odd." The moon sailed up;
    On through the shadowy land they went.
Names must be made and printed be!
Hummed the blithe Colonel. "Doc, your flask!
    Major, I drink to your good content.
        My pipe is out—enough for me!
        One's buttons shine—does Mosby see?"

"But what comes here?" A man from the front
    Reported a tree athwart the road.
"Go round it, then; no time to bide;
All right—go on! Were one to stay
    For each distrust of a nervous mood,
        Long miles we'd make in this our ride
        Through Mosby-land.—On! with the Guide!"

Then sportful to the Surgeon turned:
  "Green sashes hardly serve by night!"
"Nor bullets nor bottles," the Major sighed,
"Against these moccasin-snakes—such foes
   As seldom come to solid fight:
      They kill and vanish; through grass they glide;
      Devil take Mosby!"—his horse here shied.

"Hold! look—the tree, like a dragged balloon:
  A globe of leaves—some trickery here;
My nag is right—best now be shy."
A movement was made, a hubbub and snarl;
  Little was plain—they blindly steer.
     The Pleiads, as from ambush sly,
     Peep out—Mosby's men in the sky!

As restive they turn, how sore they feel,
  And cross, and sleepy, and full of spleen,
And curse the war. "Fools, North and South!"
Said one right out. "O for a bed!
  O now to drop in this woodland green!"
     He drops as the syllables leave his mouth
     Mosby speaks from the undergrowth—

Speaks in a volley! out jets the flame!
  Men fall from their saddles like plums from trees;
Horses take fright, reins tangle and bind;
"Steady—dismount—form—and into the wood!"
  They go, but find what scarce can please:
     Their steeds have been tied in the field behind,
     And Mosby's men are off like the wind.

Sound the recall! vain to pursue—
  The enemy scatters in wilds he knows,
To reunite in his own good time;
And, to follow, they need divide—
  To come lone and lost on crouching foes:

Maple and hemlock, beech and lime,
Are Mosby's confederates, share the crime.

"Major," burst in a bugler small,
    "The fellow we left in Loudon grass—
Sir Slyboots with the inward bruise,
His voice I heard—the very same—
    Some watchword in the ambush pass;
        Ay, sir, we had him in his shoes—
        We caught him—Mosby—but to lose!"

"Go, go!—these saddle-dreamers! Well,
    And here's another.—Cool, sir, cool!"
"Major, I saw them mount and sweep,
And one was humped, or I mistake,
    And in the skurry dropped his wool."
        "A wig! go fetch it:—the lads need sleep;
        They'll next see Mosby in a sheep!"

"Come, come, fall back! reform your ranks—
    All's jackstraws here! Where's Captain Morn?—
We've parted like boats in a raging tide!
But stay—the Colonel—did he charge?
    And comes he there? 'Tis streak of dawn;
        Mosby is off, the woods are wide—
        Hist! there's a groan—this crazy ride!"

As they searched for the fallen, the dawn grew chill;
    They lay in the dew: "Ah! hurt much, Mink?
And—yes—the Colonel!" Dead! but so calm
That death seemed nothing—even death,
    The thing we deem everything heart can think;
        Amid wilding roses that shed their balm,
        Careless of Mosby he lay—in a charm!

The Major took him by the hand—
    Into the friendly clasp it bled

(A ball through heart and hand he rued):
"Good-bye!" and gazed with humid glance;
   Then in a hollow reverie said,
      "The weakest thing is lustihood;
     But Mosby"—and he checked his mood.

"Where's the advance?—cut off, by heaven!
   Come, Surgeon, how with your wounded there?"
"The ambulance will carry all."
"Well, get them in; we go to camp.
   Seven prisoners gone? for the rest have care."
      Then to himself, "This grief is gall;
     That Mosby!—I'll cast a silver ball!"

"Ho!" turning—"Captain Cloud, you mind
   The place where the escort went—so shady?
Go, search every closet low and high,
And barn, and bin, and hidden bower—
   Every covert—find that lady!
      And yet I may misjudge her—ay,
     Women (like Mosby) mystify."

"We'll see. Ay, Captain, go—with speed!
   Surround and search; each living thing
Secure; that done, await us where
We last turned off. Stay! fire the cage
   If the birds be flown." By the cross-road spring
      The bands rejoined; no words; the glare
     Told all. Had Mosby plotted there?

The weary troop that wended now—
   Hardly it seemed the same that pricked
Forth to the forest from the camp:
Foot-sore horses, jaded men;
   Every backbone felt as nicked,
      Each eye dim as a sick-room lamp,
     All faces stamped with Mosby's stamp.

In order due the Major rode—
   Chaplain and Surgeon on either hand;
A riderless horse a negro led;
In a wagon the blanketed sleeper went;
   Then the ambulance with the bleeding band;
      And, an emptied oat-bag on each head,
      Went Mosby's men, and marked the dead.

What gloomed them? what so cast them down,
   And changed the cheer that late they took,
As double-guarded now they rode
Between the files of moody men?
   Some sudden consciousness they brook,
      Or dread the sequel. That night's blood
      Disturbed even Mosby's brotherhood.

The flagging horses stumbled at roots,
   Floundered in mires, or clinked the stones;
No rider spake except aside;
But the wounded cramped in the ambulance,
   It was horror to hear their groans—
      Jerked along in the woodland ride,
      While Mosby's clan their reverie hide.

The Hospital Steward—even he—
   Who on the sleeper kept his glance,
Was changed; late bright-black beard and eye
Looked now hearse-black; his heavy heart,
   Like his fagged mare, no more could dance;
      His grape was now a raisin dry:
      'Tis Mosby's homily—*Man must die.*

The amber sunset flushed the camp
   As on the hill their eyes they fed;
The pickets dumb looks at the wagon dart;
A handkerchief waves from the bannered tent—
   As white, alas! the face of the dead:

Who shall the withering news impart?
The bullet of Mosby goes through heart to heart!

They buried him where the lone ones lie
(Lone sentries shot on midnight post)—
A greenwood graveyard hid from ken,
Where sweet-fern flings an odor nigh—
Yet held in fear for the gleaming ghost!
Though the bride should see threescore and ten,
She will dream of Mosby and his men.

Now halt the verse, and turn aside—
The cypress falls athwart the way;
No joy remains for bard to sing;
And heaviest dole of all is this,
That other hearts shall be as gay
As hers that now no more shall spring:
To Mosby-land the dirges cling.

LEE IN THE CAPITOL

(April 1866)

Hard pressed by numbers in his strait,
   Rebellion's soldier-chief no more contends—
Feels that the hour is come of Fate,
   Lays down one sword, and widened warfare ends.
The captain who fierce armies led
Becomes a quiet seminary's head—
Poor as his privates, earns his bread.
In studious cares and aims engrossed,
   Strives to forget Stuart and Stonewall dead—
Comrades and cause, station and riches lost,
   And all the ills that flock when fortune's fled.
No word he breathes of vain lament,
   Mute to reproach, nor hears applause—
His doom accepts, perforce content,
   And acquiesces in asserted laws;
Secluded now would pass his life,
And leave to time the sequel of the strife.
   But missives from the Senators ran;
Not that they now would gaze upon a swordless foe,
And power made powerless and brought low:
   Reasons of state, 'tis claimed, require the man.
Demurring not, promptly he comes
By ways which show the blackened homes,
   And—last—the seat no more his own,
But Honor's; patriot graveyards fill
The forfeit slopes of that patrician hill,
   And fling a shroud on Arlington.
The oaks ancestral all are low;
No more from the porch his glance shall go
Ranging the varied landscape o'er,

Far as the looming Dome—no more.
One look he gives, then turns aside,
Solace he summons from his pride:
"So be it! They await me now
Who wrought this stinging overthrow;
They wait me; not as on the day
Of Pope's impelled retreat in disarray—
By me impelled—when toward yon Dome
The clouds of war came rolling home."
The burst, the bitterness was spent,
The heart-burst bitterly turbulent,
And on he fared.
                              In nearness now
      He marks the Capitol—a show
Lifted in amplitude, and set
With standards flushed with the glow of Richmond yet;
      Trees and green terraces sleep below.
Through the clear air, in sunny light,
The marble dazes—a temple white.

Intrepid soldier! had his blade been drawn
For yon starred flag, never as now
Bid to the Senate-house had he gone,
But freely, and in pageant borne,
As when brave numbers without number, massed,
Plumed the broad way, and pouring passed—
Bannered, beflowered—between the shores
Of faces, and the dinn'd huzzas,
And balconies kindling at the saber-flash,
'Mid roar of drums and guns, and cymbal-crash,
While Grant and Sherman shone in blue—
Close of the war and victory's long review.

Yet pride at hand still aidful swelled,
And up the hard ascent he held.
The meeting follows. In his mien
The victor and the vanquished both are seen—
All that he is, and what he late had been.

Awhile, with curious eyes they scan
The Chief who led invasion's van—
Allied by family to one,
Founder of the Arch the Invader warred upon:
Who looks at Lee must think of Washington;
In pain must think, and hide the thought,
So deep with grievous meaning it is fraught.

Secession in her soldier shows
Silent and patient; and they feel
    (Developed even in just success)
Dim inklings of a hazy future steal;
    Their thoughts their questions well express:
"Does the sad South still cherish hate?
Freely will Southern men with Northern mate?
The blacks—should we our arm withdraw,
Would that betray them? some distrust your law.
And how if foreign fleets should come—
Would the South then drive her wedges home?"
And more hereof. The Virginian sees—
Replies to such anxieties.
Discreet his answers run—appear
Briefly straightforward, coldly clear.

"If now," the Senators, closing, say,
"Aught else remain, speak out, we pray."
Hereat he paused; his better heart
Strove strongly then; prompted a worthier part
Than coldly to endure his doom.
Speak out? Ay, speak, and for the brave,
Who else no voice or proxy have;
Frankly their spokesman here become,
And the flushed North from her own victory save.
That inspiration overrode—
Hardly it quelled the galling load
Of personal ill. The inner feud
He, self-contained, a while withstood;
They waiting. In his troubled eye

Shadows from clouds unseen they spy;
They could not mark within his breast
The pang which pleading thought oppressed:
He spoke, nor felt the bitterness die.

"My word is given—it ties my sword;
Even were banners still abroad,
Never could I strive in arms again
While you, as fit, that pledge retain.
Our cause I followed, stood in field and gate—
All's over now, and now I follow Fate.
But this is naught. A People call—
A desolated land, and all
The brood of ills that press so sore,
The natural offspring of this civil war,
Which ending not in fame, such as might rear
Fitly its sculptured trophy here,
Yields harvest large of doubt and dread
To all who have the heart and head
To feel and know. How shall I speak?
Thoughts knot with thoughts, and utterance check.
Before my eyes there swims a haze,
Through mists departed comrades gaze—
First to encourage, last that shall upbraid!
How shall I speak? The South would fain
Feel peace, have quiet law again—
Replant the trees for homestead-shade.
    You ask if she recants: she yields.
Nay, and would more; would blend anew,
As the bones of the slain in her forests do,
Bewailed alike by us and you.
    A voice comes out from these charnel-fields,
A plaintive yet unheeded one:
'Died all in vain? both sides undone?'
Push not your triumph; do not urge
Submissiveness beyond the verge.
Intestine rancor would you bide,
Nursing eleven sliding daggers in your side?

Far from my thought to school or threat;
I speak the things which hard beset.
Where various hazards meet the eyes,
To elect in magnanimity is wise.
Reap victory's fruit while sound the core;
What sounder fruit than re-established law?
I know your partial thoughts do press
Solely on us for war's unhappy stress;
But weigh—consider—look at all,
And broad anathema you'll recall.
The censor's charge I'll not repeat,
That meddlers kindled the war's white heat—
Vain intermeddlers and malign,
Both of the palm and of the pine;
I waive the thought—which never can be rife—
Common's the crime in every civil strife:
But this I feel, that North and South were driven
By Fate to arms. For *our* unshriven,
What thousands, truest souls, were tried—
    As never may any be again—
All those who stemmed Secession's pride,
But at last were swept by the urgent tide
    Into the chasm. I know their pain.
A story here may be applied:
'In Moorish lands there lived a maid
    Brought to confess by vow the creed
    Of Christians. Fain would priests persuade
That now she must approve by deed
    The faith she kept. "What deed?" she asked.
"Your old sire leave, nor deem it sin,
    And come with us." Still more they tasked
The sad one: "If heaven you'd win—
    Far from the burning pit withdraw,
Then must you learn to hate your kin,
    Yea, side against them—such the law,
For Moor and Christian are at war."
"Then will I never quit my sire,
But here with him through every trial go,

Nor leave him though in flames below—
God help me in his fire!" '
So in the South; vain every plea
'Gainst Nature's strong fidelity;
    True to the home and to the heart,
Throngs cast their lot with kith and kin,
    Foreboding, cleaved to the natural part—
Was this the unforgivable sin?
These noble spirits are yet yours to win.
Shall the great North go Sylla's way?
Proscribe? prolong the evil day?
Confirm the curse? infix the hate?
In Union's name forever alienate?
From reason who can urge the plea—
Freemen conquerors of the free?
When blood returns to the shrunken vein,
Shall the wound of the Nation bleed again?
Well may the wars wan thought supply,
And kill the kindling of the hopeful eye,
Unless you do what even kings have done
In leniency—unless you shun
To copy Europe in her worst estate—
Avoid the tyranny you reprobate."

He ceased. His earnestness unforeseen
Moved, but not swayed their former mien;
    And they dismissed him. Forth he went
Through vaulted walks in lengthened line
Like porches erst upon the Palatine:
    Historic reveries their lesson lent,
    The Past her shadow through the Future sent.

But no. Brave though the Soldier, grave his plea—
    Catching the light in the future's skies,
Instinct disowns each darkening prophecy:
    Faith in America never dies;
Heaven shall the end ordained fulfil,
We march with Providence cheery still.

A MEDITATION

Attributed to a Northerner after Attending the Last of Two Funerals from the same Homestead—those of a National and a Confederate officer (brothers), his Kinsmen, who had died from the effects of wounds received in the closing battles.

How often in the years that close,
   When truce had stilled the sieging gun,
The soldiers, mounting on their works,
   With mutual curious glance have run
From face to face along the fronting show,
And kinsman spied, or friend—even in a foe.

What thoughts conflicting then were shared,
   While sacred tenderness perforce
Welled from the heart and wet the eye;
   And something of a strange remorse
Rebelled against the sanctioned sin of blood,
And Christian wars of natural brotherhood.

Then stirred the god within the breast—
   The witness that is man's at birth;
A deep misgiving undermined
   Each plea and subterfuge of earth;
They felt in that rapt pause, with warning rife,
Horror and anguish for the civil strife.

Of North or South they recked not then,
   Warm passion cursed the cause of war:
Can Africa pay back this blood
   Spilt on Potomac's shore?
Yet doubts, as pangs, were vain the strife to stay,
And hands that fain had clasped again could slay.

How frequent in the camp was seen
   The herald from the hostile one,
A guest and frank companion there
   When the proud formal talk was done;
The pipe of peace was smoked even 'mid the war,
And fields in Mexico again fought o'er.

In Western battle long they lay
   So near opposed in trench or pit,
That foeman unto foeman called
   As men who screened in tavern sit:
"You bravely fight" each to the other said—
"Toss us a biscuit!" o'er the wall it sped.

And pale on those same slopes, a boy—
   A stormer, bled in noonday glare;
No aid the Blue-coats then could bring,
   He cried to them who nearest were,
And out there came 'mid howling shot and shell
A daring foe who him befriended well.

Mark the great Captains on both sides,
   The soldiers with the broad renown—
They all were messmates on the Hudson's marge,
   Beneath one roof they laid them down;
And, free from hate in many an after pass,
Strove as in schoolboy rivalry of the class.

A darker side there is; but doubt
   In Nature's charity hovers there:
If men for new agreement yearn,
   Then old upbraiding best forbear:
"The South's the sinner!" Well, so let it be;
But shall the North sin worse, and stand the Pharisee?

O, now that brave men yield the sword,
   Mine be the manful soldier-view;

By how much more they boldly warred,
   By so much more is mercy due:
When Vicksburg fell, and the moody files marched
   out,
Silent the victors stood, scorning to raise a shout.

SUPPLEMENT

WERE I fastidiously anxious for the symmetry of this book, it would close with the notes. But the times are such that patriotism—not free from solicitude—urges a claim overriding all literary scruples.

It is more than a year since the memorable surrender, but events have not yet rounded themselves into completion. Not justly can we complain of this. There has been an upheaval affecting the basis of things; to altered circumstances complicated adaptations are to be made; there are difficulties great and novel. But is Reason still waiting for Passion to spend itself? We have sung of the soldiers and sailors, but who shall hymn the politicians?

In view of the infinite desirableness of Re-establishment, and considering that, so far as feeling is concerned, it depends not mainly on the temper in which the South regards the North, but rather conversely; one who never was a blind adherent feels constrained to submit some thoughts, counting on the indulgence of his countrymen.

And, first, it may be said that, if among the feelings and opinions growing immediately out of a great civil convulsion, there are any which time shall modify or do away, they are presumably those of a less temperate and charitable cast.

There seems no reason why patriotism and narrowness should go together, or why intellectual impartiality should be confounded with political trimming, or why serviceable truth should keep cloistered because not partisan. Yet the work of Reconstruction, if admitted to be feasible at all, demands little but common sense and Christian charity. Little but these? These are much.

Some of us are concerned because as yet the South shows no penitence. But what exactly do we mean by this? Since down to the close of the war she never confessed any for braving it, the only penitence now left her is that which springs solely from the sense of discomfiture; and since this evidently would be a contrition hypocritical, it would be unworthy in us to demand it. Certain it is that penitence, in the sense of voluntary humiliation, will never be displayed. Nor does this afford just ground for unreserved condemnation. It is enough, for all practical purposes, if the South have been taught by the terrors of civil war to feel that Secession, like Slavery, is against Destiny; that both now lie buried in one grave; that her fate is linked with ours; and that together we comprise the Nation.

The clouds of heroes who battled for the Union it is needless to eulogize here. But how of the soldiers on the other side? And when of a free community we name the soldiers, we thereby name the people. It was in subserviency to the slave-interest that Secession was plotted; but it was under the plea, plausibly urged, that certain inestimable rights guaranteed by the Constitution were directly menaced that the people of the South were cajoled into revolution. Through the arts of the conspirators and the perversity of fortune, the most sensitive love of liberty was entrapped into the support of a war whose implied end was the erecting in our advanced century of an Anglo-American empire based upon the systematic degradation of man.

Spite this clinging reproach, however, signal military virtues and achievements have conferred upon the Confederate arms historic fame, and upon certain of the commanders a renown extending beyond the sea—a renown which we of the North could not suppress, even if we would. In personal character, also, not a few of the military leaders of the South enforce forbearance; the memory of others the North refrains from disparaging; and some, with more or less of reluctance, she can respect. Posterity, sympathizing with our convictions, but removed from our passions, may perhaps go farther here. If George IV could, out of the graceful instinct of a gentleman, raise an honorable monument in the great fane of Christendom over the remains of the enemy of his dynasty, Charles Edward, the invader of England and victor in the rout at Prestonpans—upon whose head the king's ancestor but one reign removed had set a price—is it probable that the grandchildren of General Grant will pursue with rancor, or slur by sour neglect, the memory of Stonewall Jackson?

But the South herself is not wanting in recent histories and biographies which record the deeds of her chieftains—writings freely published at the North by loyal houses, widely read here, and with a deep though saddened interest. By students of the war such works are hailed as welcome accessories, and tending to the completeness of the record.

Supposing a happy issue out of present perplexities, then, in the generation next to come, Southerners there will be yielding allegiance to the Union, feeling all their interests bound up in it, and yet cherishing unrebuked that kind of feeling for the memory of the soldiers of the fallen Confederacy that Burns, Scott, and the Ettrick Shepherd felt for the memory of the gallant clansmen ruined through their fidelity to the Stuarts—a feeling whose passion was tempered by the poetry imbuing it, and which in no wise affected their loyalty to the Georges, and which, it may be added, indirectly contributed excellent things to literature. But, setting this view aside, dishonorable would it be in the South were she willing to abandon to shame the memory of brave men who with signal personal disinterestedness warred in her behalf, though from motives, as we believe, so deplorably astray.

Patriotism is not baseness, neither is it inhumanity. The mourners who this summer bear flowers to the mounds of the Virginian and Georgian dead are, in their domestic bereavement and proud affection, as sacred in the eye of Heaven as are those who go with similar offerings of tender grief and love into the cemeteries of our Northern martyrs. And yet, in one aspect, how needless to point the contrast.

Cherishing such sentiments, it will hardly occasion surprise that, in looking over the battle-pieces in the foregoing collection, I have been tempted to withdraw or modify some of them, fearful lest in presenting, though but dramatically and by way of a poetic record, the passions and epithets of civil war, I might be contributing to a bitterness which every sensible American must wish at an end. So, too, with the emotion of victory as reproduced on some pages, and particularly toward the close. It should not be construed into an exultation misapplied—an exultation as ungenerous as unwise, and made to minister, however indirectly, to that kind of censoriousness too apt to be produced in certain natures by success after trying reverses. Zeal is not of necessity religion, neither is it always of the same essence with poetry or patriotism.

There were excesses which marked the conflict, most of which are perhaps inseparable from a civil strife so intense and prolonged, and involving warfare in some border countries new and imperfectly civilized. Barbarities also there were, for which the Southern people collectively can hardly be held responsible, though perpetrated by ruffians in their name. But surely other qualities—exalted ones—courage and fortitude matchless, were likewise displayed, and largely; and justly may these be held the characteristic traits, and not the former.

In this view, what Northern writer, however patriotic, but must revolt from acting on paper a part anyway akin to that of the live dog to the dead lion; and yet it is right to rejoice for our triumph, so far as it may justly imply an advance for our whole country and for humanity.

Let it be held no reproach to any one that he pleads for reasonable consideration for our late enemies, now stricken down and unavoidably debarred, for the time, from speaking through authorized agencies for themselves. Nothing has been urged here in the foolish hope of conciliating those men—few in number, we trust—who have resolved never to be reconciled to the Union. On such hearts everything is thrown away except it be religious commiseration, and the sincerest. Yet let them call to mind that unhappy Secessionist, not a military man, who with impious alacrity fired the first shot of the Civil War at Sumter, and a little more than four years afterward fired the last one into his own heart at Richmond.

Noble was the gesture into which patriotic passion surprised the people in a utilitarian time and country; yet the glory of the war falls short of its pathos—a pathos which now at last ought to disarm all animosity.

How many and earnest thoughts still rise, and how hard to repress them. We feel what past years have been, and years, unretarded years, shall come. May we all have moderation; may we all show candor. Though, perhaps, nothing could ultimately have averted the strife, and though to treat of human actions is to deal wholly with second causes, nevertheless, let us not cover up or try to extenuate what, humanly speaking, is the truth— namely, that those unfraternal denunciations, continued through years, and which at last inflamed to deeds that ended in blood-shed, were reciprocal; and that, had the preponderating strength and the prospect of its unlimited increase lain on the other side, on ours might have lain those actions which now in our late op-ponents we stigmatize under the name of Rebellion. As frankly let us own—what it would be unbecoming to parade were for-eigners concerned—that our triumph was won not more by skill and bravery than by superior resources and crushing numbers; that it was a triumph, too, over a people for years politically mis-led by designing men, and also by some honestly-erring men, who from their position could not have been otherwise than broadly influential; a people who, though, indeed, they sought to per-petuate the curse of slavery, and even extend it, were not the authors of it, but (less fortunate, not less righteous than we) were the fated inheritors; a people who, having a like origin with ourselves, share essentially in whatever worthy qualities we may possess. No one can add to the lasting reproach which hopeless defeat has now cast upon Secession by withholding the recogni-tion of these verities.

Surely we ought to take it to heart that that kind of pacifica-tion, based upon principles operating equally all over the land, which lovers of their country yearn for, and which our arms, though signally triumphant, did not bring about, and which law-making, however anxious, or energetic, or repressive, never by itself can achieve, may yet be largely aided by generosity of sentiment public and private. Some revisionary legislation and adaptive is indispensable; but with this should harmoniously work another kind of prudence, not unallied with entire magnanimity. Benevolence and policy—Christianity and Machiavelli—dissuade from penal severities toward the subdued. Abstinence here is as obligatory as considerate care for our unfortunate fellow-men late in bonds, and, if observed, would equally prove to be wise forecast. The great qualities of the South, those attested in the War, we can perilously alienate, or we may make them nationally available at need.

The blacks, in their infant pupilage to freedom, appeal to the sympathies of every humane mind. The paternal guardianship which for the interval Government exercises over them was prompted equally by duty and benevolence. Yet such kindliness should not be allowed to exclude kindliness to communities who stand nearer to us in nature. For the future of the freed slaves we may well be concerned; but the future of the whole country, involving the future of the blacks, urges a paramount claim upon our anxiety. Effective benignity, like the Nile, is not narrow in its bounty, and true policy is always broad. To be sure, it is vain to seek to glide, with molded words, over the difficulties of the situation. And for them who are neither partisans, nor enthusiasts, nor theorists, nor cynics, there are some doubts not readily to be solved. And there are fears. Why is not the cessation of war now at length attended with the settled calm of peace? Wherefore in a clear sky do we still turn our eyes toward the South, as the Neapolitan, months after the eruption, turns his toward Vesuvius? Do we dread lest the repose may be deceptive? In the recent convulsion has the crater but shifted? Let us revere that sacred uncertainty which forever impends over men and nations. Those of us who always abhorred slavery as an atheistical iniquity, gladly we join in the exulting chorus of humanity over its downfall. But we should remember that emancipation was accomplished not by deliberate legislation; only through agonized violence could so mighty a result be effected. In our natural solicitude to confirm the benefit of liberty to the blacks, let us forbear from measures of dubious constitutional rightfulness toward our white countrymen—measures of a nature to provoke, among other of the last evils, exterminating hatred of race toward race. In imagination let us place ourselves in the unprecedented position of the Southerners—their position as regards the millions of ignorant manumitted slaves in their midst, for whom some of us now claim the suffrage. Let us be Christians toward our fellow-whites, as well as philanthropists toward the blacks, our fellow-men. In all things, and toward all, we are enjoined to do as we would be done by. Nor should we forget that benevolent desires, after passing a certain point, cannot undertake their own fulfillment without incurring the risk of evils beyond those sought to be remedied. Something may well be left to the graduated care of future legislation, and to heaven. In one point of view the co-existence of the two races in the South—whether the negro be bond or free—seems (even as it did to Abraham Lincoln) a grave evil. Emancipation has ridded the country of the reproach, but not wholly of the calamity. Especially in the present transition period for both races in the South, more or less of trouble may not unreasonably be anticipated; but let us not hereafter be too swift to charge the blame exclusively in any one quarter. With certain evils men must be more or less patient. Our institutions have a potent digestion, and may in time convert and assimilate to good all elements thrown in, however originally alien.

But, so far as immediate measures looking toward permanent Re-establishment are concerned, no consideration should tempt us to pervert the national victory into oppression for the vanquished. Should plausible promise of eventual good, or a deceptive or spurious sense of duty, lead us to essay this, count we must on serious consequences, not the least of which would be divisions among the Northern adherents of the Union. Assuredly, if any honest Catos there be who thus far have gone with us, no longer will they do so, but oppose us, and as resolutely as hitherto they have supported. But this path of thought leads toward those waters of bitterness from which one can only turn aside and be silent.

But supposing Re-establishment so far advanced that the Southern seats in Congress are occupied, and by men qualified in accordance with those cardinal principles of representative government which hitherto have prevailed in the land—what then? Why, the Congressmen elected by the people of the South will—represent the people of the South. This may seem a flat conclusion; but, in view of the last five years, may there not be latent significance in it? What will be the temper of those Southern members? and, confronted by them, what will be the mood of our own representatives? In private life true reconciliation

seldom follows a violent quarrel; but, if subsequent inter-
course be unavoidable, nice observances and mutual are indis-
pensable to the prevention of a new rupture. Amity itself can
only be maintained by reciprocal respect, and true friends are
punctilious equals. On the floor of Congress North and South
are to come together after a passionate duel, in which the South,
though proving her valor, has been made to bite the dust. Upon
differences in debate shall acrimonious recriminations be ex-
changed? shall censorious superiority assumed by one section
provoke defiant self-assertion on the other? shall Manassas and
Chickamauga be retorted for Chattanooga and Richmond? Un-
der the supposition that the full Congress will be composed of
gentlemen, all this is impossible. Yet, if otherwise, it needs no
prophet of Israel to foretell the end. The maintenance of Con-
gressional decency in the future will rest mainly with the North.
Rightly will more forbearance be required from the North than
the South, for the North is victor.

But some there are who may deem these latter thoughts
inapplicable, and for this reason: Since the test-oath operatively
excludes from Congress all who in any way participated in Se-
cession, therefore none but Southerners wholly in harmony
with the North are eligible to seats. This is true for the time be-
ing. But the oath is alterable; and in the wonted fluctuations
of parties not improbably it will undergo alteration, assuming
such a form, perhaps, as not to bar the admission into the Na-
tional Legislature of men who represent the populations lately
in revolt. Such a result would involve no violation of the princi-
ples of democratic government. Not readily can one perceive
how the political existence of the millions of late Secessionists
can permanently be ignored by this Republic. The years of the
war tried our devotion to the Union; the time of peace may test
the sincerity of our faith in democracy.

In no spirit of opposition, not by way of challenge, is any-
thing here thrown out. These thoughts are sincere ones; they
seem natural—inevitable. Here and there they must have sug-
gested themselves to many thoughtful patriots. And, if they be
just thoughts, ere long they must have that weight with the pub-
lic which already they have had with individuals.

For that heroic band—those children of the furnace who, in regions like Texas and Tennessee, maintained their fidelity through terrible trials—we of the North felt for them, and profoundly we honor them. Yet passionate sympathy, with resentments so close as to be almost domestic in their bitterness, would hardly in the present juncture tend to discreet legislation. Were the Unionists and Secessionists but as Guelphs and Ghibellines? If not, then far be it from a great nation now to act in the spirit that animated a triumphant town-faction in the Middle Ages. But crowding thoughts must at last be checked; and, in times like the present, one who desires to be impartially just in the expression of his views, moves as among sword-points presented on every side.

Let us pray that the terrible historic tragedy of our time may not have been enacted without instructing our whole beloved country through terror and pity; and may fulfillment verify in the end those expectations which kindle the bards of Progress and Humanity.

FROM *CLAREL*

PART I
JERUSALEM

I

THE HOSTEL

In chamber low and scored by time,
Masonry old, late washed with lime—
Much like a tomb new-cut in stone;
Elbow on knee, and brow sustained
All motionless on sidelong hand,
A student sits, and broods alone.
   The small deep casement sheds a ray
Which tells that in the Holy Town
It is the passing of the day—
The Vigil of Epiphany.
Beside him in the narrow cell
His luggage lies unpacked; thereon
The dust lies, and on him as well—
The dust of travel. But anon
His face he lifts—in feature fine,
Yet pale, and all but feminine
But for the eye and serious brow—
Then rises, paces to and fro,
And pauses, saying, "Other cheer
Than that anticipated here,
By me the learner, now I find.
Theology, art thou so blind?
What means this naturalistic knell
In lieu of Siloh's oracle
Which here should murmur? Snatched
   from grace,
And waylaid in the holy place!
Not thus it was but yesterday

Off Jaffa on the clear blue sea;
Nor thus, my heart, it was with thee
Landing amid the shouts and spray;
Nor thus when mounted, full equipped,
Out through the vaulted gate we slipped
Beyond the walls where gardens bright
With bloom and blossom cheered the sight.
The plain we crossed. In afternoon,
How like our early autumn bland—
So softly tempered for a boon—
The breath of Sharon's prairie land!
And was it, yes, her titled Rose,
That scarlet poppy oft at hand?
Then Ramleh gleamed, the sail-white town
At even. There I watched day close
From the fair tower, the suburb one;
Seaward and dazing set the sun:
Inland I turned me toward the wall
Of Ephraim, stretched in purple pall.
Romance of mountains! But in end
What change the near approach could lend.
     "The start this morning—gun and lance
Against the quarter-moon's low tide;
The thieves' huts where we hushed the ride;
Chill day-break in the lorn advance;
In stony strait the scorch of noon,
Thrown off by crags, reminding one
Of those hot paynims whose fierce hands
Flung showers of Afric's fiery sands
In face of that crusader-king,
Louis, to wither so his wing;
And, at the last, aloft for goal,
Like the ice-bastions round the Pole,
Thy blank, blank towers, Jerusalem!"
     Again he droops, with brow on hand.
But, starting up, "Why, well I knew
Salem to be no Samarcand;
'Twas scarce surprise; and yet first view

Brings this eclipse. Needs be my soul,
Purged by the desert's subtle air
From bookish vapors, now is heir
To nature's influx of control;
Comes likewise now to consciousness
Of the true import of that press
Of inklings which in travel late
Through Latin lands, did vex my state,
And somehow seemed clandestine. Ah!
These under-formings in the mind.
Banked corals which ascend from far,
But little heed men that they wind
Unseen, unheard—till lo, the reef—
The reef and breaker, wreck and grief.
But here unlearning, how to me
Opes the expanse of time's vast sea!
Yes, I am young, but Asia old.
The books, the books not all have told.

    "And, for the rest, the facile chat
Of overweenings—what was that
The grave one said in Jaffa lane
Whom there I met, my countryman,
But new-returned from travel here;
Some word of mine provoked the strain;
His meaning now begins to clear:
Let me go over it again:—

    "Our New World's worldly wit so shrewd
Lacks the Semitic reverent mood,
Unworldly—hardly may confer
Fitness for just interpreter
Of Palestine. Forgo the state
Of local minds inveterate,
Tied to one poor and casual form.
To avoid the deep saves not from storm.

    "Those things he said, and added more;
  No clear authenticated lore
I deemed. But now, need now confess
My cultivated narrowness,

Though scarce indeed of sort he meant?
'Tis the uprooting of content!"
    So he, the student. 'Twas a mind,
Earnest by nature, long confined
Apart like Vesta in a grove
Collegiate, but let to rove
At last abroad among mankind,
And here in end confronted so
By the true genius, friend or foe,
And actual visage of a place
Before but dreamed of in the glow
Of fancy's spiritual grace.

    Further his meditations aim,
Reverting to his different frame
Bygone. And then: "Can faith remove
Her light, because of late no plea
I've lifted to her source above?"
Dropping thereat upon the knee,
His lips he parted; but the word
Against the utterance demurred
And failed him. With infirm intent
He sought the house-top. Set of sun:
His feet upon the yet warm stone,
He, Clarel, by the coping leant,
In silent gaze. The mountain town,
A walled and battlemented one,
With houseless suburbs front and rear,
And flanks built up from steeps severe,
Saddles and turrets the ascent—
Tower which rides the elephant.
Hence large the view. There where he stood,
Was Acra's upper neighborhood.
The circling hills he saw, with one
Excelling, ample in its crown,
Making the uplifted city low
By contrast—Olivet. The flow
Of eventide was at full brim;

Overlooked, the houses sloped from him—
Terraced or domed, unchimnied, gray,
All stone—a moor of roofs. No play
Of life; no smoke went up, no sound
Except low hum, and that half drowned.

The inn abutted on the pool
Named Hezekiah's, a sunken court
Where silence and seclusion rule,
Hemmed round by walls of nature's sort
Base to stone structures seeming one
E'en with the steeps they stand upon.

As a three-decker's stern-lights peer
Down on the oily wake below,
Upon the sleek dark waters here
The inn's small lattices bestow
A rearward glance. And here and there
In flaws the languid evening air
Stirs the dull weeds adust, which trail
In festoons from the crag, and veil
The ancient fissures, overtopped
By the tall convent of the Copt,
Built like a light-house o'er the main.

Blind arches showed in walls of wane,
Sealed windows, portals masoned fast,
And terraces where nothing passed
By parapets all dumb. No tarn
Among the Kaatskills, high above
Farm-house and stack, last lichened barn
And log-bridge rotting in remove—
More lonesome looks than this dead pool
In town where living creatures rule.

Not here the spell might he undo;
The strangeness haunted him and grew.

But twilight closes. He descends
And toward the inner court he wends.

IV

OF THE CRUSADERS

WHEN sighting first the towers afar
Which girt the object of the war
And votive march—the Savior's Tomb,
What made the red-cross knights so shy?
And wherefore did they doff the plume
And baldrick, kneel in dust, and sigh?
     Hardly it serves to quote Voltaire
And say they were freebooters—hence,
Incapable of awe or sense
Pathetic; no, for man is heir
To complex moods; and in that age
Belief devout and bandit rage
Frequent were joined; and e'en to-day
At shrines on the Calabrian steep—
Not insincere while feelings sway—
The brigand halts to adore, to weep.
Grant then the worst—is all romance
Which claims that the crusader's glance
Was blurred by tears?
               But if that round
Of disillusions which accrue
In this our day, imply a ground
For more concern than Tancred knew,
Thinking, yet not as in despair,
Of Christ who suffered for him there
Upon the crag; then, own it true,
Cause graver much than his is ours
At least to check the hilarious heart
Before these memorable towers.
     But wherefore this? such theme why
      start?
Because if here in many a place
The rhyme—much like the knight indeed—

Abjure brave ornament, 'twill plead
Just reason, and appeal for grace.

XIII

THE ARCH

BLUE-LIGHTS sent up by ship forlorn
Are answered oft but by the glare
Of rockets from another, torn
In the same gale's inclusive snare.

'Twas then when Celio was lanced
By novel doubt, the encounter chanced
In Gihon, as recited late,
And at a time when Clarel too,
On his part, felt the grievous weight
Of those demoniacs in view;
So that when Celio advanced
No wonder that the meeting eyes
Betrayed reciprocal surmise
And interest. 'Twas thereupon
The Italian, as the eve drew on,
Regained the gate, and hurried in
As he would passionately win
Surcease to thought by rapid pace.
Eastward he bent, across the town,
Till in the Via Crucis lone
An object there arrested him.
      With gallery which years deface,
Its bulk athwart the alley grim,
The arch named Ecce Homo threw;
The same, if childlike faith be true,
From which the Lamb of God was shown
By Pilate to the wolfish crew.
And Celio—in frame how prone
To kindle at that scene recalled—

Perturbed he stood, and heart-enthralled.
       No raptures which with saints prevail,
Nor trouble of compunction born
He felt, as there he seemed to scan
Aloft in spectral guise, the pale
Still face, the purple robe, and thorn;
And inly cried—*Behold the Man!*
Yon Man it is this burden lays:
Even He who in the pastoral hours,
Abroad in fields, and cheered by flowers,
Announced a heaven's unclouded days;
And, ah, with such persuasive lips—
Those lips now sealed while doom delays—
Won men to look for solace there;
But, crying out in death's eclipse,
When rainbow none His eyes might see,
Enlarged the margin for despair—
My God, My God, forsakest Me?
       Upbraider! we upbraid again;
Thee we upbraid; our pangs constrain
Pathos itself to cruelty.
Ere yet Thy day no pledge was given
Of homes and mansions in the heaven—
Paternal homes reserved for us;
Heart hoped it not, but lived content—
Content with life's own discontent,
Nor deemed that fate ere swerved for us:
The natural law men let prevail;
Then reason disallowed the state
Of instinct's variance with fate.
But Thou—ah, see, in rack how pale
Who did the world with throes convulse;
Behold Him—yea—behold the Man
Who warranted if not began
The dream that drags out its repulse.
       Nor less some cannot break from Thee;
Thy love so locked is with Thy lore,
They may not rend them and go free:

The head rejects; so much the more
The heart embraces—what? the love?
If true what priests avouch of Thee,
The shark Thou mad'st, yet claim'st the dove.
      Nature and Thee in vain we search:
Well urged the Jews within the porch—
"How long wilt make us still to doubt?"
How long?—'Tis eighteen cycles now—
Enigma and evasion grow;
And shall we never find Thee out?
What isolation lones Thy state
That all we else know cannot mate
With what Thou teachest? Nearing Thee
All footing fails us; history
Shows there a gulf where bridge is none!
In lapse of unrecorded time,
Just after the apostles' prime,
What chance or craft might break it down?
Served this a purpose? By what art
Of conjuration might the heart
Of heavenly love, so sweet, so good,
Corrupt into the creeds malign,
Begetting strife's pernicious brood,
Which claimed for patron Thee divine?
      Anew, anew,
For this Thou bleedest, Anguished Face;
Yea, Thou through ages to accrue,
Shalt the Medusa shield replace:
In beauty and in terror too
Shalt paralyze the nobler race—
Smite or suspend, perplex, deter—
Tortured, shalt prove a torturer.
Whatever ribald Future be,
Thee shall these heed, amaze their hearts with Thee—
Thy white, Thy red, Thy fairness and Thy tragedy.

      He turned, uptorn in inmost frame,
Nor weened he went the way he came,

Till meeting two there, nor in calm—
A monk and layman, one in creed,
The last with novice-ardor warm,
Newcomer, and devout indeed,
To whom the other was the guide,
And showed the Places. "Here," he cried,
At pause before a wayside stone,
"Thou mark'st the spot where that bad Jew
His churlish taunt at Jesus threw
Bowed under cross with stifled moan:
Caitiff, which for that cruel wrong
Thenceforth till Doomsday drives along."
　　　Starting, as here he made review,
Celio winced—Am *I* the Jew?
Without delay, afresh he turns
Descending by the Way of Thorns,
Winning the Proto-Martyr's gate,
And goes out down Jehoshaphat.
Beside him slid the shadows flung
By evening from the tombstones tall
Upon the bank far sloping from the wall.
Scarce did he heed, or did but slight
The admonishment the warder rung
That with the setting of the sun,
Now getting low and all but run,
The gate would close, and for the night.

XVII

NATHAN

NATHAN had sprung from worthy stock—
Austere, ascetical, but free,
Which hewed their way from sea-beat rock
Wherever woods and winter be.
　　　The pilgrim-keel in storm and stress
Had erred, and on a wilderness.

But shall the children all be schooled
By hap which their forefathers ruled?
Those primal settlers put in train
New emigrants which inland bore;
From these, too, emigrants again
Westward pressed further; more bred more;
At each remove a goodlier wain,
A heart more large, an ampler shore,
With legacies of farms behind;
Until in years the wagons wind
Through parks and pastures of the sun,
Warm plains as of Esdraelon:
'Tis nature in her best benign.
Wild, wild in symmetry of mold,
With freckles on her tawny gold,
The lily alone looks pantherine—
The libbard-lily. Never broods
The gloom here of grim hemlock woods
Breeding the witchcraft-spell malign;
But groves like isles in Grecian seas,
Those dotting isles, the Sporades.
But who the gracious charm may tell—
Long rollings of the vast serene—
The prairie in her swimming swell
Of undulation.
                         Such glad scene
Was won by venturers from far
Born under that severer star
The landing patriarchs knew. In fine,
To Illinois—a turf divine
Of promise, how auspicious spread,
Ere yet the cities rose thereon—
From Saco's mountain wilds were led
The sire of Nathan, wife and son;
Life's lot to temper so, and shun
Mountains whose camp withdrawn was set
Above one vale he would forget.

    After some years their tale had told,

He rested; lay forever stilled
With sachems and mound-builders old.
The son was grown; the farm he tilled;
A stripling, but of manful ways,
Hardy and frugal, oft he filled
The widow's eyes with tears of praise.
An only child, with her he kept
For *her* sake part, the Christian way,
Though frequent in his bosom crept
Precocious doubt unbid. The sway
He felt of his grave life, and power
Of vast space, from the log-house door
Daily beheld. Three Indian mounds
Against the horizon's level bounds
Dim showed across the prairie green
Like dwarfed and blunted mimic shapes
Of Pyramids at distance seen
From the broad Delta's planted capes
Of vernal grain. In nearer view
With trees he saw them crowned, which drew
From the red sagamores of eld
Entombed within, the vital gum
Which green kept each mausoleum.

    Hard by, as chanced, he once beheld
Bones like sea corals; one bleached skull
A vase vined round and beautiful
With flowers; felt, with bated breath
The floral revelry over death.

    And other sights his heart had thrilled;
Lambs had he known by thunder killed,
Innocents—and the type of Christ
Betrayed. Had not such things sufficed
To touch the young pure heart with awe,
Memory's mint could move him more.
In prairie twilight, summer's own,
The last cow milked, and he alone
In barn-yard dreamy by the fence,
Contrasted, came a scene immense:

The great White Hills, mount flanked by mount,
The Saco and Ammonoosuc's fount;
Where, in September's equinox
Nature hath put such terror on
That from his mother man would run—
Our mother, Earth: the founded rocks
Unstable prove: the Slide! the Slide!
Again he saw the mountain side
Sliced open; yet again he stood
Under its shadow, on the spot—
Now waste, but once a cultured plot,
Though far from village neighborhood—
Where, nor by sexton hearsed at even,
Somewhere his uncle slept; no mound,
Since not a trace of him was found,
So whelmed the havoc from the heaven.

    This reminiscence of dismay,
These thoughts unhinged him. On a day
Waiting for monthly grist at mill
In settlement some miles away,
It chanced upon the window-sill
A dusty book he spied, whose coat,
Like the Scotch miller's powdered twill,
The mealy owner might denote.
Called off from reading, unaware
The miller e'en had left it there
A book all but forsaken now
For more advanced ones not so frank,
Nor less in vogue and taking rank;
And yet it never shall outgrow
That infamy it first incurred,
Though—viewed in light which moderns know—
Capricious infamy absurd.

    The blunt straightforward Saxon tone,
Workaday language, even his own,
The sturdy thought, not deep but clear,
The hearty unbelief sincere,
Arrested him much like a hand

Clapped on the shoulder. Here he found
Body to doubt, rough standing-ground.
After some pages brief were scanned,
"Wilt loan me this?" he anxious said.
The shrewd Scot turned his square, strong head—
The book he saw, in troubled trim,
Fearing for Nathan, even him
So young, and for the mill, may be,
Should his unspoken heresy
Get bruited so. The lad but part
Might penetrate that senior heart.
Vainly the miller would dissuade;
Pledge gave he, and the loan was made.

    Reclined that night by candle dim
He read, then slept, and woke afraid:
The White Hill's slide! the Indian skull!
But this wore off; and unto him
Came acquiescence, which tho' dull
Was hardly peace. An altered earth
Sullen he tilled, in Adam's frame
When thrust from Eden out to dearth
And blest no more, and wise in shame.
The fall! nor aught availed at need
To Nathan, not each filial deed
Done for his mother, to allay
This ill. But tho' the Deist's sway,
Broad as the prairie fire, consumed
Some pansies which before had bloomed
Within his heart; it did but feed
To clear the soil for upstart weed.

    Yes, ere long came replacing mood.
The god, expelled from given form,
Went out into the calm and storm.
Now, ploughing near the isles of wood
In dream he felt the loneness come,
In dream regarded there the loam
Turned first by him. Such mental food
Need quicken, and in natural way,

Each germ of Pantheistic sway,
Whose influence, nor always drear,
Tenants our maiden hemisphere;
As if, dislodged long since from cells
Of Thracian woodlands, hither stole—
Hither, to renew their old control—
Pan and the pagan oracles.
    How frequent when Favonius low
Breathed from the copse which mild did wave
Over his father's sylvan grave,
And stirred the corn, he stayed the hoe,
And leaning, listening, felt a thrill
Which heathenized against the will.

    Years sped. But years attain not truth,
Nor length of life avails at all;
But time instead contributes ruth:
His mother—her the garners call:
When sicklemen with sickles go,
The churl of nature reaps her low.
    Let now the breasts of Ceres swell—
In shooks, with golden tassels gay,
The Indian corn its trophies ray
About the log-house; is it well
With death's ripe harvest?—To believe,
Belief to win nor more to grieve!
But how? a sect about him stood
In thin and scattered neighborhood;
Uncanny, and in rupture new;
Nor were all lives of members true
And good. For them who hate and heave
Contempt on rite and creed sublime,
Yet to their own rank fable cleave—
Abject, the latest shame of time;
These quite repelled, for still his mind
Erring, was of no vulgar kind.
Alone, and at Doubt's freezing pole
He wrestled with the pristine forms

Like the first man. By inner storms
Held in solution, so his soul
Ripened for hour of such control
As shapes, concretes. The influence came,
And from a source that well might claim
Surprise.
          'Twas in a lake-port new,
A mart for grain, by chance he met
A Jewess who about him threw
Else than Nerea's amorous net
And dubious wile. 'Twas Miriam's race:
A sibyl breathed in Agar's grace—
A sibyl, but a woman too;
He felt her grateful as the rains
To Rephaim and the Rama plains
In drought. Ere won, herself did woo:
"Wilt join my people?" Love is power;
Came the strange plea in yielding hour.
Nay, and turn Hebrew? But why not?
If backward still the inquirer goes
To get behind man's present lot
Of crumbling faith; for rear-wall shows
Far behind Rome and Luther—what?
The crag of Sinai. Here then plant
Thyself secure: 'tis adamant.

    Still as she dwelt on Zion's story
He felt the glamor, caught the gleam;
All things but these seemed transitory—
Love, and his love's Jerusalem.
And interest in a mitred race,
With awe which to the fame belongs,
These in receptive heart found place
When Agar chanted David's songs.

      'Twas passion. But the Puritan—
Mixed latent in his blood—a strain
How evident, of Hebrew source;
'Twas that, diverted here in force,
Which biased—hardly might do less.

Hereto append, how earnestness,
Which disbelief for first-fruits bore,
Now, in recoil, by natural stress
Constrained to faith—to faith in more
Than prior disbelief had spurned;
As if, when he toward credence turned,
Distance therefrom but gave career
For impetus that shot him sheer
Beyond. Agar rejoiced; nor knew
How such a nature, charged with zeal,
Might yet overpass that limit due
Observed by her. For woe or weal
They wedded, one in heart and creed.
Transferring fields with title-deed,
From rustic life he quite withdrew—
Traded, and throve. Two children came:
Sedate his heart, nor sad the dame.
But years subvert; or he outgrew
(While yet confirmed in all the myth)
The mind infertile of the Jew.
His northern nature, full of pith,
Vigor and enterprise and will,
Having taken thus the Hebrew bent,
Might not abide inactive so
And but the empty forms fulfill:
Needs utilize the mystic glow—
For nervous energies find vent.

The Hebrew seers announce in time
The return of Judah to her prime;
Some Christians deemed it then at hand.
Here was an object: Up and do!
With seed and tillage help renew—
Help reinstate the Holy Land.

Some zealous Jews on alien soil
Who still from Gentile ways recoil,
And loyally maintain the dream,
Salute upon the Paschal day
With *Next year in Jerusalem!*

Now Nathan turning unto her,
Greeting his wife at morning ray,
Those words breathed on the Passover;
But she, who mutely startled lay,
In the old phrase found import new,
In the blithe tone a bitter cheer
That did the very speech subdue.
She kenned her husband's mind austere,
Had watched his reveries grave; he meant
No flourish mere of sentiment.
Then what to do? or how to stay?
Decry it? that would faith unsay.
Withstand him? but she gently loved.
And so with Agar here it proved,
As oft it may, the hardy will
Overpowered the deep monition still.

     Enough; fair fields and household charms
They quit, sell all, and cross the main
With Ruth and a young child in arms.
A tract secured on Sharon's plain,
Some sheds he built, and ground walled in
Defensive; toil severe but vain.
The wandering Arabs, wonted long
(Nor crime they deemed it, crime nor sin)
To scale the desert convents strong—
In sly foray leaped Nathan's fence
And robbed him; and no recompense
Attainable where law was none
Or perjured. Resolute hereon,
Agar, with Ruth and the young child,
He lodged within the stronghold town
Of Zion, and his heart exiled
To abide the worst on Sharon's lea.
Himself and honest servants three
Armed husbandmen became, as erst
His sires in Pequod wilds immersed.

Hittites—foes pestilent to God
His fathers old those Indians deemed:
Nathan the Arabs here esteemed
The same—slaves meriting the rod;
And out he spake it; which bred hate
The more imperilling his state.

    With muskets now his servants slept;
Alternate watch and ward they kept
In grounds beleaguered. Not the less
Visits at stated times he made
To them in Zion's walled recess.
Agar with sobs of suppliance prayed
That he would fix there: "Ah, for good
Tarry! abide with us, thine own;
Put not these blanks between us; should
Such space be for a shadow thrown?
Quit Sharon, husband; leave to brood;
Serve God by cleaving to thy wife,
Thy children. If come fatal strife—
Which I forebode—nay!" and she flung
Her arms about him there, and clung.

    She plead. But tho' his heart could feel,
'Twas mastered by inveterate zeal.
Even the nursling's death ere long
Balked not his purpose tho' it wrung.

    But Time the cruel, whose smooth way
Is feline, patient for the prey
That to this twig of being clings;
And Fate, which from her ambush springs
And drags the loiterer soon or late
Unto a sequel unforeseen;
These doomed him and cut short his date;
But first was modified the lien
The husband had on Agar's heart;
And next a prudence slid athwart—
After distrust. But be unsaid

That steep toward which the current led.
Events shall speak.
                    And now the guide,
Who did in sketch this tale begin,
Parted with Clarel at the inn;
And ere long came the eventide.

PART II
THE WILDERNESS

IV

OF MORTMAIN

"Our friend there—he's a little queer,"
To Rolfe said Derwent, riding on;
"Beshrew me, there is in his tone
Naught of your new world's chanticleer.
Who's the eccentric? can you say?"
        "Partly; but 'tis at second-hand.
At the Black Jew's I met with one
Who, in response to my demand,
Did in a strange disclosure run
Respecting him."—"Repeat it, pray."—
And Rolfe complied. But here receive
Less the details of narrative
Than what the drift and import may convey.

        A Swede he was—illicit son
Of noble lady, after-wed,
Who, for a cause over which be thrown
Charity of oblivion dead,—
Bore little love, but rather hate,
Even practiced to ensnare his state.
His father, while not owning, yet
In part discharged the natural debt
Of duty; gave him liberal lore
And timely income; but no more.
        Thus isolated, what to bind
But the vague bond of human kind?
The north he left, to Paris came—
Paris, the nurse of many a flame

Evil and good. This son of earth,
This Psalmanazer, made a hearth
In warm desires and schemes for man:
Even *he* was an Arcadian.
Peace and good will was his acclaim—
If not in words, yet in the aim:
Peace, peace on earth: that note he thrilled,
But scarce in way the cherubs trilled
To Bethlehem and the shepherd band.
Yet much his theory could tell;
And he expounded it so well,
Disciples came. He took his stand.

     Europe was in a decade dim:
Upon the future's trembling rim
The comet hovered. His a league
Of frank debate and close intrigue:
Plot, proselyte, appeal, denounce—
Conspirator, pamphleteer, at once,
And prophet. Wear and tear and jar
He met with coffee and cigar:
These kept awake the man and mood
And dream. That uncreated Good
He sought, whose absence is the cause
Of creeds and Atheists, mobs and laws.
Precocities of heart outran
The immaturities of brain.

     Along with each superior mind,
The vain, foolhardy, worthless, blind,
With Judases, are nothing loath
To clasp pledged hands and take the oath
Of aim, the which, if just, demands
Strong hearts, brows deep, and priestly hands.
Experience with her sharper touch
Stung Mortmain: Why, if men prove such,
Dote I? love theory overmuch?
Yea, also, whither will advance
This Revolution sprung in France
So many years ago? where end?

That current takes me. Whither tend?
Come, thou who makest such hot haste
To forge the future—weigh the past.
     Such frame he knew. And timed event
Cogent a further question lent:
Wouldst meddle with the state? Well, mount
Thy guns; how many men dost count?
Besides, there's more that here belongs:
Be many questionable wrongs:
By yet more questionable war,
Prophet of peace, these wouldst thou bar?
The world's not new, nor new thy plea.
Tho' even shouldst thou triumph, see,
Prose overtakes the victor's songs:
Victorious right may need redress:
No failure like a harsh success.
Yea, ponder well the historic page:
Of all who, fired with noble rage,
Have warred for right without reprieve,
How many spanned the wings immense
Of Satan's muster, or could cheat
His cunning tactics of retreat
And ambuscade? Oh, now dispense!
The world is portioned out, believe:
The good have but a patch at best,
The wise their corner; for the rest—
Malice divides with ignorance.
And what is stable? find one boon
That is not lackey to the moon
Of fate. The flood ebbs out—the ebb
Floods back; the incessant shuttle shifts
And flies, and wears and tears the web.
Turn, turn thee to the proof that sifts:
What if the kings in Forty-eight
Fled like the gods? even as the gods
Shall do, return they made; and sate
And fortified their strong abodes;
And, to confirm them there in state,

Contrived new slogans, apt to please—
Pan and the tribal unities.
Behind all this still works some power
Unknowable, thou 'lt yet adore.
That steers the world, not man. States drive;
The crazy rafts with billows strive.—
Go, go—absolve thee. Join that band
That wash them with the desert sand
For lack of water. In the dust
Of wisdom sit thee down, and rust.

          So mused he—solitary pined.
Tho' his apostolate had thrown
New prospects ope to Adam's kind,
And fame had trumped him far and free—
Now drop he did—a clod unknown;
Nay, rather, he would not disown
Oblivion's volunteer to be;
Like those new world discoverers bold
Ending in stony convent cold,
Or dying hermits; as if they,
Chastized to Micah's mind austere,
Remorseful felt that ampler sway
Their lead had given for old career
Of human nature.
                    But this man
No cloister sought. He, under ban
Of strange repentance and last dearth,
Roved the gray places of the earth.
And what seemed most his heart to wring
Was some unrenderable thing:
'Twas not his bastardy, nor bale
Medean in his mother pale,
Nor thwarted aims of high design;
But deeper—deep as nature's mine.
          Tho' frequent among kind he sate
Tranquil enough to hold debate,
His moods he had, mad fitful ones,

Prolonged or brief, outbursts or moans;
And at such times would hiss or cry:
"Fair Circe—goddess of the sty!"
More frequent this: "Mock worse than wrong:
The Syren's kiss—the Fury's thong!"

Such he. Tho' scarce as such portrayed
In full by Rolfe, yet Derwent said
At close: "There's none so far astray,
Detached, abandoned, as might seem,
As to exclude the hope, the dream
Of fair redemption. One fine day
I saw at sea, by bit of deck—
Weedy—adrift from far away—
The dolphin in his gambol light,
Through showery spray, arch into sight:
He flung a rainbow o'er that wreck."

XI

OF DESERTS

THO' frequent in the Arabian waste
The pilgrim, up ere dawn of day,
Inhale thy wafted musk, Cathay;
And Adam's primal joy may taste,
Beholding all the pomp of night
Bee'd thick with stars in swarms how bright;
And so, rides on alert and braced—
Tho' brisk at morn the pilgrim start,
Ere long he'll know in weary hour
Small love of deserts, if their power
Make to retreat upon the heart
Their own forsakenness.
                                        Darwin quotes
From Shelley, that forever floats
Over all desert places known,

Mysterious doubt—an awful one.
He quotes, adopts it. Is it true?
Let instinct vouch; let poetry,
Science and instinct here agree,
For truth requires strong retinue.

    Waste places are where yet is given
A charm, a beauty from the heaven
Above them, and clear air divine—
Translucent ether opaline;
And some in evening's early dew
Put on illusion of a guise
Which Tantalus might tantalize
Afresh; ironical unrolled
Like Western counties all in grain
Ripe for the sickleman and wain;
Or, tawnier than the Guinea gold,
More like a lion's skin unfold:
Attest the desert opening out
Direct from Cairo by the Gate
Of Victors, whence the annual rout
To Mecca bound, precipitate
Their turbaned frenzy.—
                     Sands immense
Impart the oceanic sense:
The flying grit like scud is made:
Pillars of sand which whirl about
Or arc along in colonnade,
True kin be to the waterspout.
Yonder on the horizon, red
With storm, see there the caravan
Straggling long-drawn, dispirited;
Mark how it labors like a fleet
Dismasted, which the cross-winds fan
In crippled disaster of retreat
From battle.—
              Sinai had renown
Ere thence was rolled the thundered Law;

Ever a terror wrapped its crown;
Never did shepherd dare to draw
Too nigh (Josephus saith) for awe
Of one, some ghost or god austere—
Hermit unknown, dread mountaineer.—

When comes the sun up over Nile
In cloudlessness, what cloud is cast
O'er Lybia? Thou shadow vast
Of Cheops' indissoluble pile,
Typ'st thou the imperishable Past
In empire posthumous and reaching sway
Projected far across to time's remotest day?
    But curb.—Such deserts in air-zone
Or object lend suggestive tone,
Redeeming them.
                For Judah here—
Let Erebus her rival own:
'Tis horror absolute—severe,
Dead, livid, honeycombed, dumb, fell—
A caked depopulated hell;
Yet so created, judged by sense,
And visaged in significance
Of settled anger terrible.
    Profoundly cloven through the scene
Winds Kedron—word (the scholar saith)
Importing anguish hard on death.
And aptly may such named ravine
Conduct unto Lot's mortal Sea
In cleavage from Gethsemane
Where it begins.
             But why does man
Regard religiously this tract
Cadaverous and under ban
Of blastment? Nay, recall the fact
That in the pagan era old,
When bolts, deemed Jove's, tore up the mound,
Great stones the simple peasant rolled

And built a wall about the gap
Deemed hallowed by the thunder-clap.
So here: men here adore this ground
Which doom hath smitten. 'Tis a land
Direful yet holy—blest tho' banned.

　　　But to pure hearts it yields no fear;
And John, he found wild honey here.

XXII

CONCERNING HEBREWS

As by the wood drifts thistle-down
And settles on soft mosses fair,
Stillness was wafted, dropped and sown;
Which stillness Vine, with timorous air
Of virgin tact, thus brake upon,
Nor with chance hint: "One can't forbear
Thinking that Margoth is—a *Jew*."
　　　Hereat, as for reponse, they view
The priest.
　　　　　"And, well, why me?" he cried;
"With one consent why turn to *me*?
Am I professional? Nay, free!
I grant that here by Judah's side
Queerly it jars with frame implied
To list this geologic Jew,
His way Jehovah's world construe:
In Gentile 'twould not seem so odd.
But here may preconceptions thrall?
Be many Hebrews we recall
Whose contrast with the breastplate bright
Of Aaron flushed in altar-light,
And Horeb's Moses, rock and rod,
Or closeted alone with God,
Quite equals Margoth's in its way:

At home we meet them every day.
The Houndsditch clothesman scarce would seem
Akin to seers. For one, I deem
Jew banker, merchant, statesman—these,
With artist, actress known to fame,
All strenuous in each Gentile aim,
Are Nature's off-hand witnesses
There's nothing mystic in her reign:
Your Jew's like wheat from Pharaoh's tomb:
Sow it in England, what will come?
The weird old seed yields market grain."
      Pleased by his wit while some recline,
A smile uncertain lighted Vine,
But died away.
               "Jews share the change,"
Derwent proceeded: "Range, they range—
In liberal sciences they roam;
They're leavened, and it works, believe;
Signs are, and such as scarce deceive.
From Holland, that historic home
Of erudite Israel, many a tome
Talmudic shipped is over sea
For antiquarian rubbish."
                  "Rest!"
Cried Rolfe; "e'en that indeed may be,
Nor less the Jew keep fealty
To ancient rites. Aaron's gemmed vest
Will long outlive Genevan cloth—
Nothing in Time's old camphor-chest
So little subject to the moth.
But Rabbis have their troublers too.
Nay, if thro' dusty stalls we look,
Haply we disinter to view
More than one bold freethinking Jew
That in his day with vigor shook
Faith's leaning tower."
              "Which stood the throe,"
Here Derwent in appendix: "look,

Faith's leaning tower was founded so:
Faith leaned from the beginning; yes,
If slant, she holds her steadfastness."

    "May be"; and paused: "but wherefore clog?—
Uriel Acosta, he was one
Who troubled much the synagogue—
Recanted then, and dropped undone:
A suicide. There's Heine, too
(In lineage crossed by blood of Jew),
Pale jester, to whom life was yet
A tragic farce; whose wild death-rattle,
In which all voids and hollows met,
Desperately maintained the battle
Betwixt the dirge and castanet.
But him leave to his Paris stone
And rail, and friendly wreath thereon.
Recall those Hebrews, which of old
Sharing some doubts we moderns rue,
Would fain Eclectic comfort fold
By grafting slips from Plato's palm
On Moses' melancholy yew:
But did they sprout? So *we* seek balm
By kindred graftings. Is that true?"

    "Why ask? But see: there lived a Jew—
No Alexandrine Greekish one—
You know him—Moses Mendelssohn."

    "Is't him you cite? True spirit staid,
He, though his honest heart was scourged
By doubt Judaic, never laid
His burden at Christ's door; he urged—
'Admit the mounting flames enfold
My basement; wisely shall my feet
The attic win, for safe retreat?'"

    "And *he* said that? Poor man, he's cold.
But was not this that Mendelssohn
Whose Hebrew kinswoman's Hebrew son,
Baptized to Christian, worthily won
The good name of Neander so?"

"If that link were, well might one urge
From such example, thy strange flow,
Conviction! Breaking habit's tether,
Sincerest minds will yet diverge
Like chance clouds scattered by mere weather;
Nor less at one point still they meet:
The selfhood keep they pure and sweet."

"But Margoth," in reminder here
Breathed Vine, as if while yet the ray
Lit Rolfe, to try his further cheer:
"But Margoth!"
               "He, poor sheep astray,
The Levitic cipher quite erased,
On what vile pig-weed hath he grazed.
Not his Spinoza's starry brow
(A non-conformer, ye'll allow),
A lion in brain, in life a lamb,
Sinless recluse of Amsterdam;
Who, in the obscure and humble lane,
Such strangers seemed to entertain
As sat by tent beneath the tree
On Mamre's plain—mysterious three,
The informing guests of Abraham.
But no, it had but ill beseemed
If God's own angels so could list
To visit one, Pan's Atheist.
That high intelligence but dreamed—
Above delusion's vulgar plain
Deluded still. The erring twain,
Spinoza and poor Margoth here,
Both Jews, which in dissent do vary:
In these what parted poles appear—
The blind man and the visionary."

    "And whose the eye that sees aright,
If any?" Clarel eager asked.
Aside Rolfe turned as overtasked;
And none responded. 'Twas like night

Descending from the seats of light,
Or seeming thence to fall. But here
Sedate a kindly tempered look
Private and confidential spoke
From Derwent's eyes, Clarel to cheer:
Take heart; something to fit thy youth
Instil I may, some saving truth—
Not best just now to volunteer.
      Thought Clarel: Pray, and what wouldst prove?
Thy faith an over-easy glove.

      Meanwhile Vine had relapsed. They saw
In silence the heart's shadow draw—
Rich shadow, such as gardens keep
In bower aside, where glow-worms peep
In evening over the virgin bed
Where dark-green periwinkles sleep—
Their bud the Violet of the Dead.

XXXI

THE INSCRIPTION

WHILE yet Rolfe's foot in stirrup stood,
Ere the light vault that wins the seat,
Derwent was heard: "What's this we meet?
A Cross? and—if one could but spell—
Inscription Sinaitic? Well,
Mortmain is nigh—*his* crazy freak;
Whose else? A closer view I'll seek;
I'll climb."
      In moving there aside
The rock's turned brow he had espied;
In rear this rock hung o'er the waste
And Nehemiah in sleep embraced
Below. The forepart gloomed Lot's wave
So nigh, the tide the base did lave.

Above, the sea-face smooth was worn
Through long attrition of that grit
Which on the waste of winds is borne.
And on the tablet high of it—
Traced in dull chalk, such as is found
Accessible in upper ground—
Big there between two scrawls, below
And over—a cross; three stars in row
Upright, two more for thwarting limb
Which drooped oblique.

                At Derwent's cry
The rest drew near; and every eye
Marked the device.—Thy passion's whim,
Wild Swede, mused Vine in silent heart.
"Looks like the *Southern Cross* to me,"
Said Clarel; "so 'tis down in chart."
"And so," said Rolfe, " 'tis set in sky—
Though error slight of place prevail
In midmost star here chalked. At sea,
Bound for Peru, when south ye sail,
Startling that novel cluster strange
Peers up from low; then as ye range
Cape-ward still further, brightly higher
And higher the stranger doth aspire,
'Till off the Horn, when at full height
Ye slack your gaze as chilly grows the night.
But Derwent—see!"

                The priest having gained
Convenient lodge the text below,
They called: "What's that in curve contained
Above the stars? Read: we would know."
"Runs thus: *By one who wails the loss,*
This altar to the Slanting Cross."
"Ha! under that?" "Some crow's-foot scrawl."
"Decipher, quick! we're waiting all."
"Patience: for ere one try rehearse,
'Twere well to make it out. 'Tis verse."
"Verse, say you? Read." " 'Tis mystical:

" 'Emblazoned bleak in austral skies—
A heaven remote, whose starry swarm
Like Science lights but cannot warm—
Translated Cross, hast thou withdrawn,
Dim paling too at every dawn,
With symbols vain once counted wise,
And gods declined to heraldries?
Estranged, estranged: can friend prove so?
Aloft, aloof, a frigid sign:
How far removed, thou Tree divine,
Whose tender fruit did reach so low—
Love apples of New Paradise!
About the wide Australian sea
The planted nations yet to be—
When, ages hence, they lift their eyes,
Tell, what shall they retain of thee?
But class thee with Orion's sword?
In constellations unadored,
Christ and the Giant equal prize?
The atheist cycles—*must* they be?
Fomentors as forefathers we?' "

    "Mad, mad enough," the priest here cried,
Down slipping by the shelving brinks;
"But 'tis not Mortmain," and he sighed.
    "Not Mortmain?" Rolfe exclaimed. "Methinks,"
The priest, " 'tis hardly in his vein."
"How? fraught with feeling is the strain?
His heart's not ballasted with stone—
He's crank." "Well, well, e'en let us own
That Mortmain, Mortmain is the man.
We've then a pledge here at a glance
Our comrade's met with no mischance.
Soon he'll rejoin us." "There, amen!"
"But now to wake Nehemiah in den
Behind here.—But kind Clarel goes.
Strange how he naps nor trouble knows

Under the crag's impending block,
Nor fears its fall, nor recks of shock."

   Anon they mount; and much advance
Upon that chalked significance.
The student harks, and weighs each word,
Intent, he being newly stirred.
   But tarries Margoth? Yes, behind
He lingers. He placards his mind:
Scaling the crag he rudely scores
With the same chalk (how here abused!)
Left by the other, after used,
A sledge or hammer huge as Thor's;
A legend lending—this, to wit:
"I, Science, I whose gain's thy loss,
I slanted thee, thou Slanting Cross."
   But sun and rain, and wind, with grit
Driving, these haste to cancel it.

XXXIV

MORTMAIN REAPPEARS

WHILE now at poise the wings of shade
Outstretched overhang each ridge and glade,
Mortmain descends from Judah's height
Through sally-port of minor glens:
Against the background of black dens
Blacker the figure glooms enhanced.
   Relieved from anxious fears, the group
In friendliness would have advanced
To greet, but shrank or fell adroop.
   Like Hecla ice inveined with marl
And frozen cinders showed his face
Rigid and darkened. Shunning parle
He seated him aloof in place,

Hands clasped about the knees drawn up
As round the cask the binding hoop—
Condensed in self, or like a seer
Unconscious of each object near,
While yet, informed, the nerve may reach
Like wire under wave to furthest beach.

By what brook Cherith had he been,
Watching it shrivel from the scene—
Or voice aerial had heard,
That now he murmured the wild word:
"But, hectored by the impious years,
What god invoke, for leave to unveil
That gulf whither tend these modern fears,
And deeps over which men crowd the sail?"

Up, as possessed, he rose anon,
And crying to the beach went down:
"Repent! repent in every land
Or hell's hot kingdom is at hand!
Yea, yea,
In pause of the artillery's boom,
While now the armed world holds its own,
The comet peers, the star dips down;
Flicker the lamps in Syria's tomb,
While Anti-Christ and Atheist set
On Anarch the red coronet!"

"Mad John," sighed Rolfe, "dost there betray
The dire *Vox Clamans* of our day?"
"Why heed him?" Derwent breathed: "alas!
Let him alone, and it will pass.—
What would he now?" Before the bay
Low bowed he there, with hand addressed
To scoop. "Unhappy, hadst thou best?"
Djalea it was; then calling low
Unto a Bethlehemite whose brow
Was wrinkled like the bat's shrunk hide—
"Your salt-song, Beltha: warn and chide."

"Would ye know what bitter drink
 They gave to Christ upon the Tree?
Sip the wave that laps the brink
 Of Siddim: taste, and God keep ye!
It drains the hills where alum's hid—
Drains the rock-salt's ancient bed;
 Hither unto basin fall
 The torrents from the steeps of gall—
Here is Hades' watershed.
 Sinner, would ye that your soul
 Bitter were and like the pool?
Sip the Sodom waters dead;
 But never from thy heart shall haste
 The Marah—yea, the after-taste."

He closed.—Arrested as he stooped,
Did Mortmain his pale hand recall?
No; undeterred the wave he scooped,
And tried it—madly tried the gall.

XXXV

PRELUSIVE

In Piranezi's rarer prints,
Interiors measurelessly strange,
Where the distrustful thought may range
Misgiving still—what mean the hints?
Stairs upon stairs which dim ascend
In series from plunged bastilles drear—
Pit under pit; long tier on tier
Of shadowed galleries which impend
Over cloisters, cloisters without end;
The height, the depth—the far, the near;
Ring-bolts to pillars in vaulted lanes,
And dragging Rhadamanthine chains;
These less of wizard influence lend

Than some allusive chambers closed.
    Those wards of hush are not disposed
In gibe of goblin fantasy—
Grimace—unclean diablerie:
Thy wings, Imagination, span
Ideal truth in fable's seat:
The thing implied is one with man,
His penetralia of retreat—
The heart, with labyrinths replete:
In freaks of intimation see
Paul's "mystery of iniquity":
Involved indeed, a blur of dream;
As, awed by scruple and restricted
In first design, or interdicted
By fate and warnings as might seem;
The inventor miraged all the maze,
Obscured it with prudential haze;
Nor less, if subject unto question,
The egg left, egg of the suggestion.
    Dwell on those etchings in the night,
Those touches bitten in the steel
By aqua-fortis, till ye feel
The Pauline text in gray of light;
Turn hither then and read aright.

    For ye who green or gray retain
Childhood's illusion, or but feign;
As bride and suite let pass a bier—
So pass the coming canto here.

XXXVI

SODOM

FULL night. The moon has yet to rise;
The air oppresses, and the skies
Reveal beyond the lake afar

One solitary tawny star—
Complexioned so by vapors dim,
Whereof some hang above the brim
And nearer waters of the lake,
Whose bubbling air-beads mount and break
As charged with breath of things alive.

  In talk about the Cities Five
Engulfed, on beach they linger late.
And he, the quaffer of the brine,
Puckered with that heart-wizening wine
Of bitterness, among them sate
Upon a camel's skull, late dragged
From forth the wave, the eye-pits slagged
With crusted salt.—"What star is yon?"
And pointed to that single one
Befogged above the sea afar.
"It might be Mars, so red it shines,"
One answered; "duskily it pines
In this strange mist."—"It is the star
Called Wormwood. Some hearts die in thrall
Of waters which yon star makes gall";
And, lapsing, turned, and made review
Of what that wickedness might be
Which down on these ill precincts drew
The flood, the fire; put forth new plea,
Which not with Writ might disagree;
Urged that those malefactors stood
Guilty of sins scarce scored as crimes
In any statute known, or code—
Nor now, nor in the former times:
Things hard to prove: decorum's wile,
Malice discreet, judicious guile;
Good done with ill intent—reversed:
Best deeds designed to serve the worst;
And hate which under life's fair hue
Prowls like the shark in sunned Pacific blue.
  He paused, and under stress did bow,

Lank hands enlocked across the brow.
    "Nay, nay, thou sea,
'Twas not all carnal harlotry,
But sins refined, crimes of the spirit,
Helped earn that doom ye here inherit:
Doom well imposed, though sharp and dread,
In some god's reign, some god long fled.—
Thou gaseous puff of mineral breath
Mephitical; thou swooning flaw
That fann'st me from this pond of death;
Wert thou that venomous small thing
Which tickled with the poisoned straw?
Thou, stronger, but who yet couldst start
Shrinking with sympathetic sting,
While willing the uncompunctious dart!
Ah, ghosts of Sodom, how ye thrill
About me in this peccant air,
Conjuring yet to spare, but spare!
Fie, fie, that didst in formal will
Plot piously the posthumous snare.
And thou, the mud-flow—evil mass
Of surest-footed sluggishness
Swamping the nobler breed—art there?
Moan, burker of kind heart: all's known
To Him; with thy connivers, moan.—
Sinners—expelled, transmuted souls
Blown in these airs, or whirled in shoals
Of gurgles which your gasps send up,
Or on this crater marge and cup
Slavered in slime, or puffed in stench—
Not ever on the tavern bench
Ye lolled. Few dicers here, few sots,
Few sluggards, and no idiots.
'Tis *thou* who servedst Mammon's hate
Or greed through forms which holy are—
Black slaver steering by a star,
'Tis *thou*—and all like thee in state.

Who knew the world, yet varnished it;
Who traded on the coast of crime
Though landing not; who did outwit
Justice, his brother, and the time—
These, chiefly these; to doom submit.
But who the manifold may tell?
And sins there be inscrutable,
Unutterable."
                          Ending there
He shrank, and like an osprey gray
Peered on the wave. His hollow stare
Marked then some smaller bubbles play
In cluster silvery like spray:
"Be these the beads on the wives'-wine,
Tofana-brew?—O fair Medea—
O soft man-eater, furry fine:
Oh, be thou Jael, be thou Leah—
Unfathomably shallow!—No!
Nearer the core than man can go
Or Science get—nearer the slime
Of Nature's rudiments and lime
In chyle before the bone. Thee, thee,
In thee the filmy cell is spun—
The mold thou art of what men be:
Events are all in thee begun—
By thee, through thee!—Undo, undo,
Prithee, undo, and still renew
The fall forever!"
                          On his throne
He lapsed; and muffled came the moan
How multitudinous in sound,
From Sodom's wave. He glanced around:
They all had left him, one by one.
Was it because he open threw
The inmost to the outward view?
Or did but pain at frenzied thought
Prompt to avoid him, since but naught

In such case might remonstrance do?
But none there ventured idle plea,
Weak sneer, or fraudful levity.

    Two spirits, hovering in remove,
Sad with inefficacious love,
Here sighed debate: "Ah, Zoima, say;
Be it far from me to impute a sin,
But may a sinless nature win
Those deeps he knows?"—"Sin shuns that way;
Sin acts the sin, but flees the thought
That sweeps the abyss that sin has wrought.
Innocent be the heart and true—
Howe'er it feed on bitter bread—
That, venturous through the Evil led,
Moves as along the ocean's bed
Amid the dragon's staring crew."

PART III
MAR SABA

V

THE HIGH DESERT

WHERE silence and the legend dwell,
A cleft in Horeb is, they tell,
Through which upon one happy day
(The sun on his heraldic track
Due sign having gained in Zodiac)
A sunbeam darts, which slants away
Through ancient carven oriel
Or window in the Convent there,
Illuming so with annual flush
The somber vaulted chamber spare
Of Catherine's Chapel of the Bush—
The Burning Bush. Brief visitant,
It makes no lasting covenant;
It brings, but cannot leave, the ray.

    To hearts which here the desert smote,
So came, so went the Cypriote.

    Derwent deep felt it; and, as fain
His prior spirits to regain;
Impatient too of scenes which led
To converse such as late was bred,
Moved to go on. But some declined.
So, for relief to heart which pined,
Belex he sought, by him sat down
In cordial ease upon a stone
Apart, and heard his stories free
Of Ibrahim's wild infantry.

    The rest abide. To these there comes,
As down on Siddim's scene they peer,

The contrast of their vernal homes—
Field, orchard, and the harvest cheer.
At variance in their revery move
The spleen of nature and her love:
At variance, yet entangled too—
Like wrestlers. Here in apt review
They call to mind Abel and Cain—
Ormuzd involved with Ahriman
In deadly lock. Were those gods gone?
Or under other names lived on?
The theme they started. 'Twas averred
That, in old Gnostic pages blurred,
Jehovah was construed to be
Author of evil, yea, its god;
And Christ divine His contrary:
A god was held against a god,
But Christ revered alone. Herefrom,
If inference availeth aught
(For still the topic pressed they home),
The twofold Testaments become
Transmitters of Chaldaic thought
By implication. If no more
Those Gnostic heretics prevail
Which shook the East from shore to shore,
Their strife forgotten now and pale;
Yet, with the sects, that old revolt
Now reappears, if in assault
Less frank: none say Jehovah's evil,
None gainsay that He bears the rod;
Scarce that; but there's dismission civil,
And Jesus is the indulgent God.
This change, this dusking change that slips
(Like the penumbra o'er the sun),
Over the faith transmitted down;
Foreshadows it complete eclipse?
        Science and Faith, can these unite?
Or is that priestly instinct right
(Right as regards conserving still

The Church's reign) whose strenuous will
Made Galileo pale recite
The Penitential Psalms in vest
Of sackcloth; which to-day would blight
Those potent solvents late expressed
In laboratories of the West?
     But in her Protestant repose
Snores faith toward her mortal close?
Nay, like a sachem petrified,
Encaved found in the mountain-side,
Perfect in feature, true in limb,
Life's full similitude in him,
Yet all mere stone—is faith dead *now*,
A petrifaction? Grant it so,
Then what's in store? what shapeless birth?
Reveal the doom reserved for earth?
How far may seas retiring go?
     But, to redeem us, shall we say
That faith, undying, does but range,
Casting the skin—the creed. In change
Dead always does some creed delay—
Dead, not interred, though hard upon
Interment's brink? At Saint Denis,
Where slept the Capets, sire and son,
Eight centuries of lineal clay,
On steps that led down into vault
The prince inurned last made a halt,
The coffin left they there, 'tis said,
Till the inheritor was dead;
Then, not till then 'twas laid away.
But if no more the creeds be linked,
If the long line 's at last extinct,
If time both creed and faith betray,
Vesture and vested—yet again
What interregnum or what reign
Ensues? Or does a period come?
The Sibyls' books lodged in the tomb?
Shall endless time no more unfold

Of truth at core? Some things discerned
By the far Noahs of India old—
Earth's first spectators, the clear-eyed,
Unvitiated, unfalsified
Seers at first hand—shall these be learned,
Though late, even by the New World, say,
Which now contemns?
                              But what shall stay
The fever of advance? London immense
Still wax for aye? A check: but whence?
How of the teeming Prairie-Land?
There shall the plenitude expand
Unthinned, unawed? Or does it need
Only that men should breed and breed
To enrich those forces into play
Which in past times could oversway
Pride at his proudest? Do they come,
The locusts, only to the bloom?
Prosperity sire them?
                              Thus they swept,
Nor sequence held, consistent tone—
Imagination wildering on
Through vacant halls which faith once kept
With ushers good.
                              Themselves thus lost,
At settled hearts they wonder most.
For those (they asked) who still adhere
In homely habit's dull delay,
To dreams dreamed out or passed away;
Do these, our pagans, all appear
Much like each poor and busy one
Who when the Tartar took Pekin
(If credence hearsay old may win),
Knew not the fact—so vast the town,
The multitude, the maze, the din?
      Still laggeth in deferred adieu
The A.D. (Anno Domini)
Overlapping into era new

Even as the Roman A.U.C.
Yet ran for time, regardless all
That Christ was born, and after fall
Of Rome itself?
                     But now our age,
So infidel in equipage,
While carrying still the Christian name—
For all its self-asserted claim,
How fares it, tell? Can the age stem
Its own conclusions? is't a king
Awed by his conquests which enring
With menaces his diadem?
Bright visions of the times to be—
Must these recoil, ere long be cowed
Before the march in league avowed
Of Mammon and Democracy?
          In one result whereto we tend
Shall Science disappoint the hope,
Yea, to confound us in the end,
New doors to superstition ope?
          As years, as years and annals grow,
And action and reaction vie,
And never men attain, but know
How waves on waves forever die;
Does all more enigmatic show?
          So they; and in the vain appeal
Persisted yet, as ever still
Blown back in sleet that blinds the eyes,
Not less the fervid Geysers rise.

          Clarel meantime ungladdened bent
Regardful, and the more intent
For silence held. At whiles his eye
Lit on the Druze, reclined half prone,
The long pipe resting on the stone
And wreaths of vapor floating by—
The man and pipe in peace as one.
How clear the profile, clear and true;

And he so tawny. Bust ye view,
Antique, in alabaster brown,
Might show like that. There, all aside,
How passionless he took for bride
The calm—the calm, but not the dearth—
The dearth or waste; nor would he fall
In waste of words, that waste of all.

For Vine, from that unchristened earth
Bits he picked up of porous stone,
And crushed in fist: or one by one,
Through the dull void of desert air,
He tossed them into valley down;
Or pelted his own shadow there;
Nor sided he with anything:
By fits, indeed, he wakeful looked;
But, in the main, how ill he brooked
That weary length of arguing—
Like tale interminable told
In Hades by some gossip old
To while the never-ending night.
Apart he went. Meantime, like kite
On Sidon perched, which doth enfold,
Slowly exact, the noiseless wing:
Each wrinkled Arab Bethlehemite,
Or trooper of the Arab ring,
With look of Endor's withered sprite
Slant peered on them from lateral height;
While unperturbed over deserts riven,
Stretched the clear vault of hollow heaven.

XXIX

ROLFE AND THE PALM

Pursued, the mounted robber flies
Unawed through Kedron's plunged demesne:

The clink, and clinking echo dies:
He vanishes: a long ravine.
And stealthy there, in little chinks
Betwixt or under slab-rocks, slinks
The dwindled amber current lean.

    Far down see Rolfe there, hidden low
By ledges slant. Small does he show
(If eagles eye), small and far off
As Mother Carey's bird in den
Of Cape Horn's hollowing billow-trough,
When from the rail where lashed they bide
The sweep of overcurling tide—
Down, down, in bonds the seamen gaze
Upon that flutterer in glen
Of waters where it sheltered plays,
While, over it; each briny height
Is torn with bubbling torrents white
In slant foam tumbling from the snow
Upon the crest; and far as eye
Can range through mist and scud which fly,
Peak behind peak the liquid summits grow.

    By chance Rolfe won the rocky stair
At base, and queried if it were
Man's work or nature's, or the twain
Had wrought together in that lane
Of high ascent, so crooked with turns
And flanked by coigns, that one discerns
But links thereof in flights encaved,
Whate'er the point of view. Up, slow
He climbed for little space; then craved
A respite, turned and sat; and, lo,
The Tree in salutation waved
Across the chasm. Remindings swell;
Sweet troubles of emotion mount—
Sylvan reveries, and they well
From memory's Bandusa fount;

Yet scarce the memory alone,
But that and question merged in one:

  "Whom weave ye in,
Ye vines, ye palms? whom now, Soolee?
Lives yet your Indian Arcady?
His sunburnt face what Saxon shows—
His limbs all white as lilies be—
Where Eden, isled, empurpled glows
In old Mendanna's sea?
Takes who the venture after me?
  "Who now adown the mountain dell
(Till mine, by human foot untrod—
Nor easy, like the steps to hell)
In panic leaps the appalling crag,
Alighting on the cloistral sod
Where strange Hesperian orchards drag,
Walled round by cliff and cascatelle—
Arcades of Iris; and though lorn,
A truant ship-boy overworn,
Is hailed for a descended god?

  "Who sips the vernal cocoa's cream—
The nereids dimpling in the darkling stream?
For whom the gambol of the tricksy dream—
Even Puck's substantiated scene,
Yea, much as man might hope and more than
    heaven may mean?
  "And whom do priest and people sue,
In terms which pathos yet shall tone
When memory comes unto her own,
To dwell with them and ever find them true:
'Abide, for peace is here:
Behold, nor heat nor cold we fear,
Nor any dearth: one happy tide—
A dance, a garland of the year:
Abide!'
  "But who so feels the stars annoy,

Upbraiding him—how far astray!—
That he abjures the simple joy,
And hurries over the briny world away?
    "Renouncer! is it Adam's flight
Without compulsion or the sin?
And shall the vale avenge the slight
By haunting thee in hours thou yet shalt win?"

    He tarried. And each swaying fan
Sighed to his mood in threnodies of Pan.

XXXII

EMPTY STIRRUPS

THE gray of dawn. A tremor slight:
The trouble of imperfect light
Anew begins. In floating cloud
Midway suspended down the gorge,
A long mist trails white shreds of shroud
How languorous toward the Dead Sea's verge.
Riders in seat halt by the gate:
Why not set forth? For one they wait
Whose stirrups empty be—the Swede.
Still absent from the frater-hall
Since afternoon and vesper-call,
He, they imagined, had but sought
Some cave in keeping with his thought,
And reappear would with the light
Suddenly as the Gileadite
In Obadiah's way. But—no,
He cometh not when they would go.
Dismounting, they make search in vain;
Till Clarel—minding him again
Of something settled in his air—
A quietude beyond mere calm—
When seen from ledge beside the Palm

Reclined in nook of Bethel stair,
Thitherward led them in a thrill
Of nervous apprehension, till
Startled he stops, with eyes avert
And indicating hand.—

     'Tis *he*—
So undisturbed, supine, inert—
The filmed orbs fixed upon the Tree—
Night's dews upon his eyelids be.
To test if breath remain, none tries:
On those thin lips a feather lies—
An eagle's, wafted from the skies.
The vow: and had the genius heard,
Benignant? nor had made delay,
But, more than taking him at word,
Quick wafted where the palm-boughs sway
In Saint John's heaven? Some divined
That long had he been undermined
In frame; the brain a tocsin-bell
Overburdensome for citadel
Whose base was shattered. They refrain
From aught but that dumb look that fell
Identifying; feeling pain
That such a heart could beat, and will—
Aspire, yearn, suffer, baffled still,
And end. With monks which round them stood
Concerned, not discomposed in mood,
Interment they provided for—
Heaved a last sigh, nor tarried more.

  Nay; one a little lingered there;
'Twas Rolfe. And as the rising sun,
Though viewless yet from Bethel stair,
More lit the mountains, he was won
To invocation, scarce to prayer:

  "Holy Morning,
What blessed lore reservest thou,

Withheld from man, that evermore
Without surprise,
But, rather, with a hurtless scorning
In thy placid eyes,
Thou viewest all events alike?
Oh, tell me, do thy bright beams strike
The healing hills of Gilead now?"
And glanced toward the pale one near
In shadow of the crag's dark brow.—
  Did Charity follow that poor bier?
It did; but Bigotry did steer:
Friars buried him without the walls
(Nor in a consecrated bed)
Where vulture unto vulture calls,
And only ill things find a friend:
There let the beak and claw contend,
There the hyena's cub be fed:
Heaven that disclaims, and him beweeps
In annual showers; and the tried spirit sleeps.

PART IV
BETHLEHEM

XX
DERWENT AND UNGAR

"NOT thou com'st in the still small voice,"
Said Derwent, "thou queer Mexican!"
And followed him with eyes: "This man,"
And turned here, "he likes not grave talk,
The settled undiluted tone;
It does his humorous nature balk.
'Twas ever too his sly rebuff,
While yet obstreperous in praise,
Taking that dusty pinch of snuff.
An oddity, he has his ways;
Yet trust not, friends, the half he says:
Not he would do a weasel harm;
A secret agent of Reform;
At least, that is my theory."

  "The quicksilver is quick to skim,"
Ungar remarked, with eye on him.

  "Yes, Nature has her levity,"
Dropped Derwent.
       Nothing might disarm
The other; he: "Your word *reform*:
What meaning's to that word assigned?
From Luther's great initial down,
Through all the series following on,
The impetus augments—the blind
Precipitation: blind, for tell
Whitherward does the surge impel?
The end, the aim? 'Tis mystery."
  "Oh, no. Through all methinks I see

The object clear: belief revised,
Men liberated—equalized
In happiness. No mystery,
Just none at all; plain sailing."

                         "Well,
Assume this: is it feasible?
Your methods? These are of the world:
Now the world cannot save the world;
And Christ renounces it. His faith,
Breaking with every mundane path,
Aims straight at heaven. To founded thrones
He says: Trust not to earthly stanchions;
And unto poor and houseless ones—
My Father's house has many mansions.
Warning and solace be but this;
No thought to mend a world amiss."

    "Ah now, ah now!" pled Derwent.

                           "Nay,
Test further; take another way:
Go ask Aurelius Antonine—
A Cæsar wise, grave, just, benign,
Lord of the world—why, in the calm
Which through his reign the empire graced—
Why he, that most considerate heart
Superior, and at vantage placed,
Contrived no secular reform,
Though other he knew not, nor balm."

    "Alas," cried Derwent (and, in part,
As vainly longing for retreat),
"Though good Aurelius was a man
Matchless in mind as sole in seat,
Yet pined he under numbing ban
Of virtue without Christian heat:
As much you intimated too,
Just saying that no balm he knew.
Howbeit, true reform goes on
By nature; doing, never done.
Mark the advance: creeds drop the hate;

Events still liberalize the state."
        "But tell: do men now more cohere
In bonds of duty which sustain?
Cliffs crumble, and the parts regain
A liberal freedom, it is clear.
And for conventicles—I fear,
Much as a hard heart aged grown
Abates in rigor, losing tone;
So sects decrepit, at death's door,
Dote into peace through loss of power."

        "You put it so," said Derwent light:
"No more developments to cite?"

        "Ay, quench the true, the mock sun fails
Therewith. Much so, Hypocrisy,
The false thing, wanes just in degree
That Faith, the true thing, wanes: each pales.
There's *one* development; 'tis seen
In masters whom not low ye rate:
What lack, in some outgivings late,
Of the old Christian style toward men—
I do not mean the wicked ones,
But Pauperism's unhappy sons
In cloud so blackly ominous,
Grimy in Mammon's English pen—
Collaterals of his overplus:
How worse than them Immanuel fed
On hill-top—helped and comforted.
Thou, Poverty, erst free from shame,
Even sacred through the Savior's claim,
Professed by saints, by sages prized—
A pariah now, and bastardized!
Reactions from the Christian plan
Bear others further. Quite they shun
A god to name, or cite a man
Save Greek, heroical, a Don:
'Tis Plato's aristocratic tone.
All recognition they forgo
Of Evil; supercilious skim

With spurious wing of seraphim
The last abyss. Freemen avow
Belief in right divine of Might,
Yet spurn at kings. This is the light—
Divine the darkness. Mark the way
The Revolution, whose first mode,
Ere yet the maniacs overrode,
Despite the passion of the dream,
Evinced no disrespect for God;
Mark how, in our denuding day,
E'en with the masses, as would seem,
It tears the fig-leaf quite away.
Contrast these incidents: The mob,
The Paris mob of 'Eighty-nine,
Haggard and bleeding, with a throb
Burst the long Tuileries. In shrine
Of chapel there, they saw the Cross
And Him thereon. Ah, bleeding Man,
The people's friend, thou bled'st for us
Who here bleed, too! Ragged they ran—
They took the crucifix; in van
They put it, marched with drum and psalm
And throned it in their Notre-Dame.
But yesterday—how did they then,
In new uprising of the Red,
The offspring of those Tuileries men?
They made a clothes-stand of the Cross
Before the church; and, on that head
Which bowed for them, could wanton toss
The sword-belt, while the gibing sped.
Transcended rebel angels! Woe
To us; without a God, 'tis woe!"

XXI

UNGAR AND ROLFE

"SUCH earnestness! such wear and tear,
And man but a thin gossamer!"
So here the priest aside; then turned,
And, starting: "List! the vesper-bell?
Nay, nay—the hour is passed. But, oh,
He must have supped, Don Hannibal,
Ere now. Come, friends, and shall we go?
This hot discussion, let it stand
And cool; to-morrow we'll remand."

    "Not yet, I pray," said Rolfe; "a word";
And turned toward Ungar; "be adjured,
And tell us if for earth may be
In ripening arts, no guarantee
Of happy sequel."

              "Arts are tools;
But tools, they say, are to the strong:
Is Satan weak? weak is the Wrong?
No blessed augury overrules:
Your arts advance in faith's decay:
You are but drilling the new Hun
Whose growl even now can some dismay;
Vindictive in his heart of hearts,
He schools him in your mines and marts—
A skilled destroyer."

              "But, need own
That portent does in no degree
Westward impend, across the sea."

    "Over there? And do ye not forebode?
Against pretences void or weak
The impieties of 'Progress' speak.
What say *these*, in effect, to God?
'How profits it? And who art Thou
That we should serve Thee? Of Thy ways

No knowledge we desire; *new* ways
We have found out, and better. Go—
Depart from us; we do erase
Thy sinecure: behold, the sun
Stands still no more in Ajalon:
Depart from us!'—And if He do?
(And that He may, the Scripture says)
Is aught betwixt ye and the hells?
For He, nor in irreverent view,
'Tis He distils that savor true
Which keeps good essences from taint;
Where He is not, corruption dwells,
And man and chaos are without restraint."
    "Oh, oh, you do but generalize
In void abstractions."
                "Hypothesize:
If be a people which began
Without impediment, or let
From any ruling which foreran;
Even striving all things to forget
But this—the excellence of man
Left to himself, his natural bent,
His own devices and intent;
And if, in satire of the heaven,
A world, a new world have been given
For stage whereon to deploy the event;
If such a people be—well, well,
One hears the kettledrums of hell!
Exemplary act awaits its place
In drama of the human race."
    "Is such act certain?" Rolfe here ran;
"Not much is certain."
                "God is—man.
The human nature, the divine—
Have both been proved by many a sign.
'Tis no astrologer and star.
The world has now so old become,
Historic memory goes so far

Backward through long defiles of doom;
Whoso consults it honestly
That mind grows prescient in degree;
For man, like God, abides the same
Always, through all variety
Of woven garments to the frame."
    "Yes, God is God, and men are men,
For ever and for aye. What then?
There's Circumstance—there's Time; and these
Are charged with store of latencies
Still working in to modify.
For mystic text that you recall,
Dilate upon, and e'en apply—
(Although I seek not to decry)
Theology's scarce practical.
But leave this: the New World's the theme,
Here, to oppose your dark extreme
(Since an old friend is good at need),
To an old thought I'll fly. Pray, heed:
Those waste-weirs which the New World yields
To inland freshets—the free vents
Supplied to turbid elements;
The vast reserves—the untried fields;
These long shall keep off and delay
The class-war, rich-and-poor-man fray
Of history. From that alone
Can serious trouble spring. Even that
Itself, this good result may own—
The first firm founding of the state."
        Here ending, with a watchful air
Inquisitive, Rolfe waited him.
And Ungar:
                "True heart do ye bear
In this discussion? or but trim
To draw my monomania out,
For monomania, past doubt,
Some of ye deem it. Yet I'll on.

Yours seems a reasonable tone;
But in the New World things make haste;
Not only men, the *state* lives fast—
Fast breeds the pregnant eggs and shells,
The slumberous combustibles
Sure to explode. 'Twill come, 'twill come!
One demagogue can trouble much:
How of a hundred thousand such?
And universal suffrage lent
To back them with brute element
Overwhelming? What shall bind these seas
Of rival sharp communities
Unchristianized? Yea, but 'twill come!"
     "What come?"
                         "Your Thirty Years (of) War."
     "Should fortune's favorable star
Avert it?"
                    "Fortune? nay, 'tis doom."
"Then what comes after? spasms but tend
Ever, at last, to quiet."
                              "Know,
Whatever happen in the end,
Be sure 'twill yield to one and all
New confirmation of the fall
Of Adam. Sequel may ensue,
Indeed, whose germs one now may view:
Myriads playing pygmy parts—
Debased into equality:
In glut of all material arts
A civic barbarism may be:
Man disennobled—brutalized
By popular science—atheized
Into a smatterer—"
                         "Oh, oh!"
     "Yet knowing all self need to know
In self's base little fallacy;
Dead level of rank commonplace:

An Anglo-Saxon China, see,
May on your vast plains shame the race
In the Dark Ages of Democracy."

     America!
               In stilled estate,
On him, half-brother and co-mate—
In silence, and with vision dim
Rolfe, Vine, and Clarel gazed on him;
They gazed, nor one of them found heart
To upbraid the crotchet of his smart,
Bethinking them whence sole it came,
Though birthright he renounced in hope,
Their sanguine country's wonted claim.
Nor dull they were in honest tone
To some misgivings of their own:
They felt how far beyond the scope
Of elder Europe's saddest thought
Might be the New World's sudden brought
In youth to share old age's pains—
To feel the arrest of hope's advance,
And squandered last inheritance;
And cry—"To Terminus build fanes!
Columbus ended earth's romance:
No New World to mankind remains!"

XXX

THE VALLEY OF DECISION

DELAY!—Shall flute from forth the Gate
Issue, to warble welcome here—
Upon this safe returning wait
In gratulation? And, for cheer,
When inn they gain, there shall they see
The door-post wreathed?
                  Howe'er it be,

Through Clarel a revulsion ran,
Such as may seize debarking man
First hearing on Coquimbo's ground
That subterranean sullen sound
Which dull foreruns the shock. His heart,
In augury fair arrested here,
Upbraided him: Fool! and didst part
From Ruth? Strangely a novel fear
Obtruded—petty, and yet worse
And more from reason too averse,
Than that recurrent haunting bier
Molesting him erewhile. And yet
It was but irritation, fret—
Misgiving that the lines he writ
Upon the eve before the start
For Siddim, failed, or were unfit—
Came short of the occasion's tone:
To leave her, leave her in grief's smart:
To leave her—her, the stricken one:
Now first to feel full force of it!
Away! to be but there, but there!
Vain goadings: yet of love true part.
But then the pledge with letter sent,
Though but a trifle, still might bear
A token in dumb argument
Expressive more than words.
                                    With knee
Straining against the saddle-brace,
He urges on; till, near the place
Of Hebrew graves, a light they see
Moving, and figures dimly trace:
Some furtive strange society.
Yet nearer as they ride, the light
Shuts down. "Abide!" enjoined the Druze;
"Waylayers these are none, but Jews,
Or I mistake, who here by night
Have stolen to do gravedigger's work.
During late outbreak in the town

The bigot in the baser Turk
Was so inflamed, some Hebrews dread
Assault, even here among their dead.
Abide a space; let me ride on."
          Up pushed he, spake, allayed the fright
Of them who had shut down the light
At sound of comers.
                    Close they draw—
Advancing, lit by fan-shaped rays
Shot from a small dark-lantern's jaw
Presented pistol-like. They saw
Mattocks and men, in outline dim,
On either ominous side of him
From whom went forth that point of blaze.
Resting from labor, each one stays
His implement on gravestones old.
New dug, between these, they behold
Two narrow pits: and (nor remote)
Twin figures on the ground they note,
Folded in cloaks.
                    "And who rest there?"
Rolfe sidelong asked.
                    "Our friends; have care!"
Replied the one that held in view
The lantern, slanting it ashift,
Plainer disclosing them, and, too,
A broidered scarf, love's first chance gift,
The student's (which how well he knew!)
Binding one mantle's slender span.
          With piercing cry, as one distraught,
Down from his horse leaped Clarel—ran,
And hold of that cloak instant caught,
And bared the face. Then (like a man
Shot through the heart, but who retains
His posture) rigid he remains—
The mantle's border in his hand,
His glazed eyes unremoved. The band
Of Jews—the pilgrims—all look on

Shocked or amazed.
                        But speech he won:
"No—yes: enchanted here!—her name?"
        "Ruth, Nathan's daughter," said a Jew
Who kenned him now—the youth that came
Oft to the close; "but, thou—forbear:
The dawn's at hand and haste is due:
See, by her side, 'tis Agar there."
        "Ruth? Agar?—*art* thou God?—But ye—
All swims, and I but blackness see.—
How happed it? speak!"
                     "The fever—grief:
'Twere hard to tell; was no relief."
        "And ye—your tribe—'twas *ye* denied
Me access to this virgin's side
In bitter trial: take my curse!—
O blind, blind, barren universe!
Now am I like a bough torn down,
And I must wither, cloud or sun!—
Had I been near, this had not been.
Do spirits look down upon this scene?—
The message? some last word was left?"
        "For thee? no, none; the life was reft
Sudden from Ruth; and Agar died
Babbling of gulls and ocean wide—
Out of her mind."
                "And here's the furl
Of Nathan's faith: then perish faith—
'Tis perjured!—Take me, take me, Death!
Where Ruth is gone, me thither whirl,
Where'er it be!"
             "Ye do outgo
Mad Korah. Boy, this is the Dale
Of Doom, God's last assizes; so,
Curb thee; even if sharp grief assail,
Respect these precincts lest thou know
An ill."
        "Give way, quit thou our dead!"

Menaced another, striding out;
"Art thou of us? turn thee about!"
     "Spurn—I'll endure; all spirit's fled
When one fears nothing.—Bear with me,
Yet bear!—Conviction is not gone
Though faith's gone: that which shall not be
Still *ought* to be!"
                    But here came on,
With heavy footing, hollow heard,
Hebrews, which bare rude slabs, to place
Athwart the bodies when interred,
That earth should weigh not on the face;
For coffin was there none; and all
Was makeshift in this funeral.
     Uncouthly here a Jew began
To readjust Ruth's cloak. Amain
Did Clarel push him; and, in hiss:
"Not thou—for me!—Alone, alone
In such bride-chamber to lie down!
Nay, leave one hand out—like to this—
That so the bridegroom may not miss
To kiss it first, when soon he comes.—
But 'tis not she!" and hid his face.

     They laid them in the under-glooms—
Each pale one in her portioned place.
The gravel, from the bank raked down,
Dull sounded on those slabs of stone,
Grave answering grave—dull and more dull,
Each mass growing more, till either pit was full.

     As up from Kedron dumb they drew,
Then first the shivering Clarel knew
Night's damp. The Martyr's port is won—
Stephen's; harsh grates the bolt withdrawn;
And, over Olivet, comes on
Ash Wednesday in the gray of dawn.

XXXI

DIRGE

Stay, Death. Not mine the Christus-wand
Wherewith to charge thee and command:
I plead. Most gently hold the hand
Of her thou leadest far away;
Fear thou to let her naked feet
Tread ashes—but let mosses sweet
Her footing tempt, where'er ye stray.
Shun Orcus; win the moonlit land
Belulled—the silent meadows lone,
Where never any leaf is blown
From lily-stem in Azrael's hand.
There, till her love rejoin her lowly
(Pensive, a shade, but all her own),
On honey feed her, wild and holy;
Or trance her with thy choicest charm.
And if, ere yet the lover's free,
Some added dusk thy rule decree—
That shadow only let it be
Thrown in the moon-glade by the palm.

XXXII

PASSION WEEK

Day passed; and passed a second one,
A third—fourth—fifth; and bound he sate
In film of sorrow without moan—
Abandoned, in the stony strait
Of mutineer thrust on wild shore,
Hearing, beyond the roller's froth,
The last dip of the parting oar.
Alone, for all had left him so;
Though Rolfe, Vine, Derwent—each was loath,

How loath to leave him, or to go
Be first. From Vine he caught new sense
Developed through fate's pertinence.
Friendly they tarried—blameless went:
Life, avaricious, still demands
Her own, and more; the world is rent
With partings.
　　　　　　　　But, since all are gone,
Why lingers he, the stricken one?
Why linger where no hope can be?
Ask grief, love ask—fidelity
In dog that by the corse abides
Of shepherd fallen—abides, abides
Though autumn into winter glides,
Till on the mountain all is chill
And snow-bound, and the twain lie still
　　　How oft through Lent the feet were led
Of this chastized and fasting one
To neutral silence of the dead
In Kedron's gulf. One morn he sate
Down poring toward it from the gate
Sealed and named Golden. There a tomb,
Erected in time's recent day,
In block along the threshold lay
Impassable. From Omar's bloom
Came birds which lit, nor dreamed of harm,
On neighboring stones. His visage calm
Seemed not the one which late showed play
Of passion's throe; but here divine
No peace; ignition in the mine
Announced is by the rush, the roar:
These end; yet may the coal burn on—
Still slumberous burn beneath the floor
Of pastures where the sheep lie down.
　　　Ere long a cheerful choral strain
He hears; 'tis an Armenian train
Embowered in palms they bear, which (green,
And shifting oft) reveal the mien

Of flamens tall and singers young
In festal robes: a rainbow throng,
Like dolphins off Madeira seen
Which quick the ship and shout dismay.
With the blest anthem, censers sway,
Whose opal vapor, spiral borne,
Blends with the heavens' own azure Morn
Of Palms; for 'twas Palm Sunday bright,
Though thereof he, oblivious quite,
Knew nothing, nor that here they came
In memory of the green acclaim
Triumphal, and hosanna-roll
Which hailed Him on the ass's foal.

But unto Clarel that bright view
Into a dusk reminder grew:
He saw the tapers—saw again
The censers, singers, and the wreath
And litter of the bride of death
Pass through the Broken Fountain's lane;
In treble shrill and bass how deep
The men and boys he heard again
The undetermined contest keep
About the bier—the bier Armenian.
Yet dull, in torpor dim, he knew
The futile omen in review.

Yet three more days, and leadenly
From over Mary's port and arch,
On Holy Thursday, he the march
Of friars beheld, with litany
Filing beneath his feet, and bent
With crosses craped to sacrament
Down in the glenned Gethsemane.
Yes, Passion Week; the altars cower—
Each shrine a dead dismantled bower.

But when Good Friday dirged her gloom
Ere brake the morning, and each light

Round Calvary faded and THE TOMB,
What exhalations met his sight:
Illusion of grief's wakeful doom:
The dead walked. There, amid the train,
White Nehemiah he saw again—
With charnel beard; and Celio passed
As in a dampened mirror glassed;
Gleamed Mortmain, pallid as wolf-bone
Which bleaches where no man hath gone;
And Nathan in his murdered guise—
Sullen, and Hades in his eyes;
Poor Agar, with such wandering mien
As in her last blank hour was seen.
And each and all kept lonely state,
Yea, man and wife passed separate.
But Ruth—ah, how estranged in face!
He knew her by no earthly grace:
Nor might he reach to her in place.
And languid vapors from them go
Like thaw-fogs curled from dankish snow.

 Where, where now He who helpeth us,
The Comforter?—Tell, Erebus!

XXXIII

EASTER

BUT on the third day Christ arose;
And, in the town He knew, the rite
Commemorative eager goes
Before the hour. Upon the night
Between the week's last day and first,
No more the Stabat is dispersed
Or Tenebræ. And when the day,
The Easter, falls in calendar
The same to Latin and the array

Of all schismatics from afar—
Armenians, Greeks from many a shore—
Syrians, Copts—profusely pour
The hymns: 'tis like the choric gush
Of torrents Alpine when they rush
To swell the anthem of the spring.

     That year was now. Throughout the fane,
Floor, and arcades in double ring
About the gala of THE TOMB,
Blazing with lights, behung with bloom—
What childlike thousands roll the strain,
The hallelujah after pain,
Which in all tongues of Christendom
Still through the ages has rehearsed
That Best, the outcome of the Worst.

     Nor blame them who by lavish rite
Thus greet the pale victorious Son,
Since Nature times the same delight,
And rises with the Emerging One;
Her passion-week, her winter mood
She slips, with crape from off the Rood.

     In soft rich shadow under dome,
With gems and robes repletely fine,
The priests like birds Brazilian shine:
And moving tapers charm the sight,
Enkindling the curled incense-fume:
A dancing ray, auroral light.

     Burn on the hours, and meet the day.
The morn invites; the suburbs call
The concourse to come forth—this way!
Out from the gate by Stephen's wall,
They issue, dot the hills, and stray
In bands, like sheep among the rocks;
And the Good Shepherd in the heaven,
To whom the charge of these is given,
The Christ, ah! counts He there His flocks?
     But they, at each suburban shrine,

Grateful adore that Friend benign;
Though chapel now and cross divine
Too frequent show neglected; nay,
For charities of early rains
Rim them about with vernal stains,
Forerunners of maturer May,
When those red flowers, which so can please
(*Christ's-Blood-Drops* named—anemones),
Spot Ephraim and the mountain-way.
      But heart bereft is unrepaid
Though Thammuz' spring in Thammuz' glade
Invite; then how in Joel's glen?
What if dyed shawl and bodice gay
Make bright the black dell? what if they
In distance clear diminished be
To seeming cherries dropped on pall
Borne graveward under laden tree?
The cheer, so human, might not call
The maiden up; *Christ is arisen*:
But Ruth, may Ruth so burst the prison?

      The rite supreme being ended now,
Their confluence here the nations part:
Homeward the tides of pilgrims flow,
By contrast making the walled town
Like a depopulated mart;
More like some kirk on week-day lone,
On whose void benches broodeth still
The brown light from November hill.

      But though the freshet quite be gone—
Sluggish, life's wonted stream flows on.

XXXIV

VIA CRUCIS

SOME leading thoroughfares of man
In wood-path, track, or trail began;
Though threading heart of proudest town,
They follow in controlling grade
A hint or dictate, Nature's own,
By man, as by the brute, obeyed.

Within Jerusalem a lane,
Narrow, nor less an artery main
(Though little knoweth it of din),
In parts suggests such origin.
The restoration or repair,
Successive through long ages there,
Of city upon city tumbled,
Might scarce divert that thoroughfare,
Whose hill abideth yet unhumbled
Above the valley-side it meets.
Pronounce its name, this natural street's:
The *Via Crucis*—even the way
Tradition claims to be the one
Trod on that Friday far away
By Him our pure exemplar shown.

'Tis Whitsuntide. From paths without,
Through Stephen's gate—by many a vein
Convergent brought within this lane,
Ere sun-down shut the loiterer out—
As 'twere a frieze, behold the train!
Bowed water-carriers; Jews with staves,
Infirm gray monks; overloaded slaves;
Turk soldiers—young, with home-sick eyes;
A Bey, bereaved through luxuries;
Strangers and exiles; Moslem dames

Long-veiled in monumental white,
Dumb from the mounds which memory claims;
A half-starved vagrant Edomite;
Sore-footed Arab girls, which toil
Depressed under heap of garden-spoil;
The patient ass with panniered urn;
Sour camels humped by heaven and man,
Whose languid necks through habit turn
For ease—for ease they hardly gain.
In varied forms of fate they wend—
Or man or animal, 'tis one:
Cross-bearers all, alike they tend
And follow, slowly follow on.

But, lagging after, who is he
Called early every hope to test,
And now, at close of rarer quest,
Finds so much more the heavier tree?
From slopes whence even Echo's gone,
Wending, he murmurs in low tone:
"They wire the world—far under sea
They talk; but never comes to me
A message from beneath the stone."

Dusked Olivet he leaves behind,
And, taking now a slender wynd,
Vanishes in the obscurer town.

XXXV

EPILOGUE

IF Luther's day expand to Darwin's year,
Shall that exclude the hope—foreclose the fear?

Unmoved by all the claims our times avow,
The ancient Sphinx still keeps the porch of shade

And comes Despair, whom not her calm may cow,
And coldly on that adamantine brow
Scrawls undeterred his bitter pasquinade.
But Faith (who from the scrawl indignant turns),
With blood warm oozing from her wounded trust,
Inscribes even on her shards of broken urns
The sign o' the cross—*the spirit above the dust!*

Yea, ape and angel, strife and old debate—
The harps of heaven and dreary gongs of hell;
Science the feud can only aggravate—
No umpire she betwixt the chimes and knell:
The running battle of the star and clod
Shall run for ever—if there be no God.

Degrees we know, unknown in days before;
The light is greater, hence the shadow more;
And tantalized and apprehensive Man
Appealing—Wherefore ripen us to pain?
Seems there the spokesman of dumb Nature's train.

But through such strange illusions have they passed
Who in life's pilgrimage have baffled striven—
Even death may prove unreal at the last,
And stoics be astounded into heaven.

Then keep thy heart, though yet but ill-resigned—
Clarel, thy heart, the issues there but mind;
That like the crocus budding through the snow—
That like a swimmer rising from the deep—
That like a burning secret which doth go
Even from the bosom that would hoard and keep;
Emerge thou mayst from the last whelming sea,
And prove that death but routs life into victory.

FROM
JOHN MARR AND
OTHER SAILORS

JOHN MARR AND OTHER SAILORS

JOHN MARR

JOHN MARR, toward the close of the last century born in America of a mother unknown, and from boyhood up to maturity a sailor under divers flags, disabled at last from further maritime life by a crippling wound received at close quarters with pirates of the Keys, eventually betakes himself for a livelihood to less active employment ashore. There, too, he transfers his rambling disposition acquired as a seafarer.

After a variety of removals, at first as a sailmaker from seaport to seaport, then adventurously inland as a rough bench-carpenter, he, finally, in the last-named capacity, settles down about the year 1838 upon what was then a frontier-prairie, sparsely sprinkled with small oak-groves and yet fewer log-houses of a little colony but recently from one of our elder inland States. Here, putting a period to his rovings, he marries.

Ere long a fever, the bane of new settlements on teeming loam, and whose sallow livery was certain to show itself after an interval in the complexions of too many of these people, carries off his young wife and infant child. In one coffin, put together by his own hands, they are committed with meager rites to the earth—another mound, though a small one, in the wide prairie, nor far from where the mound-builders of a race only conjecturable had left their pottery and bones, one common clay, under a strange terrace serpentine in form.

With an honest stillness in his general mien—swarthy and black-browed, with eyes that could soften or flash, but never harden, yet disclosing at times a melancholy depth—this kinless man had affections which, once placed, not readily could be dislodged or resigned to a substituted object. Being now arrived at middle-life, he resolves never to quit the soil that holds the only beings ever connected with him by love in the family tie.

His log-house he lets to a new-comer, one glad enough to get it, and dwells with the household.

While the acuter sense of his bereavement becomes mollified by time, the void at heart abides. Fain, if possible, would he fill that void by cultivating social relations yet nearer than before with a people whose lot he purposes sharing to the end— relations superadded to that mere work-a-day bond arising from participation in the same outward hardships, making reciprocal helpfulness a matter of course. But here, and nobody to blame, he is obstructed.

More familiarly to consort, men of a practical turn must sympathetically converse, and upon topics of real life. But, whether as to persons or events, one cannot always be talking about the present, much less speculating about the future; one must needs recur to the past, which, with the mass of men, where the past is in any personal way a common inheritance, supplies to most practical natures the basis of sympathetic communion.

But the past of John Marr was not the past of these pioneers. Their hands had rested on the plough-tail, his upon the ship's helm. They knew but their own kind and their own usages; to him had been revealed something of the checkered globe. So limited unavoidably was the mental reach, and by consequence the range of sympathy, in this particular band of domestic emigrants, hereditary tillers of the soil, that the ocean, but a hearsay to their fathers, had now through yet deeper inland removal become to themselves little more than a rumor traditional and vague.

They were a staid people; staid through habituation to monotonous hardship; ascetics by necessity not less than through moral bias; nearly all of them sincerely, however narrowly, religious. They were kindly at need, after their fashion; but to a man wonted—as John Marr in his previous homeless sojournings could not but have been—to the free-and-easy tavern-clubs affording cheap recreation of an evening in certain old and comfortable seaport towns of that time, and yet more familiar with the companionship afloat of the sailors of the same period, something was lacking. That something was geniality, the flower of life springing from some sense of joy in it, more or less. This their lot could not give to these hard-working endurers of the dispiriting malaria—men to whom a holiday never came—and they had too much of uprightness and no art at all or desire to affect what they did not really feel. At a corn-husking, their least grave of gatherings, did the lone-hearted mariner seek to divert his own thoughts from sadness, and in some degree interest theirs, by adverting to aught removed from the crosses and trials of their personal surroundings, naturally enough he would slide into some marine story or picture, but would soon recoil upon himself and be silent, finding no encouragement to proceed. Upon one such occasion an elderly man—a blacksmith, and at Sunday gatherings an earnest exhorter—honestly said to him, "Friend, we know nothing of that here."

Such unresponsiveness in one's fellow-creatures set apart from factitious life, and by their vocation—in those days little helped by machinery—standing, as it were, next of kin to Nature; this, to John Marr, seemed of a piece with the apathy of Nature herself as envisaged to him here on a prairie where none but the perished mound-builders had as yet left a durable mark.

The remnant of Indians thereabout—all but exterminated in their recent and final war with regular white troops, a war waged by the Red Men for their native soil and natural rights—had been coerced into the occupancy of wilds not very far beyond the Mississippi—wilds *then*, but now the seats of municipalities and states. Prior to that, the bisons, once streaming countless in processional herds, or browsing as in an endless battle-line over these vast aboriginal pastures, had retreated, dwindled in number, before the hunters, in main a race distinct from the agricultural pioneers, though generally their advance-guard. Such a double exodus of man and beast left the plain a desert, green or blossoming indeed, but almost as forsaken as the Siberian Obi. Save the prairie-hen, sometimes startled from its lurking-place in the rank grass; and, in their migratory season, pigeons, high overhead on the wing, in dense multitudes eclipsing the day like a passing storm-cloud; save these—there being no wide woods with their underwood—birds were strangely few.

Blank stillness would for hours reign unbroken on this prairie. "It is the bed of a dried-up sea," said the companionless sailor—no geologist—to himself, musing at twilight upon the fixed undulations of that immense alluvial expanse bounded only by the horizon, and missing there the stir that, to alert eyes and ears, animates at all times the apparent solitudes of the deep.

But a scene quite at variance with one's antecedents may yet prove suggestive of them. Hooped round by a level rim, the prairie was to John Marr a reminder of ocean.

With some of his former shipmates, *chums* on certain cruises, he had contrived, prior to this last and more remote removal, to keep up a little correspondence at odd intervals. But from tidings of anybody or any sort he, in common with the other settlers, was now cut off; quite cut off, except from such news as might be conveyed over the grassy billows by the last arrived prairie schooner—the vernacular term, in those parts and times, for the emigrant wagon arched high over with sail-cloth, and voyaging across the vast champaign. There was no reachable post-office as yet; not even the rude little receptive box with lid and leather hinges, set up at convenient intervals on a stout stake along some solitary green way, affording a perch for birds, and which, later in the unintermitting advance of the frontier, would perhaps decay into a mossy monument, attesting yet another successive overleaped limit of civilized life; a life which in America can to-day hardly be said to have any western bound but the ocean that washes Asia. Throughout these plains, now in places over-populous with towns over-opulent; sweeping plains, elsewhere fenced off in every direction into flourishing farms—pale townsmen and hale farmers alike, in part, the descendants of the first sallow settlers; a region that half a century ago produced little for the sustenance of man, but to-day launching its superabundant wheat-harvest on the world; of this prairie, now everywhere intersected with wire and rail, hardly can it be said that at the period here written of there was so much as a traceable road. To the long-distance traveller the oak-groves, wide apart, and varying in compass and form; these, with recent settlements, yet more widely separate, offered some landmarks; but otherwise he steered by the sun. In early midsummer, even going but from one log-encampment to the next, a journey it might be of hours or good part of a day, travel was much like navigation. In some more enriched depressions between the long, green, graduated swells, smooth as those of ocean becalmed receiving and subduing to its own tranquillity the voluminous surge raised by some far-off hurricane of days previous, here one would catch the first indication of advancing strangers either in the distance, as a far sail at sea, by the glistening white canvas of the wagon, the wagon itself wading through the rank vegetation and hidden by it, or, failing that, when near to, in the ears of the team, peeking, if not above the tall tiger-lilies, yet above the yet taller grass.

Luxuriant, this wilderness; but, to its denizen, a friend left behind anywhere in the world seemed not alone absent to sight, but an absentee from existence.

Though John Marr's shipmates could not all have departed life, yet as subjects of meditation they were like phantoms of the dead. As the growing sense of his environment threw him more and more upon retrospective musings, these phantoms, next to those of his wife and child, became spiritual companions, losing something of their first indistinctness and putting on at last a dim semblance of mute life; and they were lit by that aureola circling over any object of the affections in the past for reunion with which an imaginative heart passionately yearns.

He invokes these visionary ones, striving, as it were, to get into verbal communion with them, or, under yet stronger illusion, reproaching them for their silence:—

> Since as in night's deck-watch ye show,
> Why, lads, so silent here to me,
> Your watchmate of times long ago?

> Once, for all the darkling sea,
> You your voices raised how clearly,
> Striking in when tempest sung;
> Hoisting up the storm-sail cheerly,
> *Life is storm—let storm!* you rung.

Taking things as fated merely,
Childlike though the world ye spanned;
Nor holding unto life too dearly,
Ye who held your lives in hand—
Skimmers, who on oceans four
Petrels were, and larks ashore.

O, not from memory lightly flung,
Forgot, like strains no more availing,
The heart to music haughtier strung;
Nay, frequent near me, never staling,
Whose good feeling kept ye young.
Like tides that enter creek or stream,
Ye come, ye visit me, or seem
Swimming out from seas of faces,
Alien myriads memory traces,
To enfold me in a dream!

I yearn as ye. But rafts that strain,
Parted, shall they lock again?
Twined we were, entwined, then riven,
Ever to new embracements driven,
Shifting gulf-weed of the main!
And how if one here shift no more,
Lodged by the flinging surge ashore?
Nor less, as now, in eve's decline,
Your shadowy fellowship is mine.
Ye float around me, form and feature:—
Tattooings, ear-rings, love-locks curled;
Barbarians of man's simpler nature,
Unworldly servers of the world.
Yea, present all, and dear to me,
Though shades, or scouring China's sea.
Whither, whither, merchant-sailors,
Whitherward now in roaring gales?
Competing still, ye huntsman-whalers,
In leviathan's wake what boat prevails?
And man-of-war's men, whereaway?

If now no dinned drum beat to quarters
On the wilds of midnight waters—
Foemen looming through the spray;
Do yet your gangway lanterns, streaming,
Vainly strive to pierce below,
When, tilted from the slant plank gleaming,
A brother you see to darkness go?

But, gunmates lashed in shotted canvas,
If where long watch-below ye keep,
Never the shrill *"All hands up hammocks!"*
Breaks the spell that charms your sleep,
And summoning trumps might vainly call,
And booming guns implore—
A beat, a heart-beat musters all,
One heart-beat at heart-core.
It musters. But to clasp, retain;
To see you at the halyards main—
To hear your chorus once again!

TOM DEADLIGHT

(1810)

DURING a tempest encountered homeward bound from the
Mediterranean, a grizzled petty officer, one of the two captains
of the forecastle, dying at night in his hammock, swung in the
sick-bay under the tiered gundecks of the British *Dreadnought*,
98, wandering in his mind, though with glimpses of sanity, and
starting up at whiles, sings by snatches his good-bye and last in-
junctions to two messmates, his watchers, one of whom fans
the fevered tar with the flap of his old sou'-wester. Some names
and phrases, with here and there a line, or part of one; these, in
his aberration, wrested into incoherency from their original
connection and import, he involuntarily derives, as he does the
measure, from a famous old sea-ditty, whose cadences, long rife,

and now humming in the collapsing brain, attune the last flut-
terings of distempered thought.

Farewell and adieu to you noble hearties,—
    Farewell and adieu to you ladies of Spain,
For I've received orders for to sail for the Deadman,
    But hope with the grand fleet to see you again.

I have hove my ship to, with main-topsail aback, boys;
    I have hove my ship to, for to strike soundings clear—
The black scud a-flying; but, by God's blessing, dam' me,
    Right up the Channel for the Deadman I'll steer.
I have worried through the waters that are called the
        Doldrums,
    And growled at Sargasso that clogs while ye grope—
Blast my eyes, but the lightship is hid by the mist, lads:—
    Flying Dutchman—odds bobbs—off the Cape of Good
        Hope!

But what's this I feel that is fanning my cheek, Matt?
    The white goney's wing?—how she rolls!—'tis the
        Cape!—
Give my kit to the mess, Jock, for kin none is mine, none;
    And tell *Holy Joe* to avast with the crape.

Dead reckoning, says *Joe*, it won't do to go by;
    But they doused all the glims, Matt, in sky t'other night.
Dead reckoning is good for to sail for the Deadman;
    And Tom Deadlight he thinks it may reckon near right.

The signal!—it streams for the grand fleet to anchor.
    The captains—the trumpets—the hullabaloo!
Stand by for blue-blazes, and mind your shank-painters,
    For the Lord High Admiral, he's squinting at you!

But give me my *tot*, Matt, before I roll over;
    Jock, let's have your flipper, it's good for to feel;

And don't sew me up without *baccy* in mouth, boys,
    And don't blubber like lubbers when I turn up my keel.

JACK ROY

KEPT up by relays of generations young,
Never dies at halyards the blithe chorus sung;
While in sands, sounds, and seas where the storm-petrels
    cry,
Dropped mute around the globe, these halyard singers lie.
Short-lived the clippers for racing-cups that run,
And speeds in life's career many a lavish mother's-son.

But thou, manly king o' the old *Splendid*'s crew,
The ribbons o' thy hat still a-fluttering, should fly—
A challenge, and forever, nor the bravery should rue.
Only in a tussle for the starry flag high,
When 'tis piety to do, and privilege to die,

Then, only then, would heaven think to lop
Such a cedar as the captain o' the *Splendid*'s maintop:
A belted sea-gentleman; a gallant, off-hand
Mercutio indifferent in life's gay command.
Magnanimous in humor; when the splintering shot fell,
"Toothpicks a-plenty, lads; thank 'em with a shell!"

Sang Larry o' the Cannakin, smuggler o' the wine,
At mess between guns, lad in jovial recline:
"In Limbo our Jack he would chirrup up a cheer,
The martinet there find a chaffing mutineer;
From a thousand fathoms down under hatches o' your
    Hades,
He'd ascend in love-ditty, kissing fingers to your ladies!"

Never relishing the knave, though allowing for the menial,
Nor overmuch the king, Jack, nor prodigally genial.

Ashore on liberty, he flashed in escapade,
Vaulting over life in its levelness of grade,
Like the dolphin off Africa in rainbow a-sweeping—
Arch iridescent shot from seas languid sleeping.

Larking with thy life, if a joy but a toy,
Heroic in thy levity wert thou, Jack Roy.

SEA-PIECES

THE HAGLETS

By chapel bare, with walls sea-beat,
The lichened urns in wilds are lost
About a carved memorial stone
That shows, decayed and coral-mossed,
A form recumbent, swords at feet,
Trophies at head, and kelp for a winding-sheet.

I invoke thy ghost, neglected fane,
Washed by the waters' long lament;
I adjure the recumbent effigy
To tell the cenotaph's intent—
Reveal why faggoted swords are at feet,
Why trophies appear and weeds are the winding-sheet.
By open ports the Admiral sits,
And shares repose with guns that tell
Of power that smote the arm'd Plate Fleet
Whose sinking flagship's colors fell;
But over the Admiral floats in light
His squadron's flag, the red-cross Flag of the White.
    The eddying waters whirl astern,
The prow, a seedsman, sows the spray;
With bellying sails and buckling spars
The black hull leaves a Milky Way;
Her timbers thrill, her batteries roll,
She reveling speeds exulting with pennon at pole.
    But ah, for standards captive-trailed
For all their scutcheoned castles' pride—
Castilian towers that dominate Spain,
Naples, and either Ind beside;
Those haughty towers, armorial ones,
Rue the salute from the Admiral's dens of guns.

Ensigns and arms in trophy brave,
Braver for many a rent and scar,
The captor's naval hall bedeck,
Spoil that ensures an earldom's star—
Toledoes great, grand draperies too,
Spain's steel and silk, and splendors from Peru.

    But crippled part in splintering fight,
The vanquished flying the victor's flags,
With prize-crews, under convoy-guns,
Heavy the fleet from Opher drags—
The Admiral crowding sail ahead,
Foremost with news who foremost in conflict sped.

    But out from cloistral gallery dim,
In early night his glance is thrown;
He marks the vague reserve of heaven,
He feels the touch of ocean lone;
Then turns, in frame part undermined,
Nor notes the shadowing wings that fan behind.

There, peaked and gray, three haglets fly,
And follow, follow fast in wake
Where slides the cabin-luster shy,
And sharks from man a glamor take,
Seething along the line of light
In lane that endless rules the warship's flight.

    The sea-fowl here, whose hearts none know,
They followed late the flagship quelled,
(As now the victor one) and long
Above her gurgling grave, shrill held
With screams their wheeling rites—then sped
Direct in silence where the victor led.

    Now winds less fleet, but fairer, blow,
A ripple laps the coppered side,
While phosphor sparks make ocean gleam,
Like camps lit up in triumph wide;
With lights and tinkling cymbals meet
Acclaiming seas the advancing conqueror greet.

But who a flattering tide may trust,
Or favoring breeze, or aught in end?—
Careening under startling blasts
The sheeted towers of sails impend;
While, gathering bale, behind is bred
A livid storm-bow, like a rainbow dead.

    At trumpet-call the topmen spring;
And, urged by after-call in stress,
Yet other tribes of tars ascend
The rigging's howling wilderness;
But ere yard-ends alert they win,
Hell rules in heaven with hurricane-fire and din.

    The spars, athwart at spiry height,
Like quaking Lima's crosses rock;
Like bees the clustering sailors cling
Against the shrouds, or take the shock
Flat on the swept yard-arms aslant,
Dipped like the wheeling condor's pinions
    gaunt.
A lull! and tongues of languid flame
Lick every boom, and lambent show
Electric 'gainst each face aloft;
The herds of clouds with bellowings go:
The black ship rears—beset—harassed,
Then plunges far with luminous antlers vast.

    In trim betimes they turn from land,
Some shivered sails and spars they stow:
One watch, dismissed, they troll the can,
While loud the billow thumps the bow—
Vies with the fist that smites the board,
Obstreperous at each reveler's jovial word.

    Of royal oak by storms confirmed,
The tested hull her lineage shows:
Vainly the plungings whelm her prow—
She rallies, rears, she sturdier grows;
Each shot-hole plugged, each storm-sail home,
With batteries housed she rams the watery dome.

Dim seen adrift through driving scud,
The wan moon shows in plight forlorn;
Then, pinched in visage, fades and fades
Like to the faces drowned at morn,
When deeps engulfed the flagship's crew,
And, shrilling round, the inscrutable haglets flew.
  And still they fly, nor now they cry,
But constant fan a second wake,
Unflagging pinions ply and ply,
Abreast their course intent they take;
Their silence marks a stable mood,
They patient keep their eager neighborhood.
  Plumed with a smoke, a confluent sea,
Heaved in a combing pyramid full,
Spent at its climax, in collapse
Down headlong thundering stuns the hull:
The trophy drops; but, reared again,
Shows Mars' high altar and contemns the main.

Rebuilt it stands, the brag of arms,
Transferred in site—no thought of where
The sensitive needle keeps its place,
And starts, disturbed, a quiverer there;
The helmsman rubs the clouded glass—
Peers in, but lets the trembling portent pass.
  Let pass as well his shipmates do
(Whose dream of power no tremors jar)
Fears for the fleet convoyed astern:
"Our flag they fly, they share our star;
Spain's galleons great in hull are stout:
Manned by our men—like us they'll ride it out."
  To-night's the night that ends the week—
Ends day and week and month and year:
A fourfold imminent flickering time,
For now the midnight draws anear:
Eight bells! and passing-bells they be—
The Old Year fades, the Old Year dies at sea.

He launched them well. But shall the New
Redeem the pledge the Old Year made,
Or prove a self-asserting heir?
But healthy hearts few qualms invade:
By shot-chests grouped in bays 'tween guns
The gossips chat, the grizzled, sea-beat ones.

    And boyish dreams some graybeards blab:
"To sea, my lads, we go no more
Who share the Acapulco prize;
We'll all night in, and bang the door;
Our ingots red shall yield us bliss:
Lads, golden years begin to-night with this?"

    Released from deck, yet waiting call,
Glazed caps and coats baptized in storm,
A watch of Laced Sleeves round the board
Draw near in heart to keep them warm:
"Sweethearts and wives!" clink, clink, they meet,
And, quaffing, dip in wine their beards of sleet.
"Ay, let the starlight stay withdrawn,
So here her hearth-light memory fling,
So in this wine-light cheer be born,
And honor's fellowship weld our ring—
Honor! our Admiral's aim foretold:
A tomb or a trophy, and lo, 'tis a trophy and
    gold!"

    But he, a unit, sole in rank,
Apart needs keep his lonely state,
The sentry at his guarded door
Mute as by vault the sculptured Fate;
Belted he sits in drowsy light,
And, hatted, nods—the Admiral of the White.

    He dozes, aged with watches passed—
Years, years of pacing to and fro;
He dozes, nor attends the stir
In bullioned standards rustling low,
Nor minds the blades whose secret thrill
Perverts overhead the magnet's Polar will;—

Less heeds the shadowing three that ply
And follow, follow fast in wake,
Untiring wing and lidless eye—
Abreast their course intent they take;
Or sigh or sing, they hold for good
The unvarying flight and fixed inveterate mood.
    In dream at last his dozings merge,
In dream he reaps his victory's fruit:
The Flags-o'-the-Blue, the Flags-o'-the-Red,
Dipped flags of his country's fleets salute
His Flag-o'-the-White in harbor proud—
But why should it blench? Why turn to a painted shroud?
    The hungry seas they hound the hull,
The sharks they dog the haglets' flight;
With one consent the winds, the waves
In hunt with fins and wings unite,
While drear the harps in cordage sound
Remindful wails for old Armadas drowned.

Ha—yonder! are they Northern Lights?
Or signals flashed to warn or ward?
Yea, signals lanced in breakers high;
But doom on warning follows hard:
While yet they veer in hope to shun,
They strike! and thumps of hull and heart are one.
    But beating hearts a drum-beat calls
And prompt the men to quarters go;
Discipline, curbing nature, rules—
Heroic makes who duty know:
They execute the trump's command,
Or in peremptory places wait and stand.
    Yet cast about in blind amaze—
As through their watery shroud they peer:
"We tacked from land: then how betrayed?
Have currents swerved us—snared us here?"
None heed the blades that clash in place
Under lamps dashed down that lit the magnet's case.

Ah, what may live, who mighty swim,
Or boat-crew reach that shore forbid,
Or cable span? Must victors drown—
Perish, even as the vanquished did?
Man keeps from man the stifled moan;
They shouldering stand, yet each in heart how lone.
    Some heaven invoke; but rings of reefs
Prayer and despair alike deride
In dance of breakers forked or peaked,
Pale maniacs of the maddened tide;
While, strenuous yet some end to earn,
The haglets spin, though now no more astern.
    Like shuttles hurrying in the looms
Aloft through rigging frayed they ply—
Cross and recross—weave and inweave,
Then lock the web with clinching cry
Over the seas on seas that clasp
The weltering wreck where gurgling ends the gasp.

Ah, for the Plate-Fleet trophy now,
The victor's voucher, flags and arms;
Never they'll hang in Abbey old
And take Time's dust with holier palms;
Nor less content, in liquid night,
Their captor sleeps—the Admiral of the White.

        Embedded deep with shells
        And drifted treasure deep,
        Forever he sinks deeper in
        Unfathomable sleep—
        His cannon round him thrown,
        His sailors at his feet,
        The wizard sea enchanting them
        Where never haglets beat.
        On nights when meteors play
        And light the breakers' dance,
        The Oreads from the caves

With silvery elves advance;
And up from ocean stream,
And down from heaven far,
The rays that blend in dream
The abysm and the star.

MINOR SEA-PIECES

THE MAN-OF-WAR HAWK

YON black man-of-war hawk that wheels in the light
O'er the black ship's white sky-s'l, sunned cloud to the sight,
Have we low-flyers wings to ascend to his height?

No arrow can reach him; nor thought can attain
To the placid supreme in the sweep of his reign.

THE TUFT OF KELP

ALL dripping in tangles green,
    Cast up by a lonely sea,
If purer for that, O Weed,
    Bitterer, too, are ye?

THE MALDIVE SHARK

ABOUT the Shark, phlegmatical one,
Pale sot of the Maldive sea,
The sleek little pilot-fish, azure and slim,
How alert in attendance be.
From his saw-pit of mouth, from his charnel of maw,
They have nothing of harm to dread,
But liquidly glide on his ghastly flank
Or before his Gorgonian head;
Or lurk in the port of serrated teeth
In white triple tiers of glittering gates,
And there find a haven when peril's abroad,
An asylum in jaws of the Fates!
They are friends; and friendly they guide him to prey,

Yet never partake of the treat—
Eyes and brains to the dotard lethargic and dull,
Pale ravener of horrible meat.

CROSSING THE TROPICS

(From *"The Saya-y-Manto"*)

WHILE now the Pole Star sinks from sight,
    The Southern Cross it climbs the sky;
But losing thee, my love, my light,
O bride but for one bridal night,
    The loss no rising joys supply.

Love, love, the Trade Winds urge abaft,
And thee, from thee, they steadfast waft.

By day the blue and silver sea
    And chime of waters blandly fanned—
Nor these, nor Gama's stars to me
May yield delight, since still for thee
    I long as Gama longed for land.
I yearn, I yearn, reverting turn,
My heart it streams in wake astern.

When, cut by slanting sleet, we swoop
    Where raves the world's inverted year,
If roses all your porch shall loop,
Not less your heart for me will droop
    Doubling the world's last outpost drear.

O love, O love, these oceans vast:
Love, love, it is as death were past!

THE BERG
A Dream

I SAW a ship of martial build
(Her standards set, her brave apparel on)
Directed as by madness mere
Against a stolid iceberg steer,
Nor budge it, though the infatuate ship went down.
The impact made huge ice-cubes fall
Sullen, in tons that crashed the deck;
But that one avalanche was all—
No other movement save the foundering wreck.

Along the spurs of ridges pale,
Not any slenderest shaft and frail,
A prism over glass-green gorges lone,
Toppled; nor lace of traceries fine,
Nor pendant drops in grot or mine
Were jarred, when the stunned ship went down.

Nor sole the gulls in cloud that wheeled
Circling one snow-flanked peak afar,
But nearer fowl the floes that skimmed
And crystal beaches, felt no jar.
No thrill transmitted stirred the lock
Of jack-straw needle-ice at base;
Towers undermined by waves—the block
Atilt impending—kept their place.
Seals, dozing sleek on sliddery ledges
Slipt never, when by loftier edges
Through very inertia overthrown,
The impetuous ship in bafflement went down.

Hard Berg (methought), so cold, so vast,
With mortal damps self-overcast;
Exhaling still thy dankish breath—

Adrift dissolving, bound for death;
Though lumpish thou, a lumbering one—
A lumbering lubbard loitering slow,
Impingers rue thee and go down,
Sounding thy precipice below,
Nor stir the slimy slug that sprawls
Along thy dead indifference of walls.

THE ENVIABLE ISLES

(From *"Rammon"*)

THROUGH storms you reach them and from storms are free.
    Afar descried, the foremost drear in hue,
But, nearer, green; and, on the marge, the sea
    Makes thunder low and mist of rainbowed dew.
But, inland, where the sleep that folds the hills
A dreamier sleep, the trance of God, instills—
    On uplands hazed, in wandering airs aswoon,
Slow-swaying palms salute love's cypress tree
    Adown in vale where pebbly runlets croon
A song to lull all sorrow and all glee.

Sweet-fern and moss in many a glade are here,
    Where, strown in flocks, what cheek-flushed myriads lie
Dimpling in dream—unconscious slumberers mere,
    While billows endless round the beaches die.

PEBBLES

I

THOUGH the Clerk of the Weather insist,
   And lay down the weather-law,
Pintado and gannet they wist
That the winds blow whither they list
   In tempest or flaw.

II

Old are the creeds, but stale the schools,
   Revamped as the mode may veer,
But Orm from the schools to the beaches strays,
And, finding a Conch hoar with time, he delays
   And reverent lifts it to ear.
That Voice, pitched in far monotone,
   Shall it swerve? shall it deviate ever?
The Seas have inspired it, and Truth—
   Truth, varying from sameness never.

III

In hollows of the liquid hills
   Where the long Blue Ridges run,
The flattery of no echo thrills,
   For echo the seas have none;
Nor aught that gives man back man's strain—
The hope of his heart, the dream in his brain.

IV

On ocean where the embattled fleets repair,
Man, suffering inflictor, sails on sufferance there.

V

Implacable I, the old implacable Sea:
   Implacable most when most I smile serene—
Pleased, not appeased, by myriad wrecks in me.

VI

Curled in the comb of yon billow Andean,
   Is it the Dragon's heaven-challenging crest?
Elemental mad ramping of ravening waters—
   Yet Christ on the Mount, and the dove in her nest!

VII

Healed of my hurt, I laud the inhuman Sea—
Yea, bless the Angels Four that there convene;
For healed I am even by their pitiless breath
Distilled in wholesome dew named rosmarine.

FROM *TIMOLEON*, *Etc.*

TIMOLEON

(394 B.C.)

I

IF more than once, as annals tell,
  Through blood without compunction spilt,
An egotist arch rule has snatched
And stamped the seizure with his saber's hilt,
  And, legalized by lawyers, stood;
Shall the good heart whose patriot fire
Leaps to a deed of startling note,
Do it, then flinch? Shall good in weak expire?
  Needs goodness lack the evil grit
That stares down censorship and ban,
And dumbfounds saintlier ones with this—
God's will avouched in each successful man?
  Or, put it, where dread stress inspires
A virtue beyond man's standard rate,
Seems virtue there a strain forbid—
Transcendence such as shares transgression's fate?
  If so, and wan eclipse ensue,
Yet glory await emergence won,
Is that high Providence, or Chance?
And proved it which with thee, Timoleon?
  O, crowned with laurel twined with thorn,
Not rash thy life's cross-tide I stem,
But reck the problem rolled in pang
And reach and dare to touch thy garment's hem.

II

When Argos and Cleone strove
Against free Corinth's claim or right,
Two brothers battled for her well:
A footman one, and one a mounted knight.
    Apart in place, each braved the brunt
Till the rash cavalryman, alone,
Was wrecked against the enemy's files,
His bayard crippled and he maimed and thrown.
    Timoleon, at Timophanes' need,
Makes for the rescue through the fray,
Covers him with his shield, and takes
The darts and furious odds and fights at bay;
    Till, wrought to pallor of passion dumb,
Stark terrors of death around he throws,
Warding his brother from the field
Spite failing friends dispersed and rallying foes.
    Here might he rest, in claim rest here,
Rest, and a Phidian form remain;
But life halts never, life must on,
And take with term prolonged some scar or stain.
    Yes, life must on. And latent germs
Time's seasons wake in mead and man;
And brothers, playfellows in youth,
Develop into variance wide in span.

III

Timophanes was his mother's pride—
Her pride, her pet, even all to her
Who slackly on Timoleon looked:
Scarce he (she mused) may proud affection stir.
    He saved my darling, gossips tell:
If so, 'twas service, yea, and fair;

But instinct ruled and duty bade,
 In service such, a henchman e'en might share.
    When boys they were I helped the bent;
I made the junior feel his place,
Subserve the senior, love him, too;
And sooth he does, and that's his saving grace.
    But me the meek one never can serve,
Not he, he lacks the quality keen
To make the mother through the son
An envied dame of power, a social queen.
    But thou, my first-born, thou art I
In sex translated; joyed, I scan
My features, mine, expressed in thee;
Thou art what I would be were I a man.
    My brave Timophanes, 'tis thou
Who yet the world's forefront shalt win,
For thine the urgent resolute way,
Self pushing panoplied self through thick and thin.
    Nor here maternal insight erred:
Forsworn, with heart that did not wince
At slaying men who kept their vows,
Her darling strides to power, and reigns—a Prince.

IV

    Because of just heart and humane,
 Profound the hate Timoleon knew
For crimes of pride and men-of-prey
And impious deeds that perjurous upstarts do;
    And Corinth loved he, and in way
Old Scotia's clansman loved his clan,
Devotion one with ties how dear
And passion that late to make the rescue ran.
    But crime and kin—the terrorized town,
The silent, acquiescent mother—
Revulsion racks the filial heart,

The loyal son, the patriot true, the brother.
   In evil visions of the night
He sees the lictors of the gods,
Giant ministers of righteousness,
Their *fasces* threatened by the Furies' rods.
   But undeterred he wills to act,
Resolved thereon though Ate rise;
He heeds the voice whose mandate calls,
Or seems to call, peremptory from the skies.

V

   Nor less but by approaches mild,
And trying each prudential art,
The just one first advances him
In parley with a flushed intemperate heart.
   The brother first he seeks—alone,
And pleads; but is with laughter met;
Then comes he, in accord with two,
And these adjure the tyrant and beset;
   Whose merriment gives place to rage:
"Go," stamping, "what to me is Right?
I am the Wrong, and lo, I reign,
And testily intolerant too in might":
   And glooms on his mute brother pale,
Who goes aside; with muffled face
He sobs the predetermined word,
And Right in Corinth reassumes its place.

VI

   But on his robe, ah, whose the blood?
And craven ones their eyes avert,
And heavy is a mother's ban,
And dismal faces of the fools can hurt.

The whispering-gallery of the world,
Where each breathed slur runs wheeling wide
Eddies a false perverted truth,
Inveterate turning still on fratricide.
    The time was Plato's. Wandering lights
Confirmed the atheist's standing star;
As now, no sanction Virtue knew
For deeds that on prescriptive morals jar.
    Reaction took misgiving's tone,
Infecting conscience, till betrayed
To doubt the irrevocable doom
Herself had authorized when undismayed.
    Within perturbed Timoleon here
Such deeps were bared as when the sea,
Convulsed, vacates its shoreward bed,
And Nature's last reserves show nakedly.
    He falters, and from Hades' glens
By night insidious tones implore—
Why suffer? hither come and be
What Phoeion is who feeleth man no more.
    But, won from that, his mood elects
To live—to live in wilding place;
For years self-outcast, he but meets
In shades his playfellow's reproachful face.
    Estranged through one transcendent deed
From common membership in mart,
In severance he is like a head
Pale after battle trunkless found apart.

VII

    But flood-tide comes though long the ebb,
Nor patience bides with passion long;
Like sightless orbs his thoughts are rolled
Arraigning heaven as compromised in wrong:
    To second causes why appeal?

Vain parleying here with fellow clods.
To you, Arch Principals, I rear
My quarrel, for this quarrel is with gods.
    Shall just men long to quit your world?
It is aspersion of your reign;
Your marbles in the temple stand—
Yourselves as stony and invoked in vain?
    Ah, bear with one quito overborne,
Olympians, if he chide ye now;
Magnanimous be even though he rail
And hard against ye set the bleaching brow.
    If conscience doubt, she'll next recant.
What basis then? O, tell at last,
Are earnest natures staggering here
But fatherless shadows from no substance cast?
    Yea, *are* ye, gods? Then ye, 'tis ye
Should show what touch of tie ye may,
Since ye, too, if not wrung are wronged
By grievous misconceptions of your sway.
    But deign, some little sign be given—
Low thunder in your tranquil skies;
Me reassure, nor let me be
Like a lone dog that for a master cries.

VIII

    Men's moods, as frames, must yield to years,
And turns the world in fickle ways;
Corinth recalls Timoleon—ay,
And plumes him forth, but yet with schooling phrase.
    On Sicily's fields, through arduous wars,
A peace he won whose rainbow spanned
The isle redeemed; and he was hailed
Deliverer of that fair colonial land.
    And Corinth clapt: Absolved, and more!
Justice in long arrears is thine:
Not slayer of thy brother, no,

But savior of the state, Jove's soldier, man divine.
   Eager for thee thy City waits:
Return! with bays we dress your door.
But he, the Isle's loved guest, reposed,
And never for Corinth left the adopted shore.

AFTER THE PLEASURE PARTY

Lines Traced
Under an Image of
Amor Threatening

Fear me, virgin whosoever
Taking pride from love exempt,
Fear me, slighted. Never, never
Brave me, nor my fury tempt:
Downy wings, but wroth they beat
Tempest even in reason's seat.

BEHIND the house the upland falls
With many an odorous tree—
White marbles gleaming through green halls,
Terrace by terrace, down and down,
And meets the starlit Mediterranean Sea.

'Tis Paradise. In such an hour
Some pangs that rend might take release.
Nor less perturbed who keeps this bower
Of balm, nor finds balsamic peace?
From whom the passionate words in vent
After long reverie's discontent?

Tired of the homeless deep,
Look how their flight yon hurrying billows urge,
Hitherward but to reap
Passive repulse from the iron-bound verge!
Insensate, can they never know
'Tis mad to wreck the impulsion so?

An art of memory is, they tell:
But to forget! forget the glade
Wherein Fate sprung Love's ambuscade,
To flout pale years of cloistral life
And flush me in this sensuous strife.
'Tis Vesta struck with Sappho's smart.
No fable her delirious leap:
With more of cause in desperate heart,
Myself could take it—but to sleep!

Now first I feel, what all may ween,
That soon or late, if faded e'en,
One's sex asserts itself. Desire,
The dear desire through love to sway,
Is like the Geysers that aspire—
Through cold obstruction win their fervid way.
But baffled here—to take disdain,
To feel rule's instinct, yet not reign;
To dote, to come to this drear shame—
Hence the winged blaze that sweeps my soul
Like prairie fires that spurn control,
Where withering weeds incense the flame.

And kept I long heaven's watch for this,
Contemning love, for this, even this?
O terrace chill in Northern air,
O reaching ranging tube I placed
Against yon skies, and fable chased
Till, fool, I hailed for sister there
Starred Cassiopeia in Golden Chair.
In dream I throned me, nor I saw
In cell the idiot crowned with straw.

And yet, ah yet scarce ill I reigned,
Through self-illusion self-sustained,
When now—enlightened, undeceived—
What gain I barrenly bereaved!

Than this can be yet lower decline—
Envy and spleen, can these be mine?

    The peasant girl demure that trod
Beside our wheels that climbed the way,
And bore along a blossoming rod
That looked the scepter of May-Day—
On her—to fire this petty hell,
His softened glance how moistly fell!
The cheat! on briars her buds were strung;
And wiles peeped forth from mien how meek.
The innocent bare-foot! young, so young!
To girls, strong man's a novice weak.
To tell such beads! And more remain,
Sad rosary of belittling pain.

    When after lunch and sallies gay,
Like the Decameron folk we lay
In sylvan groups; and I—let be!
O, dreams he, can he dream that one
Because not roseate feels no sun?
The plain lone bramble thrills with Spring
As much as vines that grapes shall bring.

    Me now fair studies charm no more.
Shall great thoughts writ, or high themes sung
Damask wan cheeks—unlock his arm
About some radiant ninny flung?
How glad with all my starry lore,
I'd buy the veriest wanton's rose
Would but my bee therein repose.

    Could I remake me! or set free
This sexless bound in sex, then plunge
Deeper than Sappho, in a lunge
Piercing Pan's paramount mystery!
For, Nature, in no shallow surge
Against thee either sex may urge,

Why hast thou made us but in halves—
Co-relatives? This makes us slaves.
If these co-relatives never meet
Selfhood itself seems incomplete.
And such the dicing of blind fate
Few matching halves here meet and mate.
What Cosmic jest or Anarch blunder
The human integral clove asunder
And shied the fractions through life's gate?

Ye stars that long your votary knew
Rapt in her vigil, see me here!
Whither is gone the spell ye threw
When rose before me Cassiopeia?
Usurped on by love's stronger reign—
But lo, your very selves do wane:
Light breaks—truth breaks! Silvered no more,
But chilled by dawn that brings the gale
Shivers yon bramble above the vale,
And disillusion opens all the shore.

One knows not if Urania yet
The pleasure-party may forget;
Or whether she lived down the strain
Of turbulent heart and rebel brain;
For Amor so resents a slight,
And her's had been such haught disdain,
He long may wreak his boyish spite,
And boy-like, little reck the pain.

One knows not, no. But late in Rome
(For queens discrowned a congruous home)
Entering Albani's porch she stood
Fixed by an antique pagan stone
Colossal carved. No anchorite seer,
Not Thomas à Kempis, monk austere,
Religious more are in their tone;
Yet far, how far from Christian heart

That form august of heathen Art.
Swayed by its influence, long she stood,
Till surged emotion seething down,
She rallied and this mood she won:

    Languid in frame for me,
To-day by Mary's convent shrine,
Touched by her picture's moving plea
In that poor nerveless hour of mine,
I mused—A wanderer still must grieve.
Half I resolved to kneel and believe,
Believe and submit, the veil take on.
But thee, armed Virgin! less benign,
Thee now I invoke, thou mightier one.
Helmeted woman—if such term
Befit thee, far from strife
Of that which makes the sexual feud
And clogs the aspirant life—
O self-reliant, strong and free,
Thou in whom power and peace unite,
Transcender! raise me up to thee,
Raise me and arm me!
                     Fond appeal.
For never passion peace shall bring,
Nor Art inanimate for long
Inspire. Nothing may help or heal
While Amor incensed remembers wrong.
Vindictive, not himself he'll spare;
For scope to give his vengeance play
Himself he'll blaspheme and betray.

    Then for Urania, virgins everywhere,
O pray! Example take too, and have care.

THE NIGHT-MARCH

WITH banners furled, and clarions mute,
   An army passes in the night;
And beaming spears and helms salute
   The dark with bright.

In silence deep the legions stream,
   With open ranks, in order true;
Over boundless plains they stream and gleam—
   No chief in view!

Afar, in twinkling distance lost,
   (So legends tell) he lonely wends
And back through all that shining host
   His mandate sends.

THE RAVAGED VILLA

In shards the sylvan vases lie,
    Their links of dance undone,
And brambles wither by thy brim,
    Choked fountain of the sun!
The spider in the laurel spins,
    The weed exiles the flower;
And, flung to kiln, Apollo's bust
    Makes lime for Mammon's tower.

THE MARGRAVE'S BIRTHNIGHT

UP from many a sheeted valley,
From white woods as well,
Down too from each fleecy upland
Jingles many a bell

Jovial on the work-sad horses
Hitched to runners old
Of the toil-worn peasants sledging
Under sheepskins in the cold;

Till from every quarter gathered
Meet they on one ledge,
There from hoods they brush the snow off
Lighting from each sledge

Full before the Margrave's castle,
Summoned there to cheer
On his birthnight, in midwinter,
Kept year after year.

O the hall, and O the holly!
Tables line each wall;
Guests as holly-berries plenty,
But—no host withal!

May his people feast contented
While at head of board
Empty throne and vacant cover
Speak the absent lord?

Minstrels enter. And the stewards
Serve the guests; and when,

Passing there the vacant cover,
Functionally then

Old observance grave they offer;
But no Margrave fair,
In his living aspect gracious,
Sits responsive there;

No, and never guest once marvels,
None the good lord name,
Scarce they mark void throne and cover—
Dust upon the same.

Mindless as to what importeth
Absence such in hall;
Tacit as the plough-horse feeding
In the palfrey's stall.

Ah, enough for toil and travail,
If but for a night
Into wine is turned the water,
Black bread into white.

MAGIAN WINE

AMULETS gemmed, to Miriam dear,
    Adown in liquid mirage gleam;
Solomon's Syrian charms appear,
    Opal and ring supreme.
The rays that light this Magian Wine
Thrill up from semblances divine.

And, seething through the rapturous wave,
What low Elysian anthems rise:
Sibylline inklings blending rave,
    Then lap the verge with sighs.
Delirious here the oracles swim
Ambiguous in the beading hymn.

THE GARDEN OF METRODORUS

THE Athenians mark the moss-grown gate
And hedge untrimmed that hides the haven green:
    And who keeps here his quiet state?
    And shares he sad or happy fate
Where never footpath to the gate is seen?

Here none come forth, here none go in,
Here silence strange, and dumb seclusion dwell:
    Content from loneness who may win?
    And is this stillness peace or sin
Which noteless thus apart can keep its dell?

THE WEAVER

FOR years within a mud-built room
For Arva's shrine he weaves the shawl,
Lone wight, and at a lonely loom,
His busy shadow on the wall.

The face is pinched, the form is bent,
No pastime knows he nor the wine,
Recluse he lives and abstinent
Who weaves for Arva's shrine.

LAMIA'S SONG

DESCEND, descend!
      Pleasant the downward way—
From your lonely Alp
With the wintry scalp
To our myrtles in valleys of May.
      Wend then, wend:
Mountaineer, descend:
And more than a wreath shall repay.
      Come, ah come!
With the cataracts come,
That hymn as they roam
How pleasant the downward way!

IN A GARRET

Gems and jewels let them heap—
  Wax sumptuous as the Sophi:
For me, to grapple from Art's deep
  One dripping trophy!

MONODY

To have known him, to have loved him
    After loneness long;
And then to be estranged in life,
    And neither in the wrong;
And now for death to set his seal—
    Ease me, a little ease, my song!

By wintry hills his hermit-mound
    The sheeted snow-drifts drape,
And houseless there the snow-bird flits
    Beneath the fir-trees' crape:
Glazed now with ice the cloistral vine
    That hid the shyest grape.

LONE FOUNTS

Though fast youth's glorious fable flies,
View not the world with worldling's eyes;
Nor turn with weather of the time.
Foreclose the coming of surprise:
Stand where Posterity shall stand;
Stand where the Ancients stood before,
And, dipping in lone founts thy hand,
Drink of the never-varying lore:
Wise once, and wise thence evermore.

THE BENCH OF BOORS

In bed I muse on Tenier's boors,
Embrowned and beery losels all:
    A wakeful brain
    Elaborates pain:
Within low doors the slugs of boors
Laze and yawn and doze again.

In dreams they doze, the drowsy boors,
Their hazy hovel warm and small:
    Thought's ampler bound
    But chill is found:
Within low doors the basking boors
Snugly hug the ember-mound.

Sleepless, I see the slumberous boors
Their blurred eyes blink, their eyelids fall:
    Thought's eager sight
    Aches—overbright!
Within low doors the boozy boors
Cat-naps take in pipe-bowl light.

THE ENTHUSIAST

"Though He slay me yet will I trust in Him."

SHALL hearts that beat no base retreat
    In youth's magnanimous years—
Ignoble hold it, if discreet
    When interest tames to fears;
Shall spirits that worship light
    Perfidious deem its sacred glow,
    Recant, and trudge where worldlings go,
Conform and own them right?

Shall Time with creeping influence cold
    Unnerve and cow? the heart
Pine for the heartless ones enrolled
    With palterers of the mart?
Shall faith abjure her skies,
    Or pale probation blench her down
    To shrink from Truth so still, so lone
Mid loud gregarious lies?

Each burning boat in Cæsar's rear,
    Flames—No return through me!
So put the torch to ties though dear,
    If ties but tempters be.
Nor cringe if come the night:
    Walk through the cloud to meet the pall,
    Though light forsake thee, never fall
From fealty to light.

ART

In placid hours well pleased we dream
Of many a brave unbodied scheme.
But form to lend, pulsed life create,
What unlike things must meet and mate:
A flame to melt—a wind to freeze;
Sad patience—joyous energies;
Humility—yet pride and scorn;
Instinct and study; love and hate;
Audacity—reverence. These must mate
And fuse with Jacob's mystic heart,
To wrestle with the angel—Art.

BUDDHA

*"For what is your life? It is even a vapor that appeareth
for a little time and then vanisheth away."*

SWOONING swim to less and less,
   Aspirant to nothingness!
Sobs of the worlds, and dole of kinds
   That dumb endurers be—
Nirvana! absorb us in your skies,
   Annul us into thee.

C——'S LAMENT

How lovely was the light of heaven,
What angels leaned from out the sky
In years when youth was more than wine
And man and nature seemed divine
Ere yet I felt that youth must die.

Ere yet I felt that youth must die
How insubstantial looked the earth,
Aladdin-land! in each advance,
Or here or there, a new romance;
I never dreamed would come a dearth.

And nothing then but had its worth,
Even pain. Yes, pleasure still and pain
In quick reaction made of life
A lovers' quarrel, happy strife
In youth that never comes again.

But will youth never come again?
Even to his grave-bed has he gone,
And left me lone to wake by night
With heavy heart that erst was light?
O, lay it at his head—a stone!

SHELLEY'S VISION

WANDERING late by morning seas
When my heart with pain was low—
Hate the censor pelted me—
Deject I saw my shadow go.

In elf-caprice of bitter tone
I too would pelt the pelted one:
At my shadow I cast a stone.

When lo, upon that sun-lit ground
I saw the quivering phantom take
The likeness of St. Stephen crowned:
Then did self-reverence awake.

FRAGMENTS OF A LOST GNOSTIC
POEM OF THE TWELFTH CENTURY

* * * *

FOUND a family, build a state,
The pledged event is still the same:
Matter in end will never abate
His ancient brutal claim.

* * * *

Indolence is heaven's ally here,
And energy the child of hell:
The Good Man pouring from his pitcher clear,
But brims the poisoned well.

THE MARCHIONESS OF BRINVILLIERS

He toned the sprightly beam of morning
    With twilight meek of tender eve,
Brightness interfused with softness,
    Light and shade did weave:
And gave to candor equal place
With mystery starred in open skies;
And, floating all in sweetness, made
    Her fathomless mild eyes.

THE AGE OF THE ANTONINES

WHILE faith forecasts millennial years
    Spite Europe's embattled lines,
Back to the Past one glance be cast—
    The Age of the Antonines!
O summit of fate, O zenith of time
When a pagan gentleman reigned,
And the olive was nailed to the inn of the world
Nor the peace of the just was feigned.
    A halcyon Age, afar it shines,
Solstice of Man and the Antonines.

Hymns to the nations' friendly gods
Went up from the fellowly shrines,
No demagogue beat the pulpit-drum
    In the Age of the Antonines!
The sting was not dreamed to be taken from death,
No Paradise pledged or sought,
But they reasoned of fate at the flowing feast,
Nor stifled the fluent thought.
    We sham, we shuffle while faith declines—
They were frank in the Age of the Antonines.

Orders and ranks they kept degree,
Few felt how the parvenu pines,
No law-maker took the lawless one's fee
    In the Age of the Antonines!
Under law made will the world reposed
And the ruler's right confessed,
For the heavens elected the Emperor then,
The foremost of men the best.
    Ah, might we read in America's signs
The Age restored of the Antonines.

HERBA SANTA

I

AFTER long wars when comes release
Not olive wands proclaiming peace
    An import dearer share
Than stems of Herba Santa hazed
    In autumn's Indian air.
Of moods they breathe that care disarm.
They pledge us lenitive and calm.

II

Shall code or creed a lure afford
To win all selves to Love's accord?
When Love ordained a supper divine
    For the wide world of man,
What bickerings o'er his gracious wine!
    Then strange new feuds began.

Effectual more in lowlier way,
    Pacific Herb, thy sensuous plea
The bristling clans of Adam sway
    At least to fellowship in thee!
Before thine altar tribal flags are furled,
Fain wouldst thou make one hearthstone of the world.

III

To scythe, to scepter, pen and hod—
    Yea, sodden laborers dumb;

To brains overplied, to feet that plod,
In solace of the *Truce of God*
   The Calumet has come!

IV

Ah for the world ere Raleigh's find
   Never that knew this suasive balm
That helps when Gilead's fails to heal,
   Helps by an interserted charm.

Insinuous thou that through the nerve
   Windest the soul, and so canst win
   Some from repinings, some from sin,
The Church's aim that dost subserve.

The ruffled fag fordone with care
   And brooding, Gold would ease this pain:
Him soothest thou and smoothest down
   Till some content return again.

Even ruffians feel thy influence breed
   Saint Martin's summer in the mind
They feel this last evangel plead,
As did the first, apart from creed,
   Be peaceful, man—be kind!

V

Rejected once on higher plane,
O Love supreme, to come again
   Can this be thine?
Again to come, and win us too
   In likeness of a weed
That as a god didst vainly woo,
   As man more vainly bleed?

VI

Forbear, my soul! and in thine Eastern chamber
   Rehearse the dream that brings the long release:
Through jasmine sweet and talismanic amber
   Inhaling Herba Santa in the passive Pipe of Peace.

FRUIT OF TRAVEL LONG AGO

VENICE

With Pantheist energy of will
   The little craftsman of the Coral Sea
Strenuous in the blue abyss,
Upbuilds his marvelous gallery
   And long arcade,
Erections freaked with many a fringe
   Of marble garlandry,
Evincing what a worm can do.

Laborious in a shallower wave,
   Advanced in kindred art,
A prouder agent proved Pan's might
When Venice rose in reefs of palaces.

IN A BYE-CANAL

A swoon of noon, a trance of tide,
The hushed siesta brooding wide
   Like calms far off Peru;
No floating wayfarer in sight,
Dumb noon, and haunted like the night
   When Jael the wiled one slew.
A languid impulse from the oar
Plied by my indolent gondolier
Tinkles against a palace hoar,
   And, hark, response I hear!
A lattice clicks; and lo, I see
Between the slats, mute summoning me,

What loveliest eyes of scintillation,
What basilisk glance of conjuration!

    Fronted I have, part taken the span
Of portents in nature and peril in man.
I have swum—I have been
'Twixt the whale's black flukes and the white shark's fin;
The enemy's desert have wandered in,
And there have turned, have turned and scanned,
Following me how noiselessly,
Envy and Slander, lepers hand in hand.
All this. But at the latticed eye—
"Hey! Gondolier, you sleep, my man;
Wake up!" And, shooting by, we ran;
The while I mused, This, surely now,
Confutes the Naturalists, allow!
Sirens, true sirens verily be,
Sirens, waylayers in the sea.

Well, wooed by these same deadly misses,
Is it shame to run?
No! flee them did divine Ulysses,
    Brave, wise, and Venus' son.

PISA'S LEANING TOWER

THE Tower in tiers of architraves,
Fair circle over cirque,
A trunk of rounded colonnades,
The maker's master-work,
Impends with all its pillared tribes,
And, poising them, debates:
It thinks to plunge—but hesitates;
Shrinks back—yet fain would slide;
Withholds itself—itself would urge;
Hovering, shivering on the verge,
    A would-be suicide!

IN A CHURCH OF PADUA

In vaulted place where shadows flit,
An upright somber box you see:
A door, but fast, and lattice none,
But punctured holes minutely small
In lateral silver panel square
Above a kneeling-board without,
Suggest an aim if not declare.

Who bendeth here the tremulous knee
No glimpse may get of him within,
And he immured may hardly see
The soul confessing there the sin;
Nor yields the low-sieved voice a tone
Whereby the murmurer may be known.

Dread diving-bell! In thee inurned
What hollows the priest must sound,
Descending into consciences
    Where more is hid than found.

MILAN CATHEDRAL

Through light green haze, a rolling sea
    Over gardens where redundance flows,
    The fat old plain of Lombardy,
The White Cathedral shows.

    Of Art the miracles
    Its tribes of pinnacles
Gleam like to ice-peaks snowed; and higher,
Erect upon each airy spire
    In concourse without end,
Statues of saints over saints ascend
Like multitudinous forks of fire.

What motive was the master-builder's here?
Why these synodic hierarchies given,
Sublimely ranked in marble sessions clear,
Except to signify the host of heaven.

THE PARTHENON

I
Seen aloft from afar

ESTRANGED in site,
Aerial gleaming, warmly white,
You look a suncloud motionless
In noon of day divine;
Your beauty charmed enhancement takes
In Art's long after-shine.

II
Nearer viewed

Like Lais, fairest of her kind,
In subtlety your form's defined—
The cornice curved, each shaft inclined,
While yet, to eyes that do but revel
    And take the sweeping view,
Erect this seems, and that a level,
    To line and plummet true.

Spinoza gazes; and in mind
Dreams that one architect designed
        Lais—and you!

III
The Frieze

What happy musings genial went
With airiest touch the chisel lent

To frisk and curvet light
Of horses gay—their riders grave—
Contrasting so in action brave
    With virgins meekly bright,
Clear filing on in even tone
With pitcher each, one after one
    Like water-fowl in flight.

IV
The Last Tile

When the last marble tile was laid
The winds died down on all the seas;
    Hushed were the birds, and swooned the glade;
    Ictinus sat; Aspasia said
"Hist!—Art's meridian, Pericles!"

GREEK MASONRY

JOINTS were none that mortar sealed:
Together, scarce with line revealed,
The blocks in symmetry congealed.

GREEK ARCHITECTURE

NOT magnitude, not lavishness,
But Form—the Site;
Not innovating willfulness,
But reverence for the Archetype.

THE APPARITION

*(The Parthenon uplifted on its rock first challenging
the view on the approach to Athens.)*

ABRUPT the supernatural Cross,
   Vivid in startled air,
Smote the Emperor Constantine
And turned his soul's allegiance there.

With other power appealing down,
   Trophy of Adam's best!
If cynic minds you scarce convert,
You try them, shake them, or molest.

Diogenes, that honest heart,
   Lived ere your date began;
Thee had he seen, he might have swerved
In mood nor barked so much at Man.

IN THE DESERT

NEVER Pharaoh's Night,
Whereof the Hebrew wizards croon,
Did so the Theban flamens try
As me this veritable Noon.

Like blank ocean in blue calm
Undulates the ethereal frame;
In one flowing oriflamme
God flings his fiery standard out.

Battling with the Emirs fierce,
Napoleon a great victory won,
Through and through his sword did pierce:

But, bayoneted by this sun
His gunners drop beneath the gun.

Holy, holy, holy Light!
Immaterial incandescence,
Of God the effluence of the essence,
Shekinah intolerably bright!

THE GREAT PYRAMID

YOUR masonry—and is it man's?
More like some Cosmic artisan's.
Your courses as in strata rise,
Beget you do a blind surmise
                Like Grampians.

Far slanting up your sweeping flank
Arabs with Alpine goats may rank,
And there they find a choice of passes
Even like to dwarfs that climb the masses
                Of glaciers blank.

Shall lichen in your crevice fit?
Nay, sterile all and granite-knit:
Weather nor weather-stain ye rue,
But aridly you cleave the blue
                As lording it.

Morn's vapor floats beneath your peak,
Kites skim your side with pinion weak;
To sand-storms battering, blow on blow,
Raging to work your overthrow,
                You—turn the cheek.

All elements unmoved you stem,
Foursquare you stand and suffer them:

Time's future infinite you dare,
While, for the past, 'tis you that wear
            Eld's diadem.

Slant from your inmost lead the caves
And labyrinths rumored. These who braves
And penetrates (old palmers said)
Comes out afar on deserts dead
            And, dying, raves.

Craftsmen, in dateless quarries dim,
Stones formless into form did trim,
Usurped on Nature's self with Art,
And bade this dumb I AM to start,
            Imposing him.

FROM
WEEDS AND WILDINGS

CLOVER

The June day dawns, the joy-winds rush,
Your jovial fields are dressed;
Rosier for thee the Dawn's red flush,
Ruddier the Ruddock's breast.

THE LITTLE GOOD-FELLOWS

MAKE way, make way, give leave to rove
Your orchard under as above:
A yearly welcome if he love!
And all who loved us alway throve.

Love for love. For ever we
When some unfriended man we see
Lifeless under forest-eaves,
Cover him with buds and leaves;
And charge the chipmunk, mouse, and mole—
Molest not this poor human soul!

Then let us never on green floor
Where your paths wind round about,
Keep to the middle in misdoubt,
Shy and aloof, unsure of ye;
But come like grass to stones on moor
Wherever mortals be.

But toss your caps, O maids and men,
Snow-bound long in farm-house pen:
We chase Old Winter back to den.
See our red waistcoats! Alive be then—
Alive to the bridal-favors when
They blossom in your orchards every Spring,
And cock-robin curves on a bridegroom's wing!

TROPHIES OF PEACE
Illinois in 1840

FILES on files of prairie maize:
On hosts of spears the morning plays!
Aloft the rustling streamers show:
The floss embrowned is rich below.

When Asia scarfed in silks came on
Against the Greek and Marathon,
Did each plume and pennon dance
Sun-lit thus on helm and lance
Mindless of War's sickle so?

For them, a tasseled dance of death:
For these—the reapers reap them low,
Reap them low, and stack the plain
With Ceres' trophies, golden grain.

Such monuments, and only such,
O Prairie! termless yield,
Though trooper Mars disdainful flout
Nor Annals fame the field.

THE AMERICAN ALOE ON EXHIBITION

*It is but a floral superstition, as everybody knows,
that this plant flowers only once in a century. When in any
instance the flowering is for decades delayed beyond the
normal period (eight or ten years at farthest), it is owing
to something retarding in the environment or soil.*

BUT few they were who came to see
The Century-Plant in flower:
Ten cents admission—price you pay
For bon-bons of the hour.

In strange inert blank unconcern
Of wild things at the Zoo,
The patriarch let the sight-seers stare—
These seldom more than two.

But lone at night the garland sighed,
And while moaned the aged stem:
"At last, at last! but joy and pride
What part have I with them?"

Let be the dearth that kept me back
Now long from wreath decreed;
But, ah, ye Roses that have passed
Accounting me a weed!

THE NEW ROSICRUCIANS

To us, disciples of the Order
Whose Rose-Vine twines the Cross,
Who have drained the rose's chalice
Never heeding gain or loss;
For all the preacher's din
There is no mortal sin—
No, none to us but Malice.

Exempt from that, in blest recline
We let life's billows toss;
If sorrow come, anew we twine
The Rose-Vine round the Cross.

MISCELLANEOUS POEMS

THE NEW ANCIENT OF DAYS
The Man of the Cave of Engihoul

(See Lyell's The Antiquity of Man, *and Darwin's*
The Descent of the Species.*)*

THE man of bone confirms his throne
    In cave where fossils be;
Out-dating every mummy known,
Not older Cuvier's mastodon,
    Nor older much the sea:
    Old as the Glacial Period, he;
And claims he calls to mind the day
When Thule's king, by reindeer drawn,
His sleigh-bells jingling in icy morn,
Slid clean from the Pole to the Wetterhorn
Over frozen waters in May!
    O, the man of the cave of Engihoul,
    With Eld doth he dote and drule?

A wizard one, his lore is none
    Ye spell with A, B, C:
But dodo tracks, all up and down
That slate he poreth much upon,
    This algebra may be:—
    Yea, there he ciphers and sums it free;
To ages ere Indus met ocean's swell
Addeth æons ere Satan or Saturn fell.
His totals of time make an awful schism,
Cold Chronos he pitches adown the abysm
Like a pebble down Carisbrooke well.
    Yea, the man of the cave of Engihoul
    From Moses knocks under the stool.

In bas-relief he late has shown
    A terrible show, agree—
Megalosaurus, iguanodon,
Palæotherium, glyptodon—
    A Barnum's show raree;
    The vomit of slimy and sludgy sea;
Purposeless creatures, inchoate things
Which splashed thro' morasses on fleshly wings;
The cubs of Chaos, with eyes askance,
Preposterous griffins that squint at chance
And Anarch's crazed decree!
    O, the showman who dens in Engihoul,
    Would he fright us, or quit us, or fool?

But needs to own, he takes a tone,
    Satiric on nobs, pardee!
"Though in ages whose term is yet to run,
Old Adam a seraph may have for son,
    This gran'ther's a crab, d 'y 'see!
    And why cut your kinsman the ape?" adds he:
"Your trick of scratching is borrowed from him,
Grimace and cunning with many a whim,
Your fidgets and hypoes, and each megrim—
All's traced in the family tree!"
    Ha, the wag of the cave of Engihoul:
    Buss me, gorilla and ghoul!

Obstreperous grown he'd fain dethrone
    Joe Smith and e'en Jones Three;
Against even Jos and great Mahone
He flings his fossilipher's stone
    And rattles his shanks for glee.
    I'll settle these parvenu fellows, he-he!
Diluvian Ore of Ducalion's day—
A parting bake to the Phocene clay.
He swears no Ens that takes a name
Commensurate is with the vasty claim
Of the protoplastic Fegee.

O, the spook of the cave of Engihoul
He flogs us and sends us to school.

Hyena of love! Ah, beat him down,
      Great Pope, with Peter's key,
Ere the Grand Pan-Jam be overthrown
With Joe and Jos and great Mahone,
      And the firmament mix with the sea;
      And then, my masters, where should we be?
But the ogre of bone he snickers alone,
And grins for his godless glee.
"I have flung my stone, my fossil stone,
And your gods, they scamper," saith he.
      Imp of the cave of Engihoul
      Shall he grin like the Gorgon and rule?

IMMOLATED

CHILDREN of my happier prime,
When One yet lived with me, and threw
Her rainbow over life and time,
Even Hope, my bride, and mother to you!
O, nurtured in sweet pastoral air,
And fed on flowers and light and dew
Of morning meadows—spare, ah, spare
Reproach; spare, and upbraid me not
That, yielding scarce to reckless mood,
But jealous of your future lot,
I sealed you in a fate subdued.
Have I not saved you from the dread
Theft, and ignoring which need be
The triumph of the insincere
Unanimous Mediocrity?
Rest therefore, free from all despite,
Snugged in the arms of comfortable night.

THE RUSTY MAN
By a Soured One

In La Mancha he mopeth,
    With beard thin and dusty;
He doteth and mopeth
    In Library fusty—
'Mong his old folios gropeth:
    Cities' obsolete laws
    Of chivalry's laws—
    Be the wronged one's knight:
    Die, but do right.
So he rusts and musts,
While each grocer green
Thrives apace with the fulsome face
Of a fool serene.

CAMOENS

(BEFORE)

AND ever must I fan this fire?
Thus ever in flame on flame aspire?
Ever restless, restless, craving rest—
The Imperfect toward Perfection pressed!
Yea, for the God demands thy best.
The world with endless beauty teems,
And though evokes new worlds of dreams:
Hunt then the flying herds of themes!
And fan, still fan, thy fervid fire,
Until thy crucibled gold shall show
That fire can purge as well as glow.
In ordered ardor, nobly strong,
Flame to the height of epic song.

(AFTER)

CAMOENS IN THE HOSPITAL

What now avails the pageant verse,
Trophies and arms with music borne?
Base is the world; and some rehearse
Now noblest meet ignoble scorn,
Vain now thy ardor, vain thy fire,
Delirium mere, unsound desire;
Fate's knife hath ripped thy corded lyre.
Exhausted by the exacting lay,
Thou dost but fall a surer prey

To wile and guile ill understood;
While they who work them, fair in face,
Still keep their strength in prudent place,
And claim they worthier run life's race,
Serving high God with useful good.

MONTAIGNE AND HIS KITTEN

HITHER, Blanche! Come, you and I.
Now that not a fool is by,
To say we fool it—let us fool.
We, you know, in mind are one,
Alumni of no fagging school;
Superfluous business still we shun;
And ambition we let go,
The while poor dizzards strain and strive,
Rave and slave, drudge and drive,
Chasing ever, to and fro,
After ends that seldom gain
Scant exemption from life's pain.
    But preachment proses, and so I,
Blanche, round your furred neck let me tie
This Order, with brave ribbon, see—
The King he pinned it upon me.

    But, hark ye, sweeting—well-a-day!
Forever shall ye purr this way—
Forever comfortable be?
Don't you wish now 'twas for ye,
Our grandiose eternity?
Pish! what fops we humans here,
Won't admit within our sphere
The whitest doe, nor even thee—
We, the spotless humans, we!
    Preaching, preaching, scud and run,
Earnestness is far from fun,
Bless me, Blanche! we'll frisk to-night,
Hearts be ours lilt and light—
Gambol, skip, and frolic, play:
Wise ones fool it while they may!

GOLD IN THE MOUNTAIN

GOLD in the mountain,
And gold in the glen,
And greed in the heart,
Heaven having no part,
And unsatisfied men.

A SPIRIT APPEARED TO ME

A SPIRIT appeared to me, and said
"Where now would you choose to dwell?
In the Paradise of the Fool,
Or in wise Solomon's hell?"

Never he asked me twice:
"Give me the Fool's Paradise."

HEARTS-OF-GOLD

'TWERE pity, if true,
What the pewterer said—
Hearts-of-gold be few.
Howbeit, when snug in my bed,
And the firelight flickers and yellows,
I dream of the hearts-of-gold sped—
The Falernian fellows—
Hafiz and Horace,
And Beranger—all
Dexterous tumblers eluding the Fall,
Fled? can be sped?
But the marigold's morris
Is danced o'er their head;
And their memory mellows,
Embalmed and becharmed,
Hearts-of-gold and good fellows!

PONTOOSUCE

CROWNING a bluff where gleams the lake below,
Some pillared pines in well-spaced order stand,
And like an open temple show,
And here in best of seasons bland,
Autumnal noontide, I look out
From dusk arcades on sunshine all about.

Beyond the lake, in upland cheer,
Field, pastoral fields and barns appear,
They skirt the hills where lovely roads
Revealed in links through tiers of woods
Wind up to indistinct abodes
And faery-peopled neighborhoods;
While further, fainter mountains keep
Hazed in romance impenetrably deep.

Look, corn in stacks, on many a farm
And orchards ripe in langorous charm
As dreamy nature, feeling sure
Of all her genial labor done,
And the last mellow fruitage won,
Would idle out her term mature;
Reposing like a thing reclined
In kinship with man's meditative mind.

For me, within the brown arcade,
Rich life, methought; sweet here in shade,
And pleasant abroad in air!—But, nay,
A counter thought intrusive played,
A thought as old as thought itself,
And who shall lay it on the shelf!—
I felt the beauty bless the day,

I knew the opulence of Autumn's dower;
But evanescence will not stay!
A year ago was such an hour
As this, which but foreruns the blast
Shall sweep these live leaves to the dead leaves
    past.

All dies!

          I stood in reverie long,
Then to forget death's ancient wrong
I turned me in the deep arcade,
And there by chance in lateral glade
I saw low tawny mounds in lines,
Relics of trunks of stately pines,
Ranked erst in colonnades where, lo,
Erect succeeding pillars show!

          All dies! and not alone
The aspiring trees and men and grass;
The poet's forms of beauty pass,
And noblest deeds they are undone,
Even truth itself decays, and lo,
From truth's sad ashes pain and falsehood grow.

All dies!

The workman dies, and, after him, the work;
Like to those pines whose graves I trace,
Statue and statuary fall upon their face:
In every amaranth the worm doth lurk,
Even stars, Chaldæans say, fade from the starry
    space,
Andes and Appalachee tell
Of havoc ere our Adam fell,
And present Nature as a moss doth show
Of the ruins of the Nature of the æons of long ago.

But look—and hark!

     Adown the glade,
Where light and shadow sport at will,
Who cometh vocal, and arrayed
As in the first pale tints of morn—
So pure, rose-clear, and fresh and chill!
Some ground-pine sprigs her brow adorn,
The earthly rootlets tangled clinging.
Over tufts of moss which dead things made,
Under vital twigs which danced or swayed,
Along she floats, and slightly singing:

"Dies, all dies!
The grass it dies, but in vernal rain.
Up it springs, and it lives again;
Over and over, again and again,
It lives, it dies, and it lives again,
Who sighs that all dies?
Summer and winter, and pleasure and pain,
And everything everywhere in God's reign.
They end, and anon they begin again:
Wane and wax, wax and wane:
Over and over and over amain,
End, ever end, and begin again—
End, ever end, and forever and ever begin again!"

She ceased, and nearer slid, and hung
In dewy guise; then softlier sung:
"Since light and shade are equal set,
And all revolves, nor more ye know;
Ah, why should tears the pale cheek fret
For aught that waneth here below.
Let go, let go!"

With that, her warm lips thrilled me through,
She kissed me, while her chaplet cold
Its rootlets brushed against my brow,
With all their humid clinging mold.
She vanished, leaving fragrant breath
And warmth and chill of wedded life and death.

BILLY IN THE DARBIES
from *Billy Budd*

Good of the Chaplain to enter Lone Bay
And down on his marrow-bones here and pray
For the likes just o' me, Billy Budd.—But look:
Through the port comes the moon-shine astray!
It tips the guard's cutlass and silvers this nook;
But 'twill die in the dawning of Billy's last day,
A jewel-block they'll make of me to-morrow.
Pendant pearl from the yard-arm-end
Like the ear-drop I gave to Bristol-Molly—
Oh, 'tis me, not the sentence, they'll suspend.
Ay, ay, all is up; and I must up too
Early in the morning, aloft from alow.
On an empty stomach, now, never it would do.
They'll give me a nibble—bit o' biscuit ere I go.
Sure, a messmate will reach me the last parting cup;
But turning heads away from the hoist and the belay,
Heaven knows who will have the running of me up!
No pipe to those halyards—But aren't it all sham?
A blur's in my eyes; it is dreaming that I am.
A hatchet to my panzer? all adrift to go?
The drum roll to grog, and Billy never know?
But Donald he has promised to stand by the plank;
So I'll shake a friendly hand ere I sink.
But—no! It is dead then I'll be, come to think.
I remember Taff the Welshman when he sank.
And his cheek it was like the budding pink.
But me, they'll lash me in hammock, drop me deep
Fathoms down, fathoms down, how I'll dream fast asleep.
I feel it stealing now. Sentry, are you there?
Just ease these darbies at the wrist,
And roll me over fair.
I am sleepy and the oozy weeds about me twist.

Notes

BATTLE-PIECES

The Portent

John Brown and twenty-one followers captured the military arsenal at Harpers Ferry, Virginia on October 16, 1859 in an attempt to inspire a slave insurrection. He was tried on charges of treason and conspiring with slaves to commit treason and murder, convicted, and hanged on December 2, 1859.

ll.3–4. The Shenandoah Valley was known for its great beauty but also as the site of General Stonewall Jackson's diversionary campaign of May–June 1862, which halted General George B. McClellan's advance on Richmond. It was also the site of General Philip Sheridan's efforts as commander of the Middle Military Division from 1864–1865. Hence, it is a scene of pastoral peace that became crossed by war.

l.5. John Brown's capture resulted in several cuts to his head.

The Conflict of Convictions

[Melville's Note]. The gloomy lull of the early part of the winter of 1860–1, seeming big with final disaster to our institutions, affected some minds that believed them to constitute one of the great hopes of mankind, much as the eclipse which came over the promise of the first French Revolution affected kindred natures, throwing them for the time into doubt and misgivings universal.

l.10. In Milton *Paradise Lost*, the Archangel Raphael is by God sent to forewarn Adam and Eve of Satan and thereby, "to render man inexcusable." An "enthusiast" means, literally, one inspired by divinity, though Melville may be suggesting something more ironic by the phrase "white enthusiast."

l.44. An "Iron Dome" was under construction for the Capitol to re-place the old wood and brick one demolished in 1855. Melville visited Washington in March 1861 and witnessed the construction. Melville also refers to the Iron Dome as a symbol of the state in "The Scout to-ward Aldie" (ll. 32–35) and "Lee in the Capitol" (l. 33, 38).

l.61. Daniel 7:9.

Apathy and Enthusiasm

l.38. Erebus, the son of Chaos and brother of Night, personifies dark-ness, but is also the name of the cavern through which the souls of the dead pass on their journey through Hades.

The March into Virginia

The poem marks the first major engagement of the war which took place on July 21, 1861, along Bull Run near Manassas Junction, a railroad depot between Richmond and Shenandoah Valley. Confeder-ate General P. G. T. Beauregard and twenty-four thousand of his troops defeated thirty thousand Union soldiers under General Irvin McDowell.

l.23. See Milton's catalog of demons in *Paradise Lost* I: 392–393: "First *Moloch*, horrid King besmear'd with blood / Of human sacrifice, and parents' tears."

Ball's Bluff

Lincoln granted his friend and former senator Colonel Edward D. Baker permission to make a "demonstration" against Confederate positions on the fords of the Potomac near Ball's Bluff, Virginia. On October 21, 1861, Baker and many of his men were ambushed and killed, and Lin-coln was criticized severely for allowing the operation.

DuPont's Round Fight

This celebrates the Northern victory in which the Union fleet, commanded by Admiral Francis DuPont, attacked Forts Walker and

Beauregard on Port Royal Sound, South Carolina, November 7, 1861. The maneuver secured a base of operations along the South Atlantic coast. The battle plan of attack, to which Melville refers, and which was reported in *The Rebellion Record*, was for the ships to steam down the river in a circle or an ellipse and then steam up the river in a similar form.

Donelson

The Confederacy surrendered Fort Donelson on the Cumberland River near Dover, Tennessee, on February 16, 1862. More important, it became a crucial point in the war as Grant clearly rose to prominence as a victorious general. In strategic terms, Grant was able to split the South by using the Cumberland and the Mississippi as lines of operation.

The poem's shifting "aspects" include those watching the bulletin board (roman type, past tense) and those participating in battle (italics, present tense), North and South as they are afflicted by weather.

The details of Melville's poem, which begins on February 12 and continues until the following Sunday, are taken from *The Rebellion Record*.

ll.1–3. Confederate Commissioners John Slidell and James Mason were forcibly removed from the British mail steamer *Trent* by a Union warship on November 8, 1861.

l.80. William R. Morrison was wounded leading an attack on Confederate troops.

l.115. Cf. Milton, *Comus*, 428: "By grots and caverns shagged by horrid shades."

l.160. A Copperhead was Northern Democrat who favored a negotiated peace with the South.

In the Turret

The day after the Confederate ironclad *Merrimac* sank the *Cumberland*, Lieutenant John Cumberland Worden arrived commanding the Union ironclad *Monitor*. In the ensuing battle of March 9, 1862, neither ironclad was able to sink the other. The *Merrimac* did not attack the Union fleet again but did prevent McClellan's army from receiving adequate naval support. Worden received injury to his eyes when shots from the *Merrimac* forced eye and paint fragments from the eye-holes or slits of the pilot-house into his eyes. He survived. The *Monitor* eventually sank in a storm off Cape Hatteras on December 31, 1862.

ll.5–6. *Alcides* is the patronymic of Hercules. He descended into Hades to recover Alcestis who had died so that her husband might be saved.

ll.15–16. Cf. Deuteronomy 3:11: "For only Og king of Bashan remained of the giants; behold his bedstead was a bedstead of iron."

The *Temeraire*

[Melville's Note]. The *Temeraire*, that storied ship of the old English fleet, and the subject of the well-known painting by Turner, commends itself to the mind seeking for some one craft to stand for the poetic ideal of those great historic wooden warships, whose gradual displacement is lamented by none more than by regularly educated navy officers, and of all nations.

See J. M. W. Turner's *The Fighting* Temeraire. Melville saw the painting while in the National Gallery in London in 1857. The name "temeraire" means "one who dares."

l.20. [Melville's note]. Some of the canon of old times, especially the brass ones, unlike the more effective ordnance of the present day, were cast in shapes which Cellini might have designed, were gracefully enchased, generally with the arms of the country. A few of them—field-pieces—captured in our earlier wars, are preserved in arsenals and navy-yards.

A Utilitarian View of the *Monitor*'s Fight

The Union ironclad *Monitor* engaged the Confederate *Merrimac* at nine A.M. on May 9, 1862 in Hampton Roads, Virginia. It withdrew after two hours to replenish ammunition but returned to battle an hour later. The *Merrimac* fired on the *Monitor*'s sight holes and blinded its commander Lieutenant Worden (see "In the Turret"). Neither ship was sunk but the *Monitor* successfully prevented the the *Merrimac* from destroying the Federal fleet.

ll.20–22. Cf. Emerson's "Concord Hymn" l.4: "And fired the shot heard round the world."

Shiloh

The site in Tennessee of the battle that began on Sunday, April 6, 1862 when the Confederate Army, led by Albert Sidney Johnson, attacked Grant's troops as they were moving south. There were enormous casualties on both sides in the two-day battle: more than thirteen thousand Union; more than ten thousand Confederate, including Johnson. Both sides claimed victory, though the Confederate troops were forced to retreat. Melville's poem, significantly, does not emphasize the battle but the ironic reconciliation in death, the fields, the swallows. The swallows frame the poem, and the church is at the center.

Title. Cf. Judges 18: 31; 19.

l.14. Cf. Joshua 22: 11–12 And the children of Israel heard say, Behold the children of Reuben and the children of Gad and the half tribe of Manasseh have built and alter over against the land of Cannan in the borders of Jordan, at the passage of the children of Israel. And when the children of Israel heard of it, the whole congregation gathered themselves together at Shiloh to go up to war against them.

In the Biblical account of Joshua, the alleged rebellion of the tribes is seen as a misunderstanding and they become reconciled peacefully with Israel. Though it is not stated precisely when in the Bible, God eventually destroys Shiloh as punishment for the Israelites' failure to keep his covenant.

Battle of Stone River, Tennessee

Also known as the Battle of Mursfreesboro, Tennessee, this four-day battle near the Stones River began on December 30, 1862. William Rosencrans commanded the Union Army of the Cumberland against Braxton Bragg of the Confederate Army of Tennessee. The outcome was indecisive, and Bragg withdrew his troops.

The conceit of the poem is Melville's comparison of this battle with two battles of the English Wars of the Roses, Tewkesbury and Barnet

Heath. The epigraph of the poem refers to Melville's visit to Oxford on May 3–4, 1857, just prior to his return to the United States from journeying in Europe and the Levant.

l.1. In Tewkesbury on April 14, 1471 and May 3, 1471, Edward IV of York defeated the Lancastrians and ended the fratricidal Wars of the Roses.

l.6. Druids were ancient Celtic priests who worshiped the mysteries of the past within mystical tree cult.

l.23. John C. Breckenridge commanded the division that covered Bragg's retreat.

The House-top

The speaker is observing from his roof top the New York draft riots on the sweltering night of July 11, 1863. In March 1863, Congress had passed the First Conscription Act that permitted those who were financially able to purchase draft immunity for three hundred dollars. Poor New Yorkers responded by rioting, looting, and even lynching African Americans. Militia units eventually put down the riots.

l.9. Sirius in Canis Major is called the Dog Star because it follows its master Orion, the brightest star in the sky. The star's name is from the Greek *Seiros*, meaning hot or searing. Hence, the "dog days" of summer, July 3 to August 11 when Sirius, according to tradition, rises with the sun, increasing its heat. "Dog days" are also a period when dogs are vulnerable to rabies.

l.16. [Melville's Note]. "I dare not write the horrible and inconceivable atrocities committed," says Froissart, in alluding to the remarkable sedition in France during his time. The like may be hinted of some proceedings of the draft-rioters.

l.19. Draco was the first law scribe of ancient Greece and the archon eponymous for the severe laws that were transcribed in 621 B.C. The death penalty was often invoked for even minor offenses.

l.21. Calvin's doctrine of original sin and natural depravity.

l.27. Acts 16: 37–38 and 22: 25–29. Paul invoked his right as Roman citizen to exemption from scourging. The final line is, strikingly, in the hexameter of Virgilian epic.

The Armies of the Wilderness

Grant's Army of the Potomac fought Lee's Army of Northern Virginia near the Rapidan River in the foothills of the Blue Ridge Mountains on May 5–7, 1864. There were more than twelve thousand casualties but the battle was indecisive. The Virginia battleground was heavily forested and crossed by streams. It also had been the site of the battles around Chancellorsville, May 1–4, 1863, to which Melville also refers. Melville's poem is set before the battle begins and considers the unusual perspective of Union soldiers witnessing through field glasses Confederates playing baseball.

l.161. Grant's headquarters from March 26 to May 4, 1864.

l.170. Orpheus was given a lyre by his father, Apollo, and became so accomplished that he could tame wild beasts.

l.171. Stonewall Jackson was fatally wounded at Chancellorsville after outflanking the Union army.

l.210. On May 6, 1864, General James Longstreet sent his troops through an unfinished railroad cut for a successful attack on a Federal flank but was wounded by one of his own men.

ll.216–218. Cf. Exodus 13–21: "And the Lord went before them by day in a pillar of a cloud, to lead them the way; and by night in a pillar of fire, to give them light, to go by day and night."

l.220. Melville refers here not to the Sabaeans mentioned in the Old Testament but to the Sabaeans of Harran in northern Syria, a pagan sect whose transcendent theology could be characterized as astral and Neoplatonic; they became associated with hermetic religious traditions and the Egyptian priest Hermes Trismegistus. They came into conflict with Islamic Sabians in the ninth century, who characterized the Sabaeans of Harran as idol worshippers. Their name means "to turn or convert to a new God."

On the Photograph of Corps Commander

Winfield Scott Hancock commanded the Second Corps in the Spotsylvania Campaign of May 7–20, 1864. *Harper's Weekly* of May 28, 1864 featured a portrait of Hancock as its cover illustration.

l.15. 1415 the English, though outnumbered, defeated the French at Agincourt in northern France.

l.18. The Knights Templars were a military and religious order founded around 1118 in Jerusalem to protect Pilgrims visiting the Holy Land.

The Swamp Angel

[Melville's Note]. The great Parrott gun, planted in the marshes of James Island, and employed in the prolonged, though at times intermitted bombardment of Charleston, was known among our soldiers as the Swamp Angel.

St. Michael's, characterized by its venerable tower, was the historic and aristocratic church of the town.

Sheridan at Cedar Creek

The Confederate troops under General Jubal Early had nearly won the battle of Cedar Creek, Virginia until Union General Philip Sheridan made his legendary ride from twenty miles away in Winchester. Sheridan's counterattack won the battle for the Union, which still lost more than five thousand men as the Confederates lost more than three thousand. The poem first appeared in *Harper's Monthly Magazine* in April 1866 as "Philip," though it seems to celebrate the horse, Winchester, as much as the rider. It was the one poem of *Battle-Pieces* to receive some recognition and to be anthologized during Melville's lifetime. It is worth comparing with the well-known poem "Sheridan's Ride," originally published in November 1894, by Thomas Buchanan Read.

l.26. See John 26 11:1–43.

The College Colonel

William Francis Bartlett was a colonel whose 49th Regiment was being honored in Pittsfield, Massachusetts in August, 1863. Melville saw

Bartlett at an engagement in his honor hosted by Sarah Morewood. Bartlett had left Harvard College and enlisted in the Union army as private. He became a captain in the 20th Massachusetts Regiment and then lost a leg in the Peninsular Campaign in 1862. He led a regiment in the Wilderness fighting of 1864 and was known for leading his troops into battle with his crutch strapped across his saddle. The copy of *Battle-Pieces* that Melville presented him in 1867 survives.

A Dirge for McPherson

[Melville's Note]. The late Major General McPherson, commanding the Army of the Tennessee, a native of Ohio and a West Pointer, was one of the foremost spirits of the war. Young, though a veteran; hardy, intrepid, sensitive in honor, full of engaging qualities, with manly beauty; possessed of genius, a favorite with the army, and with Grant and Sherman. Both generals have generously acknowledged their professional obligations to the able engineer and admirable soldier, their subordinate and junior.

In an informal account written by the Achilles to this Sarpedon, he says: "On that day we avenged his death. Near twenty-two hundred of the enemy's dead remained on the ground when night closed upon the scene of action" (251).

It is significant of the scale on which the war was waged, that the engagement thus written of goes solely (so far as can be learned) under the vague designation of one of the battles before Atlanta.

At the Cannon's Mouth

On October 27, 1864, Lieutenant William B. Cushing and a volunteer crew of fifteen sank the Confederate ram *Albermarle* at Plymouth, North Carolina as it was about to undertake a mission against the Union fleet. They succeeded by attaching a torpedo to a spar but only Cushing, who was only twenty-one, and one other member of his crew survived or evaded capture.

l.20. Adonis spurned the love of Venus, goddess of beauty, to hunt the boar.

The March to the Sea

General William Tecumseh Sherman burned Atlanta on November 17, 1864 and began his march toward Savannah, which he reached without serious opposition on December 10. The destructive path his army cut through Georgia and South Carolina was justified as military "necessity" and "treason's retributions." Melville drew on Major George Ward Nichols's *The Story of the Great March*, of which he owned a copy, for some of the material of the poem, particularly the description of gamecocks kept as pets by Union soldiers.

l.91. Cf. *Paradise Lost*, IV, 393–94: "So spake the Fiend, and with necessity,/The Tyrant's plea, excus'd his devilish deeds."

The Frenzy in the Wake

[Melville's Note]. This piece was written while yet the reports were coming North of Sherman's homeward advance from Savannah. It is needless to point out its purely dramatic character.

Though the sentiment ascribed in the beginning of the second stanza must, in the present reading, suggest the historic tragedy of the 14th of April, nevertheless, as intimated, it was written prior to that event, and without any distinct application in the writer's mind. After consideration, it is allowed to remain.

Few need be reminded that, by the less intelligent classes of the South, Abraham Lincoln, by nature the most kindly of men, was regarded as a monster wantonly warring upon liberty. He stood for the personification of tyrannical power. Each Union soldier was called a Lincolnite.

Undoubtedly Sherman, in the desolation he inflicted after leaving Atlanta, acted not in contravention of orders; and all, in a military point of view, if by military judges deemed to have been expedient, and nothing can abate General Sherman's shining renown; his claims to it rest on no single campaign. Still, there are those who can not but contrast some of the scenes enacted in Georgia and the Carolinas, and also in the Shenandoah, with a circumstance in a great Civil War of heathen antiquity. Plutarch relates that in a military council held by Pompey and the chiefs of that party which stood for the Commonwealth, it was decided that under no plea should any city be sacked that was subject to the people of Rome. There was this difference, however, between the Roman civil conflict and the American one. The war of Pompey and Caesar divided the Roman people promiscuously; that of the North and South ran a frontier line between what for the time were distinct communities or nations. In this circumstance, possibly, and some others, may be found both the cause and the justification of some of the sweeping measures adopted.

ll.11–12. Judges 4: 2–23. Barak, encouraged by Deborah, raised an army and defeated Sisera, general of Jabin, king of Canaan, who held Israel in captivity. Sisera thought he had found refuge in the tent of Jael but she slew him as he slept by driving a nail through his temple.

The Surrender at Appomatox

Lee attempted to join forces with Gender Joseph E. Johnson, who was pressured north by Sherman. Grant blocked Lee's effort and brought about Lee's surrender at the Appomatox Courthouse, Virginia on April 9, 1865.

l.8. Grant thought that it would be an unnecessary humiliation to call upon Confederate officers to deliver their swords as part of the terms of surrender.

ll.11–12. Caesar defeated Pompey at Pharsalus, Greecein 48 B.C. and is the subject of Lucan's epic *Pharsalia*.

The Martyr

Lincoln was assassinated by John Wilkes Booth at Ford's Theater in Washington, D.C. on Good Friday, April 15, 1865 and died the next morning.

l.21. [Melville's note]. At this period of excitement the thought was by some passionately welcomed that the Presidential successor had been raised up by heaven to wreak vengeance on the South. The idea originated in the remembrance that Andrew Johnson by birth belonged to that class of Southern whites who never cherished love for the dominant: that he was a citizen of Tennessee, where the contest at times and places had been close and bitter as a Middle-Age feud; that himself and family had been hardly treated by the Secessionists.

But the expectations built hereon (if, indeed, ever soberly entertained), happily for the country, have not been verified.

Likely the feeling which would have held the entire South chargeable with the crime of one exceptional assassin, this too has died away with the natural excitement of the hour.

l.28. God to Cain Genesis 4:11: "And now art thou cursed from the earth, which hath opened her mouth to receive thy brother's blood from thy hand."

"The Coming Storm"

A landscape painting by Sanford R. Gifford that Melville saw on exhibit at the National Academy of Design in New York, shortly after the assassination of Lincoln. The catalog listed the owner as Edwin Booth, an actor famous for his interpretations of Shakespearean tragedies, particularly *Hamlet*, and also the brother of John Wilkes Booth. After Lincoln's death, John Booth retired temporarily from theater.

Rebel Color-Bearers at Shiloh

[Melville's Note]. The incident on which this piece is based is narrated in a newspaper account of the battle to be found in the "Rebellion Record." During the disaster to the national forces on the first day, a brigade on the extreme left found itself isolated. The perils it encountered are given in detail. Among others, the following sentences occur:

"Under cover of the fire from the bluffs, the rebels rushed down, crossed the ford, and in a moment were seen forming this side the creek in open fields, and within close musket-range. Their color-bearers stepped defiantly to the front as the engagement opened furiously; the rebels pouring in sharp, quick volleys of musketry, and their batteries above continuing to support them with a destructive fire. Our sharpshooters wanted to pick off the audacious rebel color-bearers, but Colonel Stuart interposed: 'No, no, they're too brave fellows to be killed.' "

The Muster

[Melville's Note]. According to a report of the Secretary of War, there were on the first day of March, 1865, 965,000 men on the army payrolls. Of these, some 200,000—artillery, cavalry, and infantry—made up from the larger portion of the veterans of Grant and Sherman, marched by the President. The total number of Union troops enlisted during the war was 2,668,000.

"Formerly a Slave."

An ecphrasis of *Jane Jackson, formerly a Slave-Drawing in oil-color* by Elihu Vedder, which was listed in the 1865 exhibition catalog of the National Academy of Design. Vedder recounts in his journals how he encountered Jackson, who was selling peanuts on a street corner near his Broadway studio. Melville became a lifelong devotee of Vedder's work, particularly his version of Kayam-Fitzgerald's *Rubaiyat*. Though he never met Vedder, Melville dedicated *Timoleon* (1891) to him.

On the Slain Collegians

[Melville's Note]. The records of Northern colleges attest what numbers of our noblest youth went from them to the battle-field. Southern members of the same classes arrayed themselves on the side of Secession; while Southern seminaries contributed large quotas. Of all these, what numbers marched who never returned except on the shield.

l.21. Saturnians refers to the golden age of the Gods and the influence of the planet Saturn. The Vale of Tempe at the base of Mount Olympus in Greece was legendary for its beauty.

ll.33–34. The Apollo Belvedere portrays the god just after he has slain Python, the serpent bred in the slime of the receding flood. The Pythian games honored Apollo's feat. Melville owned a reproduction of J. W. M. Turner's engraving *Apollo Killing Python*, which he saw in the National Gallery in London. Apollo purified himself in Tempe after killing the monster.

America

l.3. Coma Berenices is named after Berenice, the Egyptian queen who pledged her hair to Venus for safe return of her husband from war.

l.30. The Gorgons were three-snake-haired sisters so terrible that when anyone gazed upon them they were instantly turned to stone.

On the Home Guards

An outnumbered Union regiment commanded by Colonel James Mulligan surrendered to General Sterling Price on September 20, 1861, after eight days of fighting because of the weakness, as Melville's poem suggests, of the Home Guard.

The Fortitude of the North

On August 29–30, 1862, the Second Battle of Manassas was fought between the Union Army of Virginia under John Pope and the Confederate

Army of Northern Virginia under General Robert E. Lee. It was a repeat of the first Confederate victory at Manassas of July 1861.

l.5. The "Cape of Storms" was Cape Horn, which Melville himself had experienced in hellish weather in 1860.

An Uninscribed Monument

In a miserably failed attempt to drive Lee's troops from Marye's Heights, west of Fredericksberg, Virginia, General Ambrose E. Burnside, commanding the Army of the Potomac, drove his troops through the town and against a stone wall and sunken road at the base of the hill. Burnside's army had 12,700 casualties trying to drive Lee from the hill; Lee's losses were 5,300. Burnside eventually withdrew his troops.

On a Natural Monument

[Melville's Note]. Written prior to the founding of the National Cemetery at Andersonville, where 15,000 of the reinterred captives now sleep, each beneath his personal head-board, inscribed from records found in the prison-hospital. Some hundreds rest apart and without name. A glance at the published pamphlet containing the list of the buried at Andersonville conveys a feeling mournfully impressive. Seventy-four large double-columned pages in fine print. Looking through them is like getting lost among the old turbaned head-stones and cypresses in the interminable Black Forest of Scutari, over against Constantinople.

Commemorative of a Naval Victory

l.8. The Titian suggested here is "The Man with a Falcon."

l.27. See also "The Haglets," "In a Bye-Canal," "The Maldive Shark."

The Scout toward Aldie

In April of 1864, Melville had set out with his brother Allen to join his cousin Colonel Henry Gansevoort with the 13th New York Cavalry at Vienna, Virginia, which was operating against Mosby's Raiders, a guerrilla band that had been organized in 1863 by Colonel John S. Mosby to divert attention from the main Confederate army. Melville obtained a pass to go on a cavalry raid into the wilderness where Mosby's raiders were operating.

l.22. [Melville's Note]. In one of Kilpatrick's earlier cavalry fights near Aldie, a Colonel who, being under arrest, had been temporarily deprived of his sword, nevertheless, unarmed, insisted upon charging at the head of his men, which he did, and the onset proved victorious.

[Melville's Note]. Certain of Mosby's followers, on the charge of being unlicensed foragers or fighters, being hung by order of a Union cavalry commander, the Partisan promptly retaliated in the woods. In turn, this also was retaliated, it is said. To what extent such deplorable proceedings were carried, it is not easy to learn.

South of the Potomac in Virginia, and within a gallop of the Long Bridge at Washington, is the confine of a country, in some places wild, which throughout the war it was unsafe for a Union man to traverse except with an armed escort. This was the chase of Mosby, the scene of many of his exploits or those of his men. In the heart of this region at least one fortified camp was maintained by our cavalry, and from time to time expeditions were made therefrom. Owing to the nature of the country and the embittered feeling of its inhabitants, many of these expeditions ended disastrously. Such results were helped by the exceeding cunning of the enemy, born of his wood-craft, and, in some instances, by undue confidence on the part of our men. A body of cavalry, starting from camp with the view of breading up a nest of rangers, and absent say three days, would return with a number of their own forces killed and wounded (ambushed), without being able to retaliate farther than by foraging on the country, destroying a house or two reported to be haunts of the guerrillas, or capturing non-combatants accused of being secretly active in their behalf.

In the verse the name of Mosby is invested with some of those associations with which the popular mind is familiar. But facts do not warrant the belief that every clandestine attack of men who passed for Mosby's was made under his eye, or even by his knowledge.

In partisan warfare he proved himself shrewd, able, and enterprising, and always a wary fighter. He stood well in the confidence of his superior officers, and was employed by them at times in furtherance of important movements. To our wounded on more than one occasion he showed considerate kindness. Officers and civilians captured by forces under his immediate command were, so long as remaining under his orders, treated with civility. These things are well known to those personally familiar with the irregular fighting in Virginia.

Lee in the Capitol

(April 1866). Lee actually arrived in Washington on February 16, 1866 and left on February 20. Melville may have taken poetic liberty with the date because the war began and ended in the month of April.

[Melville's Note]. Among those summoned during the spring just passed to appear before the Reconstruction Committee of Congress was Robert E. Lee. His testimony is deeply interesting, both in itself and as coming from him. After various questions had been put and briefly answered, these words were addressed to him:

"If there be any other matter about which you wish to speak on this occasion, do so freely." Waiving this invitation, he responded by a short personal explanation of some point in a previous answer, and, after a few more brief questions and replies, the interview closed.

In the verse a poetical liberty has been ventured. Lee is not only represented as responding to the invitation, but also as at last renouncing his cold reserve, doubtless the cloak to feelings more or less poignant. If for such freedom warrant be necessary, the speeches in ancient histories, not to speak of those in Shakespeare's historic plays, may not unfitly perhaps be cited.

The character of the original measures proposed about time in the National Legislature for the treatment of the (as yet) Congressionally excluded South, and the spirit in which those measures were advocated—these are circumstances which it is fairly supposable would have deeply influenced the thoughts, whether spoken or withheld, of a Southerner placed in the position of Lee before the Reconstruction Committee.

l.37. John Pope was the Federal general defeated by Lee at the Second Battle of Manassas (August 29, 1862).

l.187. Lucius Cornelius Sulla was the first Roman to lead an Army against Rome. A general in the civil war against Marius (88–82 B.C.), he became a brutal dictator.

CLAREL

Part I: Jerusalem

I. *The Hostel*

Clarel, a bookish student in his chamber, is preparing to see the Holy Land for himself.

l.10. Vigil of Epiphany is a church festival on January 6 celebrating the Magi visiting the infant Jesus in Bethlehem.

l.29. Jaffa Port of entry for tourists and pilgrims going to Jerusalem.

l.39. Song of Solomon 2.1: "the Rose of Sharon."

l.65. Salem is ancient name for Jerusalem. Samarcand is an ancient city of Central Asia and a symbol of romance.

l.109. Vesta is Roman virginal divinity.

XIII. *The Arch*

While visiting Jerusalem the American millennialist Nehemiah, Clarel encounters Celio, an Italian hunchback with a beautiful face, who lives in a Franciscan monastery. Celio has challenged the Roman Church and his faith. He and Clarel have a mystical encounter at the arch across the Via Dolorosa called *Ecce Homo* (Behold the Man), where Pontius Pilate presented Jesus to the people for judgment, but they do not exchange words.

l.47. Matthew 27:46: "And about the ninth hour Jesus cried with a loud voice, saying, Eli, Eli, lama sabachthani? that is to say, My God, my God, why hast thou forsaken me?"

l.74. John 10:23-24: "And Jesus walked in the temple in Solomon's porch. Then came the Jews round about him, and said unto him, How long dost thou make us doubt? If thou be Christ, tell us plainly."

XVII. *Nathan*

Nathan is an American Gentile Zionist farmer and the father of Ruth, who was betrothed to Clarel. This canto tells his history from Puritan New England youth to Illinois farmer, which in some respects epitomizes a great deal of American social and intellectual history.

l.18. Esdraleon is the major open area of central and northern Palestine.

l.38. A river along with the Amonoosuc that rises in the White Mountains of New Hampshire (see also line 83).

l.305. The Pequods of Connecticut were a band of Algonquians who killed numerous settlers and were exterminated as a tribe in 1637.

Part II: The Wilderness

IV. Of Mortmain

A Swede and former idealistic leader of the French Revolution of 1848 who had been betrayed, Mortmain now wanders the earth an outcast and profound skeptic, convinced of the presence of evil. His name, which in legal terms signifies perpetual ownership by ecclesiastical entities and corporations, means "dead hand," and he seems plagued by the relentless and imprisoning presence of unchanging history and the material world.

l.29. George Psalmanazar (1679–1763) was the pseudonym of a French adventurer whose real identity was never revealed. His *Memoirs* were published in 1764.

l.124. Micah 6.8: ". . . and what doth the Lord require of thee . . . but to do justly, and to love mercy, and to walk, humbly with thy God?"

ll.133–134. Medea murdered her two children.

l.143. Circe turned Odysseus's men swine but was his lover for a year. She then advised him how to sail safely by the sirens by being bound to the mast.

XXII. Concerning Hebrews

The debate between the pilgrims Rolfe, Derwent, Vine, and Clarel is inspired by their fellow traveler Margoth who is a geologist and a Jew but utterly without interest in religion or religious arguments. In this light, Rolfe considers such Jews as Heinrich Heine and Baruch Spinoza.

l.63. Uriel Acosta (1585–1640) a philosopher and theologian was born a Portuguese Jew and raised a Catholic. In Amsterdam the synagogue excommunicated him but he rejoined only to be excommunicated. He rejoined and committed suicide.

l.66. Heinrich Heine (1797–1856) was a lyric poet and critic who renounced Judaism for Christianity.

l.77. The Neoplatonic School at Alexandria (300–400 A.D.) sought to reconcile Judeo-Christian and ancient Greek philosophy.

l.84. Moses Mendelsshon (1729–86) was a German Jewish philosopher and theologian.

l.96. Johann Neander (1789–1850) was an historian of Christianity and the son of a Jewish peddler named Emmanuel Mendel. He changed his name to Neander at seventeen and was baptized.

l.110. Baruch Spinoza (1632–77) philosopher of Jewish birth who lived in Amsterdam and worked as lens grinder. His *Ethics* (1677) has often been viewed as an argument for a rational love of God, divergent from the claims of scripture.

XXXI. The Inscription

The pilgrims travel south through Sodom and Gomorrah and westward along the Dead Sea, passing by the ruins of the ancient city of Petra, which Rolfe describes in great detail. The landscape is desolate but Nehemiah sleeps in the shade of a rock which bears the "Slanting Cross" and inscription.

l.97. Thor is the Norse God of thunder and armed with a magic hammer that returns to him when thrown.

XXXIV. Mortmain Reappears

The pilgrims have camped for the night near the Dead Sea. The next day they explore the shore and hear Margoth's challenges to biblical accounts of its origins. Mortmain has chosen to remain behind at Elisha's Fountain where Christ was tempted by Satan in the wilderness.

l.10. Hecla ice was created from a massive volcano in southwestern Iceland.

l.20. See 1 Kings 17:1–7 Cherith was the brook where Elijah was hid and fed by ravens.

l.40. *Vox Clamans* is the "Voice Crying" in the wilderness of John the Baptists "he that was spoken of by the prophet Esaias, saying, The voice of one crying in the wilderness, Prepare ye the way of the Lord . . ." (Matthew 3:1–3).

l.63. Exodus 15:23: The Israelites in the wilderness "could not drink of the waters of Marah, for they were bitter."

XXXV. *Prelusive*

A meditation on the "Imaginary Prisons," (*Carceri*) a set of sixteen haunting etchings executed in the 1740s by Giovanni Battista Piranesi (1720–78). They represented for Melville "the mystery of iniquity." The canto is "prelusive" to his vision expressed in the next canto of what brought about the destruction of Sodom.

XXXVI. *Sodom*

l.23. Revelations 8:10–11: "And the third angel sounded, and there fell a great star from heaven, burning as it were a lamp, and it fell upon the third part of the rivers, and upon the fountains of the waters;

"And the name of the star is called Wormwood, and the third part of the waters became wormwood; and many men died of the waters, because they were made bitter."

Part III: Mar Saba

V. *The High Desert*

l.26. Ibrahim Pasha (1789–1848) was a brutal Egyptian general who controlled Syria from 1832–1841.

l.40. Gnosticism was a heretical religion forged of western and eastern elements that developed in the first century of Christianity and emphasized a dualistic cosmology and *gnosis*, a form of knowledge used to penetrate divine mysteries. It viewed the created world as the work of an evil demiurge, often represented as the God of the Old Testament. Any form of salvation must be regarded in complete antithesis to this God through *gnosis*. Melville's interest in Gnosticism and its related formulations such as Manichaeanism and Zoroastrianism can be seen in *Moby-Dick* (particularly "The Candles," but not only), *Pierre: or, The Ambiguities*, and "Bartleby, the Scrivener." See also the poem "Fragments of a Lost Gnostic Poem of the Twelfth Century." Followers of such heretical views such as the Cathars were at times subjected to persecution by the Roman Catholic Church. Cf. "Fragments of a Lost Gnostic Poem of the Twelfth Century."

l.68. In 1616, the Inquisition forced Galileo to recant his advocacy of the Copernican system.

l.89. The Capet kings (987–1328), with four exceptions, are buried in the cathedral of St. Denis along with all of the later kings of France through the nineteenth century.

l.103. The Sibylline Books contained oracles from the Cumaean Sibyl on all matters of Roman religious worship and law and were kept in Rome until A.D. 405.

l.133. The Tartar invasion, fall of Pekin and end of the Ming dynasty occurred in 1644.

l.140. A.U.C.: *Anno urbis conditae*—from the founding of the city (namely, Rome), in 753 B.C.

l.201. The witch of Endor whom Saul consulted (I Samuel 28. 7–14).

XXIX. Rolfe and the Palm

The pilgrims have traveled up the mountains of Judah to the monastery of Mar Saba where they rest, wander about the convent, and meditate on a palm tree jutting from a ledge as a possible sign of grace. While the others meditate Rolfe has an elaborate reverie of a lost arcadia. Mortmain has disappeared.

l.11. Mother-Cary's bird is a sailor's term for a small petrel.

l.38. The *Fons Bandusia* are celebrated in Horace's Odes.

l.47. Alvarro Mendana de Neira was sixteenth-century explorer who discovered and named the Marquesas Islands.

XXXII. Empty Stirrups

ll.15–16. 1 Kings 18.7: "And as Obadiah was in the way, behold Elijah met him: and he knew him, and fell on his face, and said, Art thou that my Lord Elijah?"

Part IV: Bethlehem

XX. Derwent and Ungar

Derwent has been debating Don Hannibal, a disillusioned *reformado* (reformed) from the Mexican revolution (1858–61). Derwent believes in liberation and the possibilities of revolution, reform, progress, and democracy. Ungar, who has joined the travelers, disagrees. He is a part Native American ex-officer of the Southern Confederacy who has arrived in Mar Saba, "a wandering Ishmael of the West," to perform mercenary military services for the Egyptians and Turks.

l.1. God spoke to Elijah, unlike Moses or Job, in a "still small voice." (1 Kings 19:11–12).

l.45. Marcus Aurelius Antoninus (121–80), Roman Emperor and author of *Meditations*. See also Melville's poem "The Age of the Antonines" in *Timoleon*.

l.117. The Palais des Tuileries, formerly the royal residence, near the Louvre. Its main wing was burned in the revolution of 1871.

XXX. The Valley of Decision

The pilgrims ride toward the Cistern of Kings, where the Magi watered their camels. Clarel discovers the bodies of Ruth, his betrothed, and her mother, Agar, who have died in grief over the drowning of their father and husband, Nathan.

Title. Joel 3:16: "Multitudes, multitudes in the valley of decision: for the day of the Lord is near in the valley of decision.

The sun and the moon shall be darkened, and the stars shall withdraw their shining.

The Lord also shall roar out of Zion, and utter his voice from Jerusalem; and the heavens and the earth shall shake: but the Lord will be the hope of his people, and the strength of the children of Israel."

l.9. Coquimbo is a province in Chile.

XXXII. Passion Week

Passion week or Holy Week is the week before Easter. Palm Sunday is the first day of Holy Week, followed by Holy Thursday and Good Friday.

l.104. John 14:16: "And I will pray the Father, and he shall give you another Comforter, that he may abide with you forever."

l.104. Erebus is the son of Chaos.

XXXIII. Easter

ll.57–58. Thammuz is a Syrian deity celebrated in the seasonal resurrection of nature.

l.65. Matthew 28.6: "He is not here: for he is arisen, as he said."

XXXIV. Via Crucis

The *Via Crucis* or Way of the Cross is also known as *Via Dolorosa* (Way of Sorrow), along which Jesus passed to his crucifixion.

l.34. Whitsunday is the seventh Sunday after Easter when the apostles were visited by cloven tongues of fire. (Acts 2:1–14)

JOHN MARR AND OTHER SAILORS

Tom Deadlight

Ship decks had thick panes of glass set in them called deadlights designed to provide light below.

Jack Roy

The subject of the poem recalls Jack Chase, the captain of the U.S.S. *United States* with whom Melville served in 1843–44. Melville also describes him as the captain of the maintop of the frigate *Neversink* in *White-Jacket* (see chapter 4). He also dedicated *Billy Budd* to him.

The Haglets

The poem first appeared in *The New York Daily Tribune* in a shorter version as "The Admiral of the White," dedicated to his recently deceased brother Tom. The original title refers to the white ensign with the red cross of St. George flown by a British admiral's ship. The revised title refers to the birds that are flying above the doomed ship (sometimes called kittiwakes). A similar story appears in *Clarel* as "The Timoneer's Story."

The Maldive Shark

The Maldive Sea is southwest of India.

TIMOLEON, ETC.

Timoleon

Melville's sources for this poem about fratricide included both Plutarch and Pierre Bayle's *Dictionary*. Timoleon was the younger brother of Timophanes, a ruthless Corinthian tyrant. He participated in the assassination of his brother but was denounced by his mother and his people, and the poem focuses on his twenty years of exile.

After the Pleasure Party

The poem from lines 1–110 is a monologue spoken by Urania, who in classical mythology is a daughter of Zeus and Mnemosyne, and one of the Nine Muses and the Muse of Astronomy. Nathanial Philbrick (1991) has argued that the speaker may have been modeled on Maria Mitchell (1818–89), the first woman American astronomer, whom Melville met on Nantucket in 1852. She has been at a party at a Mediterranean Villa and attempts to resolve the conflict between her love of science and her erotic desires. From lines 111–130, the poet speaks of Urania as she stands in the statue garden of the Villa Albani in Rome. The next stanza returns to the voice of Urania as she contemplates entering a nunnery and prays to the "armed Virgin." The concluding stanzas, lines 148–157, return to the voice of the poet and the question of art as form of salvation from desire. It is apparent from several drafts of the poem in Melville's hand, and that of his wife, that he considered several titles including "Urania," "A Boy's Revenge," and "A Boy's Revenge, or After the Pleasure Party."

The Garden of Metrodorus

Metrodorus of Chios was a radically skeptical ancient Greek philosopher known for such statements as "We nothing, no, not even whether we know or not," from the opening of his treatise *On Nature*. Melville may also have had in mind Metrodorus of Lampascus, a disciple of Epicurus.

The Bench of Boors

The poem is likely based on a painting of a tavern scene by Flemish painter David Teniers (1610–90).

Art

l.10. Genesis 32:24–32.

C——'s Lament

"C" is Samuel Taylor Coleridge, and Melville refers to, among other works, the poet's "Dejection: An Ode" (1802).

Fragments of a Lost Gnostic Poem of the Twelfth Century

Gnosticism was a heretical religion that developed in the first century of Christianity and combined elements of eastern and western thought. Its cosmology is decidedly dualistic, the world being the work of an evil demiurge often represented as the God of the Old Testament. Transcendence can be achieved only through knowledge or *gnosis* of a realm in opposition to the worldly. Cf. *Clarel* Part III: iv.

The Marchioness of Brinvilliers

Marie Marguerite d'Aubray, marquise de Brinvilliers (1630–76) was a French aristocrat who poisoned her father and brothers and was executed. Melville visited the Louvre in November 1849 and probably saw a famous crayon sketch of her execution by Charles Le Brun that was displayed there.

The Age of the Antonines

The two Antonines were the Roman Emperor Antoninus Pius, the adopted son of the Emperor Hadrian, who reigned from A.D. 138–161 and his adopted son Marcus Aurelius, who ruled until A.D. 180. Melville's primary source for discussion of this period of sound government was Edward Gibbon's *Decline and Fall of the Roman Empire*.

Herba Santa

Title is Spanish for "Holy Weed." Melville loved tobacco.

In a Bye-Canal

l.6. Judges 4:2–23

The Apparition

During his 1857 journey in Athens, Melville noted in his journal that "the Parthenon elevated like a cross of Constantine." The poem recalls how the Parthenon dominates Athens from the citadel of the acropolis and that this had been supplanted by the cross that converted Roman Emperor Constantine (A.D. 272?–337) to Christianity.

l.9. Diogenes (412?–323 B.C.) was a Cynic philosopher, a school of thought that believed virtue to be the only good and achievable through self-control. Melville puns on "cynic" which in Greek means "dog."

In the Desert

l.1. Exodus 10:21–29.

l.3. Priests of Thebes on the upper Nile.

l.10. At the Battle of the Pyramids, July 1798, when the French defeated the Malmuke Army.

l.16. See *Paradise Lost*, Book III, 11:1–6.

l.17. Shekinah is the majestic presence or manifestation of God that has descended to dwell with man.

MISCELLANEOUS POEMS

The New Ancient of Days

The occasion of the poem is the discovery in 1835 by paleontologist Philippe Charles Schmerling of human fossil remains in the Engihoul cavern in Belgium. The title derives from the Book of Daniel 7:9, "I beheld till the thrones were cast down, and the Ancient of days did sit." Melville conflates the titles of two of Darwin's books, *The Descent of Man* and *On the Origin of Species*.

Camoens

Melville was an admirer of Luis de Camoens's (1524–80) epic *Os Lusiads*, which recounts the voyages of Vasco de Gama. Camoens died impoverished in Lisbon.

Montaigne and His Kitten

The essayist Michel de Montaigne (1533–92), who was awarded the Order of St. Michel by Charles IX in 1571, had a kitten named Blanche.

Pontoosuce

A lake north of Pittsfield, Massachusetts. Melville's manuscript reveals he considered giving it the title of "The Lake."

Index of First Lines

FOR THE BEST IN PAPERBACKS, LOOK FOR THE

In every corner of the world, on every subject under the sun, Penguin represents quality and variety—the very best in publishing today.

For complete information about books available from Penguin—including Penguin Classics, Penguin Compass, and Puffins—and how to order them, write to us at the appropriate address below. Please note that for copyright reasons the selection of books varies from country to country.

In the United States: Please write to *Penguin Group (USA), P.O. Box 12289 Dept. B, Newark, New Jersey 07101-5289* or call 1-800-788-6262.

In the United Kingdom: Please write to *Dept. EP, Penguin Books Ltd, Bath Road, Harmondsworth, West Drayton, Middlesex UB7 0DA.*

In Canada: Please write to *Penguin Books Canada Ltd, 90 Eglinton Avenue East, Suite 700, Toronto, Ontario M4P 2Y3.*

In Australia: Please write to *Penguin Books Australia Ltd, P.O. Box 257, Ringwood, Victoria 3134.*

In New Zealand: Please write to *Penguin Books (NZ) Ltd, Private Bag 102902, North Shore Mail Centre, Auckland 10.*

In India: Please write to *Penguin Books India Pvt Ltd, 11 Panchsheel Shopping Centre, Panchsheel Park, New Delhi 110 017.*

In the Netherlands: Please write to *Penguin Books Netherlands bv, Postbus 3507, NL-1001 AH Amsterdam.*

In Germany: Please write to *Penguin Books Deutschland GmbH, Metzlerstrasse 26, 60594 Frankfurt am Main.*

In Spain: Please write to *Penguin Books S. A., Bravo Murillo 19, 1° B, 28015 Madrid.*

In Italy: Please write to *Penguin Italia s.r.l., Via Benedetto Croce 2, 20094 Corsico, Milano.*

In France: Please write to *Penguin France, Le Carré Wilson, 62 rue Benjamin Baillaud, 31500 Toulouse.*

In Japan: Please write to *Penguin Books Japan Ltd, Kaneko Building, 2-3-25 Koraku, Bunkyo-Ku, Tokyo 112.*

In South Africa: Please write to *Penguin Books South Africa (Pty) Ltd, Private Bag X14, Parkview, 2122 Johannesburg.*